Contents at a Glance

Prologue	Getting Started with the iMac	**1**
Chapter 1	Managing Your Desktop	**19**
Chapter 2	Making the Most of Your Screen Space	**57**
Chapter 3	Connecting Your Mac to a Network	**81**
Chapter 4	Setting Up iCloud Services and Internet Accounts	**105**
Chapter 5	Accessing Email and the Web	**127**
Chapter 6	Sharing Files, Devices, and Services	**179**
Chapter 7	Being Social with Messages, FaceTime, Twitter, and Facebook	**215**
Chapter 8	Managing Who, Where, When, and What	**251**
Chapter 9	Entertainment on the (Big) Little Screen	**311**
Chapter 10	Installing and Managing Software on Your Mac	**371**
Chapter 11	Making the Most of Your Mac Hardware	**387**
Chapter 12	Connecting Devices to Your Mac	**419**
Chapter 13	Securing and Protecting Your Mac	**447**
Chapter 14	Troubleshooting Your System	**479**
Chapter 15	Upgrading Your Mac	**online**
	Index	**500**

Register your book at quepublishing.com/register for access to an online-only, bonus chapter: Chapter 15, "Upgrading Your Mac."

Find this bonus chapter and other helpful information on this book's website at quepublishing.com/title/9780789751713.

Table of Contents

Prologue: Getting Started with the iMac   **1**

Getting to Know the iMac Hardware 2

    Special Keyboard Keys 4

What You Need to Know 4

    The Menu Bar 5

    The Dock 5

    The Finder 6

    Tags 6

    The Launchpad 8

    Mission Control 8

    The App Store (and Security) 9

    The Notification Center 10

    System Preferences 10

    Window Controls 11

    Contextual Menus 12

    Gestures 12

    Dictation 12

Understanding iCloud and Apple ID 13

Windows Compatibility 14

    Boot Camp 14

    Virtualization 15

1   Managing Your Desktop   **19**

Organizing in the Dock 20

    Adding and Removing Items from the Dock 20

    Using Folders and Stacks in the Dock 21

    Customizing the Dock's Appearance 24

Customizing Finder Windows 25

    Configuring the Sidebar's System Shortcuts 26

    Manually Modifying the Sidebar 27

    Modifying the Finder Toolbar 28

    Using Finder Window Tabs 29

    Opening Tabs with a Click 30

My
iMac®

MAVERICKS EDITION

John Ray

Que®

800 East 96th Street,
Indianapolis, Indiana 46240 USA

My iMac® Mavericks Edition

Copyright © 2014 by Pearson Education, Inc.

ISBN-13: 978-0-7897-5171-3
ISBN-10: 0-7897-5171-2

Library of Congress Control Number: 2013951119

Printed in the United States of America

First Printing: November 2013

Trademarks

All terms mentioned in this book that are known to be trademarks or service marks have been appropriately capitalized. Que Publishing cannot attest to the accuracy of this information. Use of a term in this book should not be regarded as affecting the validity of any trademark or service mark.

Warning and Disclaimer

Every effort has been made to make this book as complete and as accurate as possible, but no warranty or fitness is implied. The information provided is on an "as is" basis. The author(s) and the publisher shall have neither liability nor responsibility to any person or entity with respect to any loss or damages arising from the information contained in this book.

Special Sales

For information about buying this title in bulk quantities, or for special sales opportunities (which may include electronic versions; custom cover designs; and content particular to your business, training goals, marketing focus, or branding interests), please contact our corporate sales department at corpsales@pearsoned.com or (800) 382-3419.

For government sales inquiries, please contact governmentsales@pearsoned.com.

For questions about sales outside the U.S., please contact international@pearsoned.com.

Editor-in-chief
Greg Wiegand

Senior Acquisitions Editor
Laura Norman

Development Editor
Charlotte Kughen

Managing Editor
Kristy Hart

Project Editor
Lori Lyons

Proofreader
Debbie Williams

Indexer
Erika Millen

Editorial Assistant
Cindy Teeters

Cover Designer
Mark Shirar

Compositor
Kim Scott,
Bumpy Design

Technical Editor
Anne Groves

Graphics Technician
Tammy Graham

Arranging and Grouping Files 31

   Using All My Files 31

   Arranging a Finder View 32

   Assigning Tags 33

   Removing Tags 34

   Viewing Tags 34

   Managing Tags 35

Previewing Document Contents with Quick Look 37

   Viewing a File with Quick Look 38

   Previewing Files Using Finder Icons 40

Using Instant-Access Utilities in the Dashboard 40

   Activating the Dashboard 41

   Adding and Removing Dashboard Widgets 42

   Configuring Dashboard Widgets 43

Finding Information with Spotlight 44

   Searching for Files and Information 45

   Customizing Spotlight Searching 46

   Saving Searches as Smart Folders in the Finder 47

Keeping Track of System Events with Notifications 48

   Receiving Notifications 49

   Viewing the Notification Center 49

   Customizing the Notification Display 51

   Activating Do Not Disturb Mode 53

   Customizing Do Not Disturb Mode 54

2 Making the Most of Your Screen Space   57

Swimming in a Sea of Application Windows with
Mission Control 58

   Opening and Closing Mission Control 58

   Navigating Applications and Windows 59

   Creating and Populating a New Space 60

   Closing a Space 63

   Creating Full-Screen Application Spaces 64

   Choosing Between Application Windows 65

   Showing the Desktop 66

   Configuring Mission Control Features and Shortcuts 67

Managing and Launching Applications with Launchpad . . 69

Starting Launchpad 69

Navigating Launchpad 70

Searching Launchpad 71

Rearranging Icons 72

Creating New Folders 73

Deleting Folders 74

Deleting Applications 75

Managing Auto Open and Save Features 76

Toggling Application Auto Open 76

Setting Window Restoration 77

Enabling Manual File Saving 78

3 **Connecting Your Mac to a Network** **81**

Connecting to a Wired Network 82

Making an Ethernet (Wired) Connection 82

Connecting to a Wireless Network 84

Making a Wireless Connection 84

Authenticating on a Wireless Network 87

Disabling (and Enabling) Wireless Networking 88

Manually Configuring Network Settings 89

Configuring TCP/IP and Proxy Settings 89

Activating PPPoE for DSL Connections 92

Creating Virtual Private Network Connections 94

Creating a VPN Connection 94

Managing Multiple Connections with Locations
and Configurations 96

Creating Configurations 97

Adding and Using Locations 98

Seeking Automated Network Assistance 100

Launching Diagnostics 100

Launching the Setup Assistant 101

4   Setting Up iCloud Services and Internet Accounts   105

Setting Up iCloud 106

Configuring iCloud for the First Time 106

Activating iCloud Services 108

Exploring Unique iCloud Services 110

Accessing iCloud Applications Online 110

Using Find My Mac 111

Using Documents and Data 113

Using Photo Sharing 118

Getting Started with Accounts 122

Adding an Account 123

5   Accessing Email and the Web   127

Using Mail 128

Things You Need Before Setting Up an Email
Connection 128

Adding an Email Account 129

Configuring Advanced Account Settings 131

Finding Your Way Around Mail 134

Reading Email 135

Composing Email 142

Managing Your Email 146

Web Browsing in Safari 155

Managing Your Bookmarks, Top Sites,
and Reading List 156

Advanced Browsing Features 162

Adding Web Content to the Dashboard 173

Extending Safari's Capabilities with Extensions 175

6   Sharing Files, Devices, and Services   179

File Sharing on Your Mac 180

Using AirDrop to Wirelessly Share Files and Folders . . 180

Configuring Traditional File and Folder Sharing 184

Sharing Files via Share Sheets 194

    Sharing Files via Messages 194

    Uploading Files to an Online Service 195

Sharing Printers 197

    Enabling Network Printer Sharing 198

    Setting Printer Sharing Permissions 199

    Accessing a Network Printer 200

Sharing an Optical Drive 202

    Enabling DVD and CD Sharing 202

    Accessing a Shared Optical Drive 203

Sharing Your Mac Screen 204

    Enabling Screen Sharing 204

    Setting Screen Sharing Permissions 205

    Accessing the Screen of a Local Mac 207

    Accessing Remote Computers and Non-Macs 209

Sharing Your Internet Connection 211

    Sharing Your Connection 211

7 Being Social with Messages, FaceTime, Twitter, and Facebook   215

Instant Messaging with Messages 216

    Adding Accounts to Messages 216

    Logging into (and out of) Your IM Account 221

    Configuring Your IM Identity 222

    Managing Your IM Buddy List 225

    Communicating with IM and iMessages 227

    Starting an IM Audio or IM Video Chat 231

    Sharing Your Files and Screen 232

Video Calls with FaceTime 235

    Setting Up FaceTime 236

    Placing FaceTime Calls 237

    Receiving a FaceTime Call 240

    Accessing Your Call List 241

    Disabling FaceTime 241

    Updating Account Information and FaceTime
        Addresses 242

Using the Mavericks Twitter and Facebook Posting
Support 243

Enabling Twitter 244

Enabling Facebook 246

Posting Tweets and Facebook Updates 247

8   Managing Who, Where, When, and What   251

Managing Contacts in Contacts 252

Adding Groups 253

Using iCloud and Server-Based Contacts 261

Sharing Contacts via Email and Messages 265

Printing Addresses 266

Finding Your Way with Maps 267

Starting and Navigating Maps 267

Using Map Views 268

Finding Places 270

Working with Points of Interest 272

Traveling with Maps 275

Working with Schedules in Calendar 277

Adding Calendars 278

Connecting to iCloud and Server-Based Calendars ... 280

Viewing Calendars 285

Working with Events 285

Printing Calendars 293

Remembering with Reminders 294

Creating a List 295

Setting Reminder Attributes, Including Location 296

Completing Reminders 298

Finding Reminders 298

Using iCloud and Server-Based Reminders 300

Keeping Track with Notes 301

Managing Folders 301

Adding Notes 303

Moving Notes Between Folders 304

Searching and Displaying Notes 304

Sharing Notes via Email and Messages 306

Using iCloud and Server-Based Notes 307

9 Entertainment on the (Big) Little Screen   311

Creating a Media Library in iTunes 311

Running iTunes for the First Time 312

Finding Your Way Around iTunes 313

Building Your Media Library 315

Searching the Library 324

Using Playlists 326

Using the Mini Player 330

Using iTunes Radio 331

Syncing Media Between Devices 336

Keeping an iCloud Library with iTunes Match 341

Reading Your iBooks 345

Starting iBooks and Authorizing Your Mac 345

Purchasing Books 347

Viewing and Arranging Your Library 349

Reading iBooks 353

Getting Your Game on with Game Center 357

Signing into Game Center 358

Navigating the Me Screen 360

Managing Friends and Friend Requests 361

Sizing Up Your Friends 364

Browsing by Game 366

Making and Taking a Challenge 367

10 Installing and Managing Software on Your Mac   371

Mac App Store 372

Logging into the App Store 372

Browsing for Apps 373

Searching for Apps 374

Purchasing an App 375

Reinstalling Apps and Installing Purchases on
Other Macs 376

Hiding Apps You No Longer Want 377

Installing Non–App Store Applications 378

Unarchiving Zip Files 379

Accessing Disk Images 380

Keeping Your Applications and Operating System
Up-To-Date 382

Configuring Software Updates and Auto
Downloads 383

Manually Applying Software Updates 384

11   Making the Most of Your Mac Hardware   387

Going Green with Energy Saver 388

Configuring Display, Computer, and Hard
Disk Sleep 388

Creating a Sleep/Wake Schedule 390

Updating Keyboard and Dictation Settings 391

Setting Keyboard Repeat Rate 391

Creating Keyboard Shortcuts 392

Activating Dictation 396

Changing Trackpad and Mouse Options 398

Setting the Trackpad Speed 398

Controlling Trackpad Gestures 399

Configuring the Magic Mouse Speed 401

Configuring Magic Mouse Gestures 401

Adjusting Your Display 402

Setting Display Resolution 403

Controlling Display Brightness 404

Choosing a Color Profile 405

Calibrating the Display 406

Setting Sound Input and Output 408

Setting the Output Volume 408

Configuring Alert Sounds 409

Choosing and Adjusting an Output Device 410

Picking and Calibrating an Input Device 411

Recording Audio and Video 413

Recording Audio 413

Recording with the FaceTime HD Video Camera 414

12 Connecting Devices to Your Mac   419

Connecting USB Input Devices 419

Configuring a USB Keyboard 420

Configuring a USB Mouse 421

Using Bluetooth Devices 422

Pairing a Bluetooth Mouse or Trackpad 422

Pairing a Bluetooth Keyboard 424

Connecting a Bluetooth Headset 425

Adding and Using the Bluetooth Status Menu 426

Using External Displays and Projectors 427

Extending Your Desktop to Another Monitor 428

Setting Monitor Arrangements 428

Adding the Display Mirroring Menu to Your
Menu Bar 430

Using Mirrored Displays 431

Connecting to an Apple TV (or Other Device)
with AirPlay 431

Mirroring Your Display to an Apple TV 432

Setting the AirPlay Apple TV Resolution 433

Extending Your Desktop to an Apple TV 434

Sharing Multimedia to an Apple TV 435

Sending System Audio to an Apple TV 435

Connecting and Using a Printer 436

Adding a Printer 436

The Printing Process 440

Connecting and Using a Scanner 442

Adding a Scanner 442

Scanning in Preview 443

13 Securing and Protecting Your Mac **447**

Working with Users and Groups 448

Creating User Accounts 448

Adding Accounts 449

Enabling the Guest Account 450

Applying Parental Controls 450

Creating Groups 453

Configuring General Account Security 454

Assigning File Permissions for Users and Groups . . . 455

Tracking Passwords with Keychain Access 456

Viewing Keychain Items 457

Adding Data to the Keychain 458

Creating a New Keychain 459

Adding a Keychain Menu Item 460

Encrypting Your Mavericks Disk 460

Activating FileVault 461

Limiting Application Execution 463

Adding Network Security with the Built-In Firewall 464

Activating the Mavericks Firewall 464

Configuring Incoming Services 465

Hiding Location Information and Application Data . . 466

Backing Up Important Information 467

Using Time Machine 467

Activating Time Machine 468

Customizing the Time Machine Backups 469

Adding a Time Machine Menu Item 470

Recovering Data 471

Restoring a Machine from Scratch 473

Using File Versions 474

Manually Saving a Version 474

Restoring a File Version 475

14 **Troubleshooting Your System**   **479**

   Dealing with Troublesome Software 480

      Force Quitting Applications 480

      Testing with the Guest Account 481

      Removing Corrupted Application Files 482

   Restarting and Correcting a Frozen Machine 484

      Starting in Safe Mode 485

      Changing Login Applications 486

      Removing Startup Applications and Launch
         Daemons 487

      Disabling Extensions 488

      Removing System Preference Panes 490

   Fixing Disk Problems with Disk Utility 490

      Repairing Permission Problems 491

      Verifying and Repairing Common Disk Errors 492

      Verifying Your Disk Has an Error 492

      Repairing Your Disk 493

   Gathering Information About Your Mac 495

      Monitoring System Activity 495

      Generating a System Profiler Report 496

      Viewing the System Logs 498

   Remember Your Backups! 499

      Viewing System Support Options 499

15 **Upgrading Your Mac**   **online**

      Index   **500**

About the Author

John Ray is a life-long fan of Apple products; he has been an avid Mac user since its inception in 1984. He relies on OS X both at work and at home because it is a robust, flexible platform for programming, networking, and design. Over the past 15 years, John has written books on OS X, iOS development, Linux, web development, networking, and computer security. He currently serves as the Director of the Office of Research Information Systems at The Ohio State University. When he isn't writing, he is either re-creating a marine disaster in his living room, or planning a highly elaborate electronics project that will quadruple his carbon footprint.

Dedication

This book is dedicated to Maddy. She's my dog. She died this year.
I was very sad. I promise my next dedication will be happier.

Acknowledgments

Thanks to the team at Que Publishing: Laura Norman, Charlotte Kughen, Todd Brakke, Lori Lyons, and Kim Scott for pulling this together in record time. Thanks also go to Anne Groves for figuring out the figures and keeping me honest. It takes an amazing team effort to make this happen. Thank you all.

We Want to Hear from You!

As the reader of this book, *you* are our most important critic and commentator. We value your opinion and want to know what we're doing right, what we could do better, what areas you'd like to see us publish in, and any other words of wisdom you're willing to pass our way.

We welcome your comments. You can email or write to let us know what you did or didn't like about this book—as well as what we can do to make our books better.

Please note that we cannot help you with technical problems related to the topic of this book.

When you write, please be sure to include this book's title and author as well as your name, email address, and phone number. We will carefully review your comments and share them with the author and editors who worked on the book.

Email: feedback@quepublishing.com

Mail: Que Publishing
ATTN: Reader Feedback
800 East 96th Street
Indianapolis, IN 46240 USA

Reader Services

Visit our website and register this book at quepublishing.com/register for convenient access to any updates, downloads, or errata that might be available for this book.

Prologue: Getting Started with the iMac

This book explains how your iMac and the latest edition of the OS X operating system, Mavericks, are used to create your ideal working environment. If you've never worked with a Mac before, OS X is the name applied to Apple's desktop operating system—like "Windows" on a PC. iPhones and iPads run iOS, and Macintosh computers run OS X.

Apple has a long tradition of naming the releases of OS X after large cats, but has started something new with Mavericks—place names. In case you're interested, Mavericks refers to a prime surfing spot in California. It was named after a dog—Maverick—and is meant as a possessive (that is, Maverick's spot).

Thankfully, surfing experience is not necessary to use an operating system. But, before we jump in (did I just type that?), let's get our feet wet (seriously?) by reviewing the hardware capabilities of your system and the prerequisites necessary to use this book.

Getting to Know the iMac Hardware

The iMac family has always included a wide array of ports and plugs for connecting to other computers, handheld devices, and peripherals such as printers and external displays. As of 2013, two different models of the iMac are available: the 21.5" iMac and the 27" iMac. These (and future) models drop support for optical drives but can easily be expanded with external CD, DVD, and Blu-ray drives. To understand the hardware options that are included in your system, let's review the different expansion options that Apple has shipped in the iMac since 2010.

- **Ethernet**—Ethernet provides high-speed wired network connections with greater speeds and reliability than wireless service. Your iMac supports a very fast version of Ethernet, Gigabit Ethernet, that makes it a first-class citizen on any home or corporate network.

- **FireWire 800**—FireWire 800 is a fast peripheral connection standard that is frequently used to connect external storage and video devices. This was dropped as of the 2012 models, but an adapter is available from Apple.

- **Mini DisplayPort**—The DisplayPort enables you to connect external monitors to your iMac. Although few monitors support the DisplayPort standard, you can get adapters from Apple for connecting to both VGA and DVI interface standards. DisplayPort was dropped in favor of Thunderbolt in 2011 and later iMacs.

- **Thunderbolt**—The highest-speed interconnect available on a personal computer, Thunderbolt makes it possible for monitors, storage units, and other devices to be daisy-chained together. This means that each device connects to the next device, rather than all having to plug into a separate port on your iMac.

- **USB 2.0/3.0**—Universal Serial Bus is a popular peripheral connection standard for everything from mice, to scanners, to hard drives. iMac models released in 2012 or later support USB 3.0, the next, much faster, evolution of USB.

- **SD Card Slot**—SD (Secure Digital) RAM cards are a popular Flash RAM format used in many digital cameras. Using the built-in SD RAM slot, you can create a bootable system "disk" that you can use to start your computer in an emergency.

- **Audio In**—A connection for an external microphone.

- **Audio Out**—An output for headphones, speakers, or a home theater/amplifier system.

- **802.11ac**—The fastest standard currently available for consumer wireless network connections. Your iMac's wireless hardware can connect to any standards-based wireless access point for fast, long-range Internet access.

- **Bluetooth**—Bluetooth connects peripheral devices wirelessly to your Mac. Unlike 802.11ac, Bluetooth has a more limited range (about 30 feet, in most cases), but it is easier to configure and doesn't require a specialized base station.

- **SuperDrive**—An optical drive that can be used to write CDs and DVDs. In 2012 and later iMac models, optical drives are no more.

So what does your computer have? Apple's iMac lineup changes throughout the year, so your features depend on the model and the date it was made. Be sure to consult your owner's manual for a definitive description of what is included in your system.

Special Keyboard Keys

Take a look across the top of your keyboard. Notice that even though there are "F" (function) designations on the keys, there are also little icons. The keys marked with icons provide system-wide control over important Mavericks features.

- **F1, F2**—Dim and brighten the display, respectively

- **F3**—Start Mission Control and display all application windows

- **F4**—Open the Launchpad

- **F7, F8, F9**—Act as Rewind, Play, and Fast Forward controls during media playback

- **F10, F11, F12**—Mute, decrease, and increase volume

The Eject key is located in the farthest-right corner of the keyboard and is used to eject any media in your iMac's SuperDrive—if you have one!

Accessing the Function Keys

If you are using an application that requires you to press a function key, hold down the Fn button in the lower-left corner of the keyboard and then push the required function key.

What You Need to Know

If you're holding this book in your hand, you can see that it contains a few hundred pages packed with information about using your iMac with Mavericks. You might also notice books dedicated to the same topic and sitting on the same shelf at the bookstore that include a thousand pages or more! So what's the difference?

My iMac doesn't cover the basics of using a computer; you already know how to drag windows around the screen and move files by dragging them from folder to folder. Instead, this book focuses on using and configuring the core features of OS X—file sharing, Internet access, social networking, calendaring, and entertainment.

If you're switching from Windows, you might encounter a few unique features of OS X. Review these features in the next few sections.

The Menu Bar

The menu bar is universally accessible across all running applications and contains a combination of the Apple menu, which is used to access common system functions; the active application's menus; and menu items, which are global utilities for controlling and monitoring system functions.

Apple menu   **Application menus**   **Menu items**

The Dock

The Mavericks Dock is the starting point for many of your actions when using the iMac. Part application launcher, part file manager, and part window manager, the Dock gives you quick access to your most frequently used applications and documents without requiring that you navigate the Finder to find things on your hard drive.

The Dock

The Finder

In Windows, Explorer provides many of your file management needs. In OS X, you work with files within an ever-present application called Finder. The Finder starts as soon as you log into your computer and continues to run until you log out.

To switch to the Finder at any time, click the blue smiling icon at the left end of the Dock.

Tags

Don't like trying to fit all your files in a folder structure that doesn't make sense? In Mavericks, you don't have to. Create tags that represent different attributes of your files (Projects, Important, Personal, and so on) and then apply as many or as few as you'd like. Once applied, you to view your files by tag, rather than having to dig through folders.

The Launchpad

Applications are installed in folders, nested in folders, or even just lumped together with no organization at all. For simple setups, this is fine; after you've accumulated a few years of downloads, however, finding what you're looking for becomes difficult. The Launchpad offers a consolidated view of all your applications and even lets you group them logically, without having to worry about what folders they're in.

Mission Control

Mission Control is a power-user feature that is easy for anyone to use. With Mission Control, you can manage all your running applications and their windows in a single consolidated display. You can even create new workspaces to hold specific apps or navigate between existing workspaces.

**Application and
associated windows**   **Workspaces**   **Current workspace**

The App Store (and Security)

If you've used a modern smartphone or tablet, you've almost certainly used an "app store" of some sort. The Mac App Store is fully integrated with the operating system and provides fast access to screened and safe applications that are installed, updated, and even removed through a simple point-and-click process. Mavericks also implements security controls to prevent undesirable software installation.

The Notification Center

Does Mavericks need to tell you something? If so, it lets you know in the Notification Center. The Notification Center, activated by clicking the far right side of the menu bar, shows alerts from your applications that help you stay on top of important events. New mail, software updates, meeting invitations, and more are consolidated in this area and presented in a unified fashion.

Notification
Center

System Preferences

Many configuration options for features in this book require you to access the Mavericks System Preferences. The System Preferences application (accessible from the Dock or the Apple menu) is the central hub for system configuration. You can do everything from setting your password to choosing a screen saver in the System Preferences application.

Window Controls

Mavericks provides up to four controls at the top of each window. On the left are the Close, Minimize, and Resize controls. The Close control shuts the window; Minimize slides the window off the screen and into the Dock; and Resize changes the size of the window to best fit the content being displayed.

On the right side of the window is the Fullscreen control. Clicking the Fullscreen control switches an app to full screen, if available. You might not expect it, but full-screen applications can take on a completely different appearance from their windowed selves.

Contextual Menus

If you're new to OS X, you might find it hard to believe that the Mac has a "right-click" (also known as the "secondary click") menu in its operating system—and it's been there for a long time! You can invoke contextual menus by right-clicking using a mouse, Ctrl-clicking with your trackpad, or clicking with two fingers simultaneously.

Contextual menus are rarely required in any application, but they can give you quick access to features that might otherwise take more clicks.

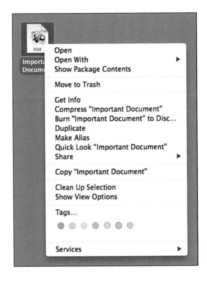

Gestures

Gestures are motions that you can make on an Apple Magic Trackpad to control your computer. In Mavericks, gestures are used heavily to navigate between applications and access special features. Gestures can help you navigate web pages, resize images, and do much more with just your fingertips. In fact, without a trackpad, you'll likely miss out on all Mavericks has to offer.

Dictation

Don't like typing? With Mavericks, you don't have to. Mavericks supports dictation into any application where you would normally type—performed either "in the cloud" or locally on your Mac (with an optional install). You learn more about activating dictation in Chapter 11.

DON'T LIKE A GESTURE? CHANGE IT!

If you don't like a touch, a click, or a swipe that you find in Mavericks (including how contextual menus are activated), it's likely that there is an alternative. The Trackpad System Preferences panel provides complete control over your "touching" OS X experience—something covered Chapter 11's "Changing Trackpad and Mouse Options" section.

Understanding iCloud and Apple ID

Apple's iCloud and its corresponding Apple ID deserve special attention during your foray into Mavericks. iCloud provides services such as calendars, notes, and reminders that you can use to synchronize information across multiple Macs and multiple iOS devices. It also offers free email, a means of locating your Mac (if you lose it), a tool for controlling your system from remote locations, and even an online office application suite! You don't need to use iCloud, but you'll see references to it, like the one shown here, as you navigate the operating system.

To use iCloud, you must establish an Apple ID to authenticate with the service. If you've installed Mavericks, chances are you've created an Apple ID in the process and already have everything you need to start using iCloud. If you aren't sure whether you have an Apple ID or you want to generate a new one, I recommend visiting https://appleid.apple.com/ and using the web tools to verify, or start, your setup.

You learn more about configuring iCloud in Chapter 4, "Setting Up iCloud Services and Internet Accounts."

iCloud Everywhere

Because iCloud makes many of your Mavericks features more useful, it is referenced throughout this book. The information doesn't fit into a single category, so I discuss it in the places where I hope you'll find it most useful.

Windows Compatibility

If you have an Mac, you have a powerful Intel-based computer in your hands—a computer that is capable of natively running the Windows operating system. The goal of this book is to make you comfortable using your Mac with Mavericks, but I'd be remiss in my authoring duties if I didn't mention the options available for running Windows on your hardware.

Boot Camp

Boot Camp is included with Mavericks and gives you the capability to install and boot Windows directly on your iMac. Put simply, when you do this, your Mac becomes a Windows computer. Switching between Mavericks and Windows requires a reboot, so this option is best if you need to work in Windows for extended periods of time.

Apple's Boot Camp Assistant (found in the Utilities folder within the Applications folder) guides you through the process of partitioning your iMac for Windows and burning a CD of drivers for Windows, and configuring your system to boot into Windows or OS X.

You can install Boot Camp at any time, as long as you have enough room (about 28GB) for a Windows installation. Boot Camp even works correctly with the iMac's fusion drive—just install using the Boot Camp drivers and go.

Virtualization

Another solution to the Windows compatibility conundrum is the use of virtualization software. Through virtualization, you can run Windows at near-native speeds at the same time you run Mavericks. Some virtualization solutions even go so far as to mix Mac and Windows applications on the same screen, blurring the lines between the operating systems.

Unlike Boot Camp, virtualization runs operating systems simultaneously. Virtualization requires more resources and has lower performance than a Boot Camp solution, but it is more convenient for running an occasional application or game.

Consider three options for virtualizing Windows on your iMac:

- **VMWare Fusion (www.vmware.com)**—A stable solution from a leader in virtualization software. VMWare Fusion is rock solid and fully compatible with a wide range of virtual "appliances" available for VMWare on Windows.

- **Parallels Desktop (www.parallels.com)**—The widest range of features available of any virtualization solution for OS X, including near-seamless integration with Mac applications.

- **VirtualBox (www.virtualbox.org)**—Free virtualization software that offers many of the same features of VMWare and Parallels. VirtualBox is not as polished as the commercial solutions, but it's well supported and has excellent performance.

Other Operating Systems

Virtualization isn't limited to running Windows. You can also run other operating systems, such as Linux, Chrome, and Solaris, using any of these solutions. In fact, if you have enough memory, you can run two, three, or more operating systems simultaneously.

Use the sidebar
to quickly access
locations, files, and
set tags.

Navigate and
customize your
workspace in the
Finder.

Receive important
information in
the Notification
Center.

The Dock serves as a
launching point for
common applications
and documents.

In this chapter, you learn how to make efficient use of your screen space.

- → Organizing files using the Dock
- → Navigating folders within the Dock's Grid view mode
- → Customizing the Finder sidebar and toolbar
- → Creating Finder tabs
- → Organizing with File Tags
- → Viewing the contents of files with Quick Look
- → Searching for files and information with Spotlight
- → Keeping track of application events with Notifications

Managing Your Desktop

Your Mac is a powerful machine, capable of working with hundreds of different types of files and managing gigabytes upon gigabytes of data. Back when I got my first 128K Mac (w/ floppy), you barely needed folders because only a few files fit on a disk. Today, if you try to count the number of files on your system at any given point in time, the numbers will come back in the hundreds of thousands. The world is more complex, and so are our computers.

To keep things tidy, you can take advantage of a variety of time- and space-saving tools built into Mavericks that will help keep your desktop clean, make working with files and applications fun and efficient, and keep you up-to-date on how your system and applications are performing. You'll see that, no matter the size of your screen, Mavericks can make working with your computer easier and more intuitive.

Organizing in the Dock

The Mavericks Dock serves as application launcher, filer, and process manager. It enables you to launch applications and documents with a single click, place documents in folders, and even navigate the contents of folders without using the Finder. It also displays running applications so you can easily switch between them. Configuring your Dock to suit your working style and habits can be a big time saver because you don't have to dig through folders within folders just to find a single file.

The Dock is divided into two parts—applications, and files and folders. Applications are on the left of the faint broken line; files and folders are on the right (or top/bottom, if the Dock is oriented vertically).

Applications

Files, folders, minimized windows

Running applications

Trash

Adding and Removing Items from the Dock

Adding files and folders to the Dock is a simple process of dragging and dropping.

1. Use the Finder to locate the icon you want to add to the Dock.

2. Drag the item from the Finder window to the appropriate side of the Dock (apps on the left, docs and folders on the right). As you drag the icon into the Dock, the existing icons move to make room for the addition. Release your mouse when you're happy with the new location.

3. You can rearrange Dock items at any time by dragging them to another position in the Dock.

4. To remove an icon from the Dock, click and drag the icon out of the Dock.

Keep Your Apps Handy

If you start an application and decide you want to keep it in the Dock, click and hold the icon of the running application, and then choose Options, Keep in Dock from the menu that appears.

Using Folders and Stacks in the Dock

Folders that are added to the Dock behave differently from files or applications. When you click a folder residing on the Dock, the contents of the folder are displayed above it in one of three different styles—a Fan, Grid, or List. Additionally, the folder icons themselves can be shown as a simple folder or a stack of files, with your most recent file at the top.

Configuring Folders and Stacks

You can dramatically change the behavior of folders and stacks in the Dock by using the configuration options.

1. After adding a folder to the Dock, right-click or Control-click the folder to open the menu to configure its behavior.

2. Choose to Display as a Folder or Stack to customize the appearance of the icon on the Dock.

3. Choose Fan, Grid, List, or Automatic to set how the content will be displayed when you click the icon in the Dock. The Automatic setting will choose the best option based on the number of items in the folder.

4. Finally, to customize the sorting of the displayed items, choose an option from the Sort By menu.

Navigating Files and Folders in Grid Mode

In Mavericks, the Folder Grid mode offers the most functionality for navigating your files. You can navigate through a scrolling list of files, and you can open additional folders.

1. Click a Folder in the Dock that has been configured to Grid mode. A grid popover appears above the folder icon.

2. Scroll through the available files, if needed.

3. To navigate into a folder, click the folder's icon.

4. The Grid refreshes to show the contents of the folder.

5. Click the back arrow in the upper-left corner to return to the previous "parent" folder.

6. Click Open in Finder if you wish to open the current folder as a window in the Finder.

Customizing the Dock's Appearance

The Dock helps keep your desktop nice and tidy by giving you a place to put your commonly used files and folders, but it also takes up a bit of screen space. You can easily customize the Dock's appearance to make it as unobtrusive as possible.

1. Open the System Preferences panel, and click the Dock icon.

2. Use the Size slider to change the size of the Dock.

3. Click the Magnification checkbox. Use the corresponding slider to set the magnification of the icons as you mouse over them in the Dock.

4. Use the radio buttons to control the position of the Dock on the screen.

5. To control the way windows animate to and from the Dock, click the Minimize Windows Using drop-down menu to choose between the Genie and Scale effects.

6. Choose Double-click a Window's Title Bar to provide a quick means of minimizing a window into the Dock without having to click the minimize button.

7. Check the Minimize Windows into Application Icon checkbox to help conserve space in the Dock by putting minimized windows into their applications' Dock icons.

8. By default, application icons "bounce" in the Dock while they're opening. Uncheck the Animate Opening Applications checkbox to disable this behavior.

9. Click Automatically Hide and Show the Dock if you'd like the Dock to disappear altogether when you're not using it.

10. Check Show Indicator Lights for Open Applications if you'd like a dot to appear under applications that are running.

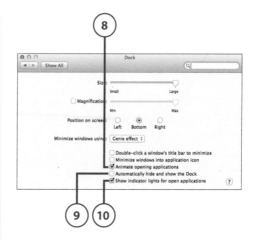

Hiding the Dock

To quickly hide the Dock, press Command+Option+D. You can also easily toggle the position and magnification of the Dock using the Dock submenu from the Apple menu.

Customizing Finder Windows

Like the Dock, Finder windows provide an opportunity to configure shortcuts to information that are accessible via a single click. The Finder sidebar and toolbar can be customized with your own files as well as default system shortcuts.

Configuring the Sidebar's System Shortcuts

To change the sidebar's default shortcuts, you need to use the Finder preferences.

1. Open the Finder using its icon in the Dock and choose Finder, Preferences.

2. Click the Sidebar icon at the top of the Finder Preferences window.

3. Use the checkboxes beside Favorites, Shared, Devices, and Tags to configure which folders, network computers, connected hardware, and file tags should be displayed.

4. Close the Finder Preferences window.

Manually Modifying the Sidebar

In addition to the predefined short-cuts, you can easily add your own icons to the sidebar.

1. To add an icon to the sidebar, first make sure the item's icon is vis-ible in a Finder window.

2. Drag the icon to the Favorites area in the sidebar.

3. A blue line appears to show where the item will be placed. Release your mouse button to add the item to the list.

4. The icon appears in the sidebar.

5. Rearrange the icons in the sidebar by clicking and dragging them up and down.

6. Remove existing sidebar entries by right-clicking (or Control-clicking) their icons and choosing Remove from Sidebar. Alterna-tively, just click and drag them from the sidebar.

Modifying the Finder Toolbar

Like the sidebar, the Finder window's toolbar can hold shortcuts to files, folders, and applications.

1. Open the Finder window containing the file or folder you want to work with.

2. Drag the icon you wish to add into the toolbar. The other interface elements shift to make room for the new addition.

3. To move an icon to a new location on the toolbar, hold the Command key down, and then click and drag. Drag the icon off the toolbar to remove it altogether.

Dragging Allowed!

Toolbar and sidebar items can serve as drag destinations as well as clickable shortcuts. For example, to file a document in a folder, you can drag it to a folder in the sidebar. To save a document to a file server, you can drag it onto a shared drive, and so on.

Using Finder Window Tabs

For years your web browser has had tabs to help you browse without having dozens of windows open at a time. In Mavericks, the Finder offers the same feature. You can open a new tab in a Finder window by following these steps.

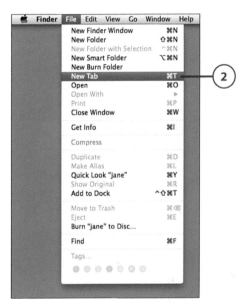

1. Make sure that a Finder window is open. It doesn't matter what view it is showing.

2. Choose File, New Tab (Command+T) from the menu bar.

3. A new tab appears in the Finder window.

4. After the first tab appears, you can add new tabs by clicking the + icon at the right of the tab bar.

5. You can use each tab as a unique window, browsing different parts of the file system in each.

6. Close a tab by positioning your cursor near its left side and clicking the X box that appears.

Ever-Present Tabs

If you like seeing the tab bar all the time (even if you don't have multiple tabs open), you can choose Show Tab Bar from the Finder's View menu. This makes the + icon always visible, so adding new tabs becomes easier.

Opening Tabs with a Click

In the Safari web browser (read about it in Chapter 5, "Accessing Email and the Web"), you can open new tabs just by holding Command and clicking. You can do the same with the right preferences set in the Finder. To do this, just complete the following:

1. Choose Finder, Preferences from the menu bar.

2. Make sure the General tab is selected.

3. Check Open Folders in Tabs Instead of New Windows

4. Close the Finder Preferences window.

5. From this point forward, when you hold Command while clicking a folder, the folder opens in a new tab rather than a window.

Tabs Are a Drag

Although it may not seem intuitive, you can drag files from one tab to another. Just drag the file into the tab where you want to drop it, keep holding, and after a few seconds the other tab opens, enabling you to continue your drag. Additionally, when you grab a tab itself and drag it out of the window, a new Finder window is created.

Arranging and Grouping Files

You might have noticed that this book doesn't take a bunch of time to tell you about how to sort files, open folders, and all the typical things you do on a computer. Why? Because they work exactly the way you'd expect on a modern operating system. That said, Mavericks has some interesting ways of looking at files that you might not be aware of.

Using All My Files

If you've ever wanted to view all the files you have, the All My Files group will help you. This feature displays, quite literally, *all* your files in your personal account, including files stored in iCloud (see Chapter 4, "Setting Up iCloud Services and Internet Accounts," for more details). To view your files, follow these steps:

1. Make sure the Favorites section of the Finder sidebar is expanded.

2. Click the All My Files icon, or choose Go, All My Files from the menu bar.

3. All the files that belong to you are shown in the Finder window.

4. Use the view icons to change between icon, list, column, and coverflow views, respectively.

Granted, this isn't the most exciting feature in the world, but when coupled with the Arrange By feature (covered in the next task), it becomes far more interesting.

Arranging a Finder View

You're probably used to clicking a column heading and sorting files by name, date, modified, or other attributes. This is expanded in OS X with the Arrange By feature. Using Arrange By, you can view your files arranged by more "human" categories, such as the files you've opened today, in the last week, and so on.

1. Open the finder view you want to arrange.

2. Use the Arrange By menu to select a category for grouping your files.

3. Different groups are separated by horizontal lines.

4. When in icon view mode, swipe left or right on a multitouch trackpad or Magic Mouse to scroll through a coverflow-like view of the icons within a grouping.

5. Click the Show All link to turn off the Cover Flow scrolling and show all the items within the window.

Making Arrangements

To set a default arrangement (among other things) for a folder, choose View, Show View Options from the menu bar when viewing the folder.

Assigning Tags

When choosing an arrangement for a view, you may notice a Tags category. This is a new feature to Mavericks that offers the ability to assign tags to your files and folders. These can be anything you want—"Important," "Projects," and so on. They are arbitrary text descriptions that you establish and can use to label any of your files or folders, no matter where they exist on your system.

1. Select a file or folder in a Finder window.

2. Click the Tags button in the Finder toolbar.

3. Either type in a new tag, or choose an existing tag from the menu.

4. Click outside the menu to assign the tags.

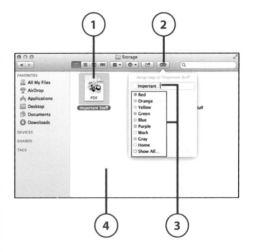

Mavericks *Loves* Tags

Truth be told, there are a million and one ways to assign tags in Mavericks. You can do it using the method just described; you can add tags by clicking the file name on a window in many Mavericks applications; you can assign tags by choosing Finder, Get Info when a file or folder is selected. I could write a whole chapter on adding tags, but I suggest you find a method you prefer and stick with it.

Removing Tags

After you start adding tags in Mavericks, you'll quickly discover that you can add as many tags to an individual file or folder as you want. As a result, you might want to remove a tag you added in error.

1. Select a file or folder in a Finder window.

2. Click the Tags button in the Finder toolbar.

3. All of the assigned tags appear in the field at the top of the drop-down menu.

4. Click to highlight a tag, and either press delete or drag it to the trash.

5. Click outside of the menu to save the new tag list.

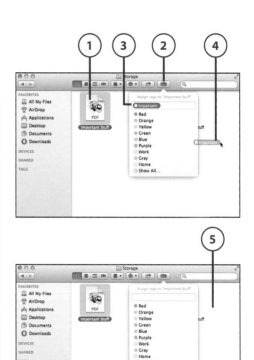

Viewing Tags

After you've assigned tags, you can view them using the Tags section in the Finder sidebar.

1. Make sure the Tags section is visible.

2. Click the tag you want to view or All Tags if your tag list is long and the one you want isn't visible.

3. Files and folders matching the tag are displayed. Note that if the tag has an assigned color, it will be displayed as a color-coded dot beside the file in many of the standard finder views.

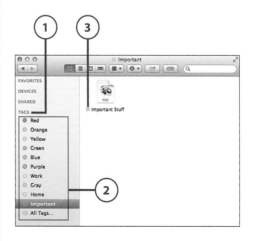

4. You can drag new files and folders into the window to assign them to the tag. (I told you there were a million ways to assign tags!)

Tags—Seriously, They're Everywhere

When you open files, notice that Tags now appear in the sidebar within the File Open dialog box. You can use these to quickly view all the files matching a tag and open a file without having to find its folder.

The "Finding Information with Spotlight" section later in this chapter explains how Spotlight can be used to search for files matching certain tags and other criteria (for example, "All images with the tag 'Vacation' created between the dates of June 2014 and August 2014").

Managing Tags

To see, edit, and assign colors to your tags, use the Finder preferences.

1. Choose Finder, Preferences from the menu bar.

2. Click the Tags tab at the top of the Preferences window.

3. Use the checkboxes to control which tags are visible in the Finder sidebar.

4. Click the circle beside a tag to choose a color for it.

5. Click a tag's name to edit it.

6. Drag Tags to the rectangular list of Tags at the bottom to have quick access to them through Finder contextual menus or the Finder's File menu (yet *another* way to add tags to files and folders!).

Missing Tags?

If the Tags section is missing from your Finder sidebar, you might have disabled it accidentally. You can add the Tags section back using the Sidebar Finder preferences (Finder, Preferences).

Previewing Document Contents with Quick Look

Launching applications takes time and resources. Frequently, when you want to open a file, all you really want is to see the contents of the file. Using the equivalent of X-Ray vision, called Quick Look, you can view many of your documents without the need to open an application.

Viewing a File with Quick Look

Using Quick Look doesn't require anything more than your mouse and a press of the spacebar.

1. Select a file from the Finder or Desktop by clicking once, but don't open it!

2. Press the spacebar to open Quick Look.

3. Click the double arrows to expand Quick Look to fullscreen.

4. Some files might show additional controls above the preview or below when in fullscreen mode. An image, for example, includes a button to open in the Preview application, or, when in fullscreen mode, add the file to iPhoto.

5. Press the spacebar again to exit Quick Look (not shown). Note that if you are in fullscreen mode, you need to push Escape (Esc) on your keyboard or press the onscreen X button to exit fullscreen mode before exiting Quick Look.

Instant Slideshows!

If you start Quick Look on multiple files, you can run a slideshow. The fullscreen Quick Look window includes play, forward, and backward arrows to start and control the slideshow. You can also use an index sheet icon (four squares) to show previews of all the files in a single Quick Look window (also available in windowed mode).

Quick Look even works on music and video files, enabling you to play back media without opening a dedicated application.

Previewing Files Using Finder Icons

The Finder includes Quick Look-like capability for some files just by mousing over them.

1. To preview a file using icons in Mavericks, make sure you're in icon view mode.

2. Mouse over the file, and use the controls that appear to navigate the contents of the file. As with Quick Look, even media files can be played in this manner.

Adjust Icon Size

For quick access to a slider for changing your icon sizes, choose View, Show Status Bar from the menu bar. Alternatively, you can adjust a window's icon size by choosing View, Show View Options from the menu bar.

Using Instant-Access Utilities in the Dashboard

Sometimes it is handy to be able to access information and simple utilities without moving your windows around or digging through your Applications folder to find what you need. For simple tasks, you can to use a Dashboard widget.

The Dashboard is an overlay of useful tools, called widgets, which you can call up and dismiss with a single keystroke. Widgets that you add to the Dashboard persist between reboots, so when you've configured your Dashboard the way you like it, it's there to stay!

Activating the Dashboard

The Mavericks Dashboard appears and disappears with a keystroke or a click.

1. To activate the Dashboard, click the Dashboard icon in the Dock (or in the Applications folder), or, even easier, swipe with four fingers to the right across your Magic Trackpad (not shown).

2. The desktop slides out of the way and a default set of Dashboard widgets displays.

3. You can now interact with any of the widgets, including dragging them around to rearrange them, just as you would with normal applications.

4. Exit Dashboard by clicking the arrow in the lower right of the Dashboard or swiping with four fingers to the left.

Tweaking Your Shortcuts

To configure additional shortcuts to the Dashboard, you can visit the Mission Control system preference panel. Read more in Chapter 2, "Making the Most of Your Screen Space."

Adding and Removing Dashboard Widgets

One of the best things about widgets is that you can keep adding them to your screen, and they'll always be there until you choose to remove them.

1. To add (or remove) a widget in the Dashboard, start the Dashboard and click the + icon in the lower-left corner. A screen of widgets displays.

2. If you have many widgets, use the search field, if needed, to find what you are looking for.

3. To add a widget to your desktop, click its icon. The list of widgets disappears and you return to the Dashboard with the new widget visible.

4. To remove a single widget, hold Option, position your mouse over the widget, and click the X icon in the widget's upper-left corner.

5. To remove several widgets, click the – icon in the lower-left corner, and all the widgets display the X icon in their corner. Tap the X for each widget you want to remove.

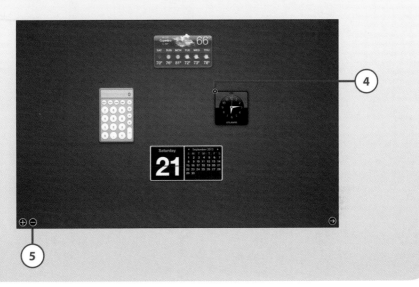

Configuring Dashboard Widgets

Widgets are unique applications that each behave differently; but, in general, you configure them one of two ways.

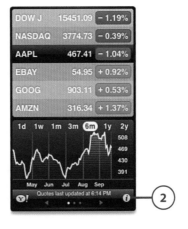

1. Some widgets, when you add them to your screen, automatically prompt you with the information they are expecting. Other widgets must be configured in order to show the proper results.

2. Mouse over a widget you want to configure. A small "i" appears in the corner of the widget. Click the "i" icon.

3. The widget flips over, revealing the configuration details.

Get More Widgets!

To find new widgets outside of the Dashboard, visit www.apple.com/ downloads/dashboard/Widgets to download a file in your Downloads folder. You can install them by double-clicking their icons.

Launchpad in Disguise

The view for adding widgets to the Dashboard is really just a feature called Launchpad, but customized to only show Dashboard widgets. You can use the same techniques you'll learn about Launchpad in Chapter 2 to organize and manage your widget library.

Finding Information with Spotlight

When the Finder's file organization features can't help you find what you want, the amazing Spotlight search system in Mavericks makes it simple. Spotlight can search across files, email messages, and even the built-in dictionary to find information.

Searching for Files and Information

Spotlight searches can be started at any time, without needing to launch any additional applications.

1. To start a search, press Command+Space, or click the magnifying glass icon in the upper-right corner of your screen. A search field appears.

2. Begin typing in the search field.

3. As you type, files, images, folders, and even definitions that match your terms are displayed in a list.

4. Hover your mouse over a result to see a preview.

5. Click a matched item in the list to open the item.

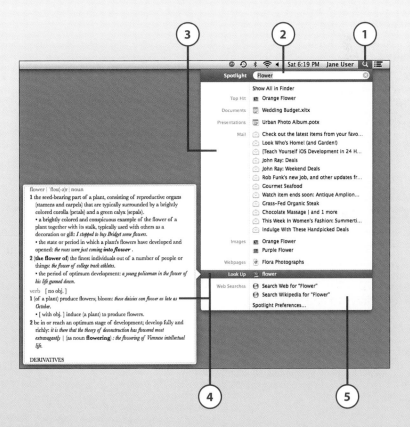

Customizing Spotlight Searching

Spotlight searches can turn up tons of information. More, perhaps, than you'd like. To choose exactly what you want to display, you need to configure the Spotlight System Preferences panel.

1. Open the Spotlight System Preferences panel.

2. Within the Search Results panel, check items you want to be returned as part of the search results. Uncheck the items you want to exclude.

3. To restrict what volumes are searched, click the Privacy button. You can choose to have Spotlight ignore specific folders or disks.

4. Click the + button to choose a folder or disk that you don't want to be searchable. Alternatively, drag folders directly from the Finder into the Privacy list.

5. Use the checkboxes to change how Spotlight is started or disable keyboard shortcuts altogether.

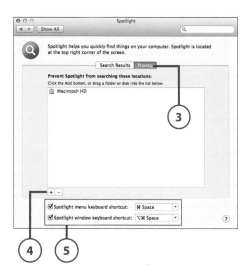

Saving Searches as Smart Folders in the Finder

Spotlight searches for files can be saved and reused in the form of Smart Folders. If you'd like to create a search that shows all your image files—regardless of where they are stored, for example—you can create and save a Show All Images search.

1. Use a Finder window's search field to type the name or content of a file you want to find.

2. Choose what the search should include (such as a file name). The default is to include file content, kinds, and other metadata.

3. Adjust whether you want to search your entire Mac (indicated by the words "This Mac") or just the folder you're currently in.

4. Use the + and – buttons below the search field to add or subtract additional search criteria lines.

5. Use the pop-up menu at the start of each search line to configure search attributes such as file, kinds, or size.

6. To add even more search criteria, choose Other. A window listing the available search attributes displays. Choose an attribute and click OK.

7. When you're satisfied with your search, click the Save button.

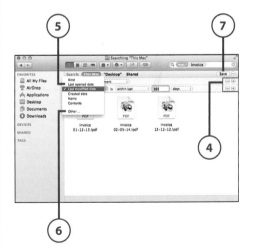

8. You are prompted for a name for the search and where it should be saved.

9. Click Add to Sidebar.

10. Click Save.

11. If you choose to add the search to your sidebar, it is accessible immediately from your Finder window. Otherwise you need to navigate to the saved location and double-click the search's Smart Folder icon to run it again.

Less Is More

After you've configured a few search criteria beyond the text for the file name or file content, you can erase the search text and Mavericks includes all of the files that match your other criteria.

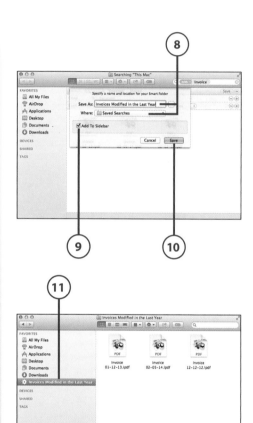

Keeping Track of System Events with Notifications

At any given time, your computer has quite a bit going on—mail being checked, potential FaceTime invites, software updates, and more. To keep you in the loop, applications have traditionally displayed alert messages, made sounds, or used any number of other methods to get your attention. In Mavericks, applications that you purchase from the App Store (and OS X itself) can present notifications to you in a simple, unified manner.

Receiving Notifications

To receive a notification, you technically don't need to do anything, but you should know what to expect:

1. Notifications, as they occur, appear along the right side of the display.

2. Most notifications go away after a few seconds and require no interaction. Some might include options to immediately react to the notification. Clicking the buttons performs the action described.

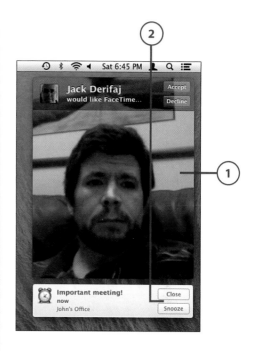

Viewing the Notification Center

If a notification "goes away" before you have a chance to read it, you can catch up with the latest notifications in the Notification Center.

1. Click the bulleted list icon in the upper-right corner of the menu bar. You can also open the Notification Center with a trackpad gesture by sliding two fingers to the left, starting off the right side of the trackpad.

2. The desktop slides over to reveal the Notification Center.

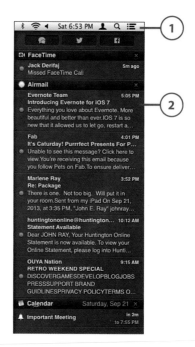

3. Clicking a notification reacts appropriately—clicking an event reminder, for example, opens the Calendar application and high-lights the event.

4. To dismiss an application's noti-fications, click the X icon in the upper-right corner of its list of notifications.

5. To close the Notification Center, click on the Desktop, or slide two fingers to the right on the trackpad.

Customizing the Notification Display

How each application presents notifications (or if they present notifications
at all) can be customized in OS X.

1. Open the Notifications System
   Preferences panel.

2. Choose an Application to customize from the list on the left.

3. Use the alert style buttons to
   choose from None (no visual at
   all), Banners (automatically close),
   and Alerts (stay on the screen
   until manually dismissed).

4. Check Show Notifications on Lock
   Screen if you want to see the notifications when your Mac's screen
   is locked.

5. Uncheck Show in Notification
   Center if you prefer to not receive
   any notifications (visual or audio)
   from the application.

6. Use the Recent Items pop-up
   menu to choose how many notifications are shown at a time.

7. Check the Badge App Icon with
   Notification Count to show the
   count of notifications (such as
   new messages) on the application's icon.

8. Check Play Sound for Notifications to enable the application to provide an audio alert.

9. Select whether to Sort Notification Center manually or according to the time a notification was received. If sorting manually, you can drag the icons up and down in the application list to choose how they appear in the Notification Center.

Gone but Not Lost

If you uncheck "Show in Notification Center" for an application, it disappears from the list of applications to configure. What if you want to get it back? Never fear—it didn't really disappear—it was just placed at the bottom of the app list, in a section titled "Not In Notification Center."

Quick Settings Access Within Notification Center

In the lower-right corner of the Notification Center is a button labeled with a small gear icon. Clicking this button opens the Notification Center preferences.

Activating Do Not Disturb Mode

If you're like me, you probably have a zillion different things happening on your computer and (potentially) several dozen apps wanting to tell you something via notification. For the times you'd prefer not to hear all the sounds and see the notification windows, you can activate a Do Not Disturb mode that lasts until the next morning. Begin by opening the Notification Center, and then follow these steps:

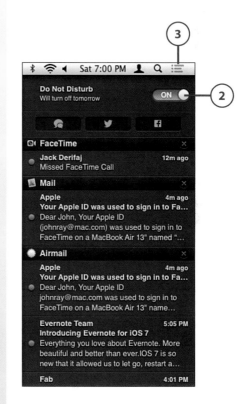

1. Scroll the Notification Center content down.

2. An On/Off button is revealed. Click Off to quiet your notifications or On to let them be seen and heard.

3. The Notification Center icon becomes dimmed when in Do Not Disturb mode.

Do Not Disturb Me NOW!

Want to activate Do Not Disturb mode in a flash? Just hold the option key and click the Notification Center icon in the menubar. The icon will gray to show it is disabled. Repeat the process to turn it back on.

Customizing Do Not Disturb Mode

It's simple to activate Do Not Disturb when you need it, but you can customize the feature to automatically activate in situations where you typically don't want notifications to be appearing.

1. Open the Notifications System Preferences Panel.

2. Select the Do Not Disturb option.

3. Provide a time range (and check the checkbox) to automatically apply Do Not Disturb during a common time period (for example, night time).

4. Check When Mirroring to TVs and Projectors to keep notifications from showing up when you're displaying content on a TV or a projector.

5. Use the Allow FaceTime calls drop-down menu and checkbox to choose a group of people that should be allowed to call you during Do Not Disturb hours.

6. Click the Allow Repeated Calls checkbox to disable Do Not Disturb for individuals who have called repeatedly (in case of potential emergencies).

Navigate Desktop spaces and applications.

Create new spaces to make room for your work.

View active applications and windows in Mission Control.

In this chapter, you learn how to take control of your applications and windows, including:

→ Finding your way around Mission Control
→ Managing applications and windows
→ Creating new spaces
→ Launching applications with Launchpad
→ Creating application groups in Launchpad
→ Uninstalling applications through Launchpad
→ Managing auto open and save features

Making the Most of Your Screen Space

As applications become more complex, so does the task of managing them. Software is installed everywhere, windows are spread out over your desktop, and just trying to find your way through the maze of information overload can be nightmarish. Mavericks attempts to bring the madness under control by way of Mission Control.

Mission Control, combined with features such as Spaces, Launchpad, full-screen apps, auto application, and window restoration, makes it easy to navigate the most cluttered computer. The biggest problem? Many of these features are hidden until you invoke them. In this chapter, you learn how to do just that!

Swimming in a Sea of Application Windows with Mission Control

One of the big benefits of modern operating systems is that they enable you to run multiple applications at once. Unfortunately, no matter how much screen space we have, we always need more! To help manage the ever-expanding collection of windows that you need to work within, Apple provides Mission Control as part of OS X Mavericks. Mission Control helps you view your running apps, see the windows they have open, and even expand the amount of desktop real estate you have available.

Opening and Closing Mission Control

To manage Mission Control and access its features, follow these instructions:

1. Slide three fingers up your trackpad, double-tap two fingers on the Magic Mouse, or press the Mission Control key (F3) on your keyboard. Mission Control opens. Spaces appear on the top; the current space is in the center of the screen.

2. Slide three fingers down on the trackpad, double-tap two fingers on the mouse, or press the Mission Control key again. Mission Control closes.

In Mission Control terms, a "space" is a single screenful of information. It can be your Dashboard screen, your typical desktop, a full-screen app, or even additional desktop views that you create.

Docking Mission Control

If you prefer to start Mission Control by clicking, you can use the Mission Control icon. It's in the Dock on machines without a multitouch trackpad—but you can add it from the Applications folder on any Mac.

Navigating Applications and Windows

When you start Mission Control, your current space (probably your desktop, if you're starting Mission Control for the first time) is front and center, along with representations of each app running in the space and its windows.

To switch between applications and their windows, do the following:

1. Start Mission Control.

2. Click an application icon to exit Mission Control and bring the application to the front.

3. Click a window to exit Mission Control and bring the chosen window to the front.

4. To preview the contents of a window, position your pointer over the window and then press the spacebar. Press the spacebar again to hide the preview.

Creating and Populating a New Space

Modern applications look like the cockpit controls of advanced aircraft; it can be overwhelming finding your way around a single application—let alone 10. With Mission Control, however, you can create new desktop spaces dedicated to whatever applications you'd like. To do so, start Mission Control and follow these steps:

1. Move your mouse to the upper-right corner. A + button appears as your mouse approaches the corner; click it.

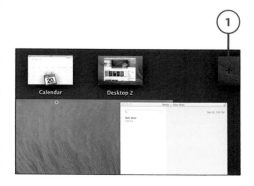

2. A new space is created and a thumbnail of its contents is added to the top of Mission Control.

3. Drag application icons or even individual windows from the current space to the thumbnail of the new space.

Switching Between Spaces

After you've created a new space, you can switch to it via Mission Control or using a trackpad gesture:

1. Start Mission Control.

2. Click the space thumbnail you want to display, or swipe left or right with three fingers to move between spaces.

3. Click on the background to exit Mission Control.

Even Faster Space Switching

The fastest way to switch between Mission Control spaces is without even starting Mission Control. Swipe left or right with three fingers on your trackpad (or two fingers on the Magic Mouse) at any time to move between spaces.

Closing a Space

It's so easy to create spaces, you might find yourself with some extra ones you need to get rid of. To close out a space, follow these steps:

1. Start Mission Control.

2. Position your cursor over a space.

3. After a few seconds, an X appears in the upper-left corner of the space thumbnail. Click the X to close the space. Any windows within it move back to the primary desktop space.

Creating Full-Screen Application Spaces

Spaces are great for providing more, um, space for your windowed applications, but they also serve as a "container" for your full-screen apps. Rather than a full-screen application eating up one of your desktop spaces, it automatically creates a new dedicated space when it starts and removes it when it stops.

1. Click the double-arrow icon in the upper-right corner of the application window to enter full-screen mode.

2. A new space is created and is visible in Mission Control.

3. Switch to and from the space exactly as you would any other. When you're done using the full-screen app, either quit the application or exit full-screen mode. The space is automatically removed from Mission Control.

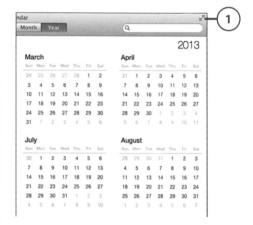

Choosing Between Application Windows

When you just need to navigate your windows, the Mission Control Application windows option comes in handy. Using this, you can show all your application windows, or just the windows for a specific program, with a single click.

1. To display all the windows open within an application, click and hold an active application's icon in the dock and choose Show All Windows. Alternatively, press Control+down arrow.

2. The screen refreshes to show miniature versions of your windows. Minimized windows appear in the bottom portion of the display; active windows appear at the top.

3. Press the Tab key to switch between active applications, limiting the miniaturized windows to the highlighted application.

4. Click a window to select it and move it to the front.

Showing the Desktop

Sometimes you need quick access to the files on your desktop, and rearranging windows (or using the Finder's Hide menu) isn't very efficient. Mission Control's Show Desktop feature comes in handy here:

1. To clear all the windows off the screen so that you can temporarily work with the desktop, press F11 (you need to hold down the function key).

2. You can now work within the desktop with no obstructions. Press F11 again to return the windows to their original positions.

If Only Real Life Were So Easy...

To quickly drop a file from the Finder into another application (such as an attachment into an email message), start dragging a file while the desktop is cleared, press F11 to return the windows to the screen, and then finish dragging and dropping the file into an application.

Configuring Mission Control Features and Shortcuts

If you have a specific way of working and want to customize how Mission Control or any of its features is activated, just follow these steps:

1. Open the System Preferences application, and click the Mission Control panel icon.

2. If you'd like Dashboard to appear on top of your current space rather than in its own space, uncheck Show Dashboard As a Space.

3. Uncheck Automatically Rearrange Spaces Based on Most Recent Use if you prefer that Mavericks keeps your spaces in the same order you add them, regardless of your usage patterns.

4. In most cases, leave When Switching to an Application, Switch to a Space with Open Windows for the Application checkbox checked. This indicates that when you switch to an application (using the Dock or Command+Tab), you automatically switch to the space that contains its open windows.

5. If you prefer application windows to not be grouped under their application icon in the Mission Control display, uncheck Group Windows by Application.

6. If you're lucky enough to have multiple monitors connected to your Mac, check Displays Have Separate Spaces to have each display act as a separate work area with its own collection of fullscreen apps and workspaces. To use the monitors as a single unified space, uncheck this option.

7. At the bottom of the panel, use the pop-up menus to configure keyboard and mouse button combinations to invoke the Mission Control features and Dashboard.

8. To trigger these features by moving the mouse to the screen corners, click the Hot Corners button.

9. Use the pop-up menus beside each screen corner to choose among the different options. After you've made a selection, just move the mouse into that corner to invoke the feature.

10. Click OK when finished.

11. Close the System Preferences.

Remember Your Gestures!

As you know, you control Mission Control through gestures, and these aren't set in stone! Use the trackpad or Mouse System Preferences panels to configure the gestures used by Mission Control.

Managing and Launching Applications with Launchpad

Whereas Mission Control helps you find your way through your windows, the Launchpad eliminates the need to open them. Launchpad brings iOS-like application management to your Mac. Instead of digging through folders to launch an application, you simply start Launchpad and all your installed apps are visible in one place. No digging required.

Starting Launchpad

Like Mission Control, Apple wants to keep Launchpad at the ready. Unlike other applications, it takes no time to start and can be invoked through a gesture:

1. Open Launchpad by performing a pinching gesture with your thumb and three fingers on your trackpad. Alternatively, press the Launchpad key (F4), or click the Launchpad icon in the Dock or in the Applications folder.

2. The Launchpad appears, blurring out your background.

3. Reverse the pinching gesture, or click on the background to exit Launchpad.

Navigating Launchpad

If you've used an iPad or an iPhone, you immediately know how to navigate Launchpad. If you haven't, don't worry—it takes about a minute to learn everything you'll need to know.

1. Open Launchpad to access your applications.

2. Click an application icon to launch it.

3. Click a folder icon to open it.

4. Click outside the folder to close it.

5. There can be multiple pages of icons, represented by the dots at the center bottom of the screen.

6. Move between pages by swiping left or right with your fingers, clicking the dots, or clicking and dragging left or right.

Searching Launchpad

If you can't find an application you're looking for, you can easily search for it directly in Launchpad.

1. Open Launchpad.

2. Click to type in the search field.

3. Enter a few characters of the name of the application you're looking for.

4. Launchpad refreshes to show the search results. The best match is highlighted.

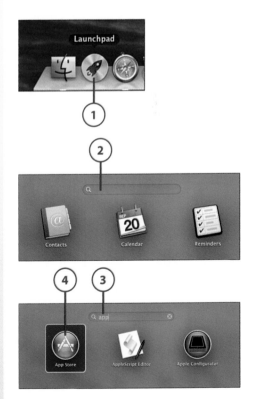

Rearranging Icons

The Launchpad display is completely customizable. To rearrange the icons on your screen, follow these instructions:

1. Open Launchpad.

2. Click and drag the icon to a new location—even a new page. Release the mouse to place the icon.

It's Not All Good

A MAC DISGUISED AS AN iPAD

Launchpad suffers from a bit of an identity crisis. It follows the same "click and hold to enter icon wiggle mode," just like iOS. This behavior, however, isn't necessary for rearranging or even deleting icons as it is in iOS. Whether you use it is up to you and completely superficial. You can even make the icons wiggle manually by pressing and holding the Option key on your keyboard.

Creating New Folders

Unlike folders in the Finder, Launch-pad folders are created on the fly and automatically disappear when all their contents are removed. To create a folder in Launchpad, follow these steps:

1. Open Launchpad.

2. Drag an icon on top of another icon that you want to group it with.

3. A new folder is created and opened, and the icons are added.

4. Click the title of the folder to rename it.

5. Click on the background outside the folder to close it.

The Folder That Wasn't There

Folders you create or delete in Launchpad do not alter your file system. They are purely logical group-ings and do not affect the location of your actual files.

Deleting Folders

To remove a folder from Launchpad, follow these instructions:

1. Open Launchpad.

2. Click the folder that you want to remove.

3. The folder opens.

4. Drag each item out of the folder.

5. When you reach the last item, the folder vanishes automatically.

Deleting Applications

In addition to providing a quick way to access your applications, Launchpad offers an easy way to uninstall applications that you've installed from the Mac App Store. (See Chapter 10, "Installing and Managing Software on Your Mac," for details.)

1. Open Launchpad.

2. Drag an application you want to uninstall to the trash. Alternatively, click and hold on the icon until an X appears in the upper left, and click the X.

3. You are prompted to confirm the deletion.

4. Click Delete. The application is uninstalled from your system. You can reinstall it through the App Store if needed.

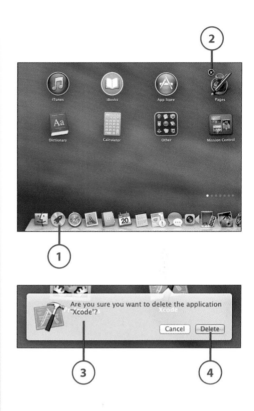

Are you sure you want to delete the application "Xcode"?

Cancel   Delete

It's Not All Good

THE NOT-SO-UNIVERSAL UNINSTALLER

You can only use Launchpad for uninstalling applications you've added through the Mac App Store. To remove other apps, you need to revert to the old-school method of using an uninstaller (if one came with the application) or manually dragging the application files to the trash.

Managing Auto Open and Save Features

Mavericks offers some unique features that save you time when you're booting your system after some downtime, starting an application you use frequently, or even just saving files. Although these can be useful, they can also be disconcerting to users who expect more conventional behavior—such as explicitly choosing when to open applications and save files.

Toggling Application Auto Open

By default, applications and windows open at login exactly as you had them when you shut down your computer. This is a nifty feature, but it also means you might have software starting at boot that you didn't intend. You can toggle this feature on and off by following these steps:

1. Choose Log Out from the Apple menu.

2. Uncheck Reopen Windows When Logging Back In to disable automatic application startup, or check the box to re-enable it.

3. Click Log Out or Cancel. Your preference will be maintained regardless of your choice.

Setting Window Restoration

In addition to restoring applications, Mavericks can restore the open files and windows that you were using when you quit an application. By default, this feature is turned off, but you can easily toggle it on.

1. Open the System Preferences application and click the General icon.

2. Uncheck Close Windows When Quitting an Application. This causes your applications to save their current state when they quit. Check the box to disable the behavior.

3. Close the System Preferences.

Temporarily Enable or Disable Window Saving

If you're not sure you want to use the window restoration feature, or you don't want to use it with specific applications, you can temporarily toggle it on and off. To do this, just hold down the Option key when quitting your application. The Quit menu selection changes to Quit and Keep Windows or Quit and Close All Windows, depending on your setting in the General preference panel.

Enabling Manual File Saving

When you start working in Mavericks, you'll notice something "missing" when you work with files: Frequently, you aren't asked to save them when you close them. Mavericks automatically saves your files, even if you prefer that it didn't. To change this, complete these steps:

1. Open the System Preferences application and click the General icon.

2. Check Ask to Keep Changes When Closing Documents.

3. Close the System Preferences.

Configure and control your network interfaces in the Network System Preference Panel.

Use the Wi-Fi status menu to find and join wireless networks.

In this chapter, you learn how to get your Mac online, including tasks like:

→ Connecting to wired networks
→ Connecting to secure wireless networks
→ Configuring network address, DNS, and routing information
→ Verifying network connections
→ Creating VPN connections
→ Managing multiple connections with Locations

3

Connecting Your Mac to a Network

Being connected to a network gives you access to information, files, and services such as email or the Web. Your Mac comes with the latest networking technology—802.11ac Wi-Fi and gigabit Ethernet, making it a snap to connect to existing wired or wireless networks.

In this chapter, we explore the connection options available to you on your Mac.

Connecting to a Wired Network

The most common type of network connection in the business world is a wired Ethernet connection. The cables used to connect to the network look like oversized phone connectors and, as luck has it, plug directly into your Mac's Ethernet port. Your system supports gigabit Ethernet—capable of exchanging information at extremely high speeds.

It's Not All Good

There aren't many things that upset a network administrator more than a person who attempts to guess at the proper configuration of his computer when attaching it to a network. An improperly configured computer can potentially disrupt an entire network, so please make sure you have all the information you need from your administrator or ISP before attempting the things in this chapter!

Making an Ethernet (Wired) Connection

On a network that is set up to auto-matically configure your computer using DHCP, the most complicated thing you need to do is plug in the network cable!

1. Open the System Preferences panel and click the Network icon.

2. The network preference panel displays. All of the active network interfaces are listed here. Red dots indicate that no connection is present on the interface.

3. Plug the network cable into the back of your Mac. After a few seconds, the interface should update, showing a green dot for an active connection. The pane to the right of the interfaces displays the information that your computer is using to communicate online.

Things Not Working?

If your network connection is showing a yellow dot, you might have to configure your settings manually, or if you're using a DSL connection, you might have to use PPPoE to make your connection. If this is the case, skip ahead to "Manually Configuring Network Settings."

If, however, you see a red dot, you need to check your cable or the device you're plugging into because your Macintosh can't detect *any* type of network.

Connecting to a Wireless Network

When wireless network cards first started appearing, they were limited to portable computers. Over the past decade, however, Wi-Fi has taken off as a networking standard for both laptops and desktop computers. Current wireless network speeds are approaching wired connections, so, slowly but surely, wireless is taking over.

Using the built-in AirPort wireless card in your Mac, you can connect to almost any type of wireless network.

>>>Go Further
WHAT TYPE OF WIRELESS NETWORKS CAN MY MAC USE?

The latest Macs can make use of 802.11ac, 802.11n, 802.11a, 802.11b, and 802.11g networks! This represents the full range of consumer and business wireless networking standards. Your Mac is also capable of talking to a wide range of 802.1x authentication protocols and encryption methods. Setup is usually automatic, so you won't need to know the specifics unless your administrator tells you otherwise.

To learn more about wireless security, read http://en.wikipedia.org/wiki/Wireless_security.

Making a Wireless Connection

Apple makes life easy. Your Mac comes ready (and able) to connect to wireless networks with a minimal amount of fuss.

Finding and Connecting to a Network

If you haven't already made a wired connection, your Mac's Wi-Fi (wireless) card will be active and searching for networks that it can connect to.

1. If your Mac finds an available network, it prompts you to make a connection.

2. Choose the network name to connect to. Note that the network signal strength and security are denoted by icons to the right of the name. If a lock is present, the network requires authentication. This is covered in "Authenticating on a Wireless Network" later in this chapter.

3. Click Join to connect to the selected network.

4. If you've been given the specific name of a network (called an SSID) by a network administrator and it doesn't appear in the available networks list, click the Join Other button to enter the name and attempt to find the network.

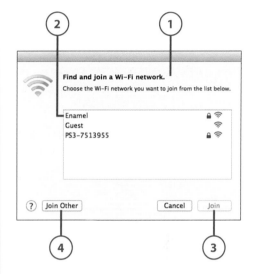

Things Not Working?

If you've successfully connected to a wireless network, but it doesn't seem to work, you might need to configure the network settings manually. Keep in mind that you need to get those settings from your wireless network administrator.

If this is the case, skip ahead to the "Manually Configuring Network Settings" task.

Manually Choosing a Wireless Connection

If you want to manually choose a wireless network connection, you can use the Wi-Fi menu in your menu bar.

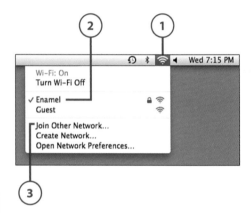

1. The Wi-Fi menu displays a list of all of the available wireless access points, their signal strengths, and their security requirements.

2. Choose the network name to which you want to connect from the list. If you're connecting to a network that shows a lock icon, it requires authentication. This topic is covered in "Authenticating on a Wireless Network" later in this chapter.

3. If you want to connect to a network using only its name, choose Join Other Network to enter the name and attempt the connection.

Alternative Wi-Fi Configuration

If you'd prefer to manage all your network connection information in one place, you can access these same options by opening the Network System Preference panel and selecting the Wi-Fi interface.

You can also use the Show Wi-Fi Status in Menu Bar checkbox to remove or add (if it's missing) the Wi-Fi status menu item.

Authenticating on a Wireless Network

When your Mac connects to an open (unsecured) network, it works immediately. If you're connecting to a network that is secure, however, you need to authenticate, which means you need to provide a password or other identifying information. This requirement is usually denoted by a lock icon next to the network's signal strength icon.

1. If you attempt to connect to a network that has a security requirement, you are prompted for a password.

2. Enter the password (or other information, depending on the security settings).

3. Click Show Password if you'd like to see the password instead of dots while you type.

4. To make sure that the network can be used again in the future without requiring that you retype the password, check the Remember This Network button.

5. Click Join to finish and authenticate to the network.

Disabling (and Enabling) Wireless Networking

Not everyone *wants* to have wireless networking always enabled. It can potentially expose you to network attacks on poorly secured wireless networks. Disabling the Wi-Fi network interface, and re-enabling it, is just a menu option away.

1. To disable the Wi-Fi card, choose Turn Wi-Fi Off from the Wi-Fi status menu.

2. The Wi-Fi menu updates to an outline of the usual multiline symbol. The Wi-Fi hardware is now powered down.

3. To re-enable the Wi-Fi card, choose Turn Wi-Fi On from the Wi-Fi status menu.

Need More Wi-Fi detail? No Problem.

To see all the stats about your Wi-Fi connection, hold Option while clicking the Wi-Fi menu. You'll see signal strength, speed, and more!

Manually Configuring Network Settings

Network connections, when automatically configured, seem to work almost like magic. Your computer finds a signal (wired or wireless), makes a connection, and everything just "works." Behind the scenes, however, there are a handful of network settings that make this happen. If a network doesn't support auto-configuration, using a protocol known as DHCP, you need to make these settings manually.

Your network administrator needs to provide the following settings in order to manually set up your network:

- **IP Address**—A numerical address that uniquely identifies your computer.

- **Subnet Mask**—A value that helps your computer determine what network it is on.

- **Router**—The address of a device that moves network traffic between other local computers and remote networks (such as the Internet).

- **DNS**—The address of a device providing domain name lookups to your network. This service translates human-readable names (such as www.apple.com) into IP addresses and vice-versa.

- **Proxy Settings**—A device that sends and receives network traffic on your behalf, acting as a middleman for services.

Configuring TCP/IP and Proxy Settings

To manually change your TCP/IP and Proxy settings, follow these simple steps:

1. Open System Preferences and click the Network panel icon.

2. The network panel opens, showing all the available interfaces. Click the interface you want to configure (usually Ethernet or Wi-Fi).

3. Click the Advanced button to view the full manual interface for network settings.

4. The Advanced configuration screen appears. Click TCP/IP in the button bar to access the common TCP/IP network settings.

5. Use the Configure IPv4 drop-down menu to change your settings to be configured Manually.

6. Enter the IP address, Subnet Mask, and Router, as provided by your network administrator.

7. Click DNS in the button bar to change your domain name server settings.

8. Click the + button below the DNS Servers list to add a new server to the list. Your ISP or network administrator usually provides at least two addresses to use; be sure to type it exactly as provided. (Use the – button to remove unused DNS Servers. Search Domains are not required unless specified by your administrator.)

9. If your network requires the use of a proxy, click the Proxies button in the button bar. If not, skip ahead to step 13.

10. Click the checkboxes beside the protocols that you want to configure.

11. Click the protocol names to configure each proxy. Setup fields appear to the right of the protocol list.

12. Enter the proxy information as provided by your network administrator.

13. Click OK to exit advanced setup.

14. Click Apply to activate and begin using your new network settings.

Switching to Automatic Configuration

To revert back to the default "automatic" configuration of a network interface, you need to select Using DHCP from the Configure IPv4 drop-down menu.

Activating PPPoE for DSL Connections

In some cases, most typically when using a DSL modem, you need to activate PPPoE (Point-to-Point Protocol over Ethernet) in order to make a connection.

1. Open System Preferences and click the Network panel icon.

2. Select your active Ethernet Interface.

3. Choose Create PPPoE Service from the Configure IPv4 drop-down menu.

4. Choose a name for the connection. (The default, PPPoE, is fine.)

5. Click Done.

6. Enter the PPPoE information as provided by your ISP. Choose to remember the password if desired.

7. Click the Show PPPoE Status in Menu Bar checkbox to add a convenient menu option for connecting and disconnecting to the service.

8. Click the Advanced button.

9. Click PPP to open a variety of options for configuring your connection.

10. To help maintain a stable connection, check Connect Automatically When Needed and uncheck the Disconnect checkboxes if desired.

11. If required by your ISP, configure the TCP/IP settings manually as described in the "Configuring TCP/IP and Proxy Settings" task.

12. Click OK to close the Advanced settings.

13. Click Connect to begin using the PPPoE interface you've configured.

Creating Virtual Private Network Connections

In the modern world, it's difficult not to bring your work home with you. Your Mac makes an excellent workstation for both business and school use and is more than capable of handling serious tasks. Unfortunately, network security requirements frequently force businesses and schools to disable direct access to their networks. This limits your ability to access printers, file servers, and other critical resources that you might need to work remotely.

Thankfully, many organizations also provide Virtual Private Network (VPN) servers. Using a VPN server, your Mac can use its current network connection (wired or wireless) to securely connect to your company's network. You can access all of the same resources that you see when you're sitting in your office chair.

Creating a VPN Connection

Mavericks supports three types of VPN connections—L2TP, PPTP, and Cisco IPSec. You need to find out from your network administrator which option is right for you, along with the settings you need to make the connection.

1. Create a new VPN connection by opening the System Preferences and clicking the Network icon.

2. Click the + button at the bottom of the interfaces pane.

3. Choose VPN as the interface.

4. Set the VPN type to the type specified by your network administrator.

5. Enter a meaningful name for the VPN service, such as "Work VPN."

6. Click Create.

7. A new VPN interface is created and added to the list of network interfaces. Make sure the VPN interface is highlighted.

8. Configuration options appear on the right side of the network preference panel. Enter the server address and account information provided by your network administrator.

9. Click the Show VPN Status in Menu Bar checkbox. This adds a menu item to the menu bar so you can quickly connect and disconnect from a VPN.

10. Click the Authentication Settings button.

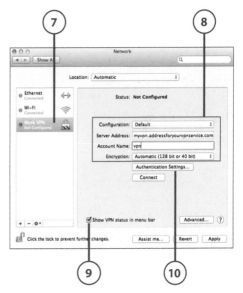

11. You are prompted for a method of authentication. Enter a password or choose one of the other available options as directed by your network administrator

12. Click OK.

13. If you have been given specific network settings by your network administrator, click the Advanced button and enter the options as described in "Manually Configuring Network Settings."

14. Click the Connect button to connect to the VPN.

Managing Your VPN Connection

If you've chosen to show the VPN status in your menu bar, you can use the menu item to quickly connect and disconnect at any time. In addition, you can show the amount of time you've been connected, in case connection charges apply.

Managing Multiple Connections with Locations and Configurations

If you work in a business or academic environment, you might find that you need to juggle network settings depending on what you are trying to accomplish. My workplace, for example, includes a wired network and three wireless networks—each providing a different level of access and a different way of viewing network resources. Depending on the day, I might need to connect to the intranet wireless, guest wireless, or just use a wired connection.

To help keep things straight, Mavericks includes Configurations and Locations—two important tools for keeping multiple sets of network information.

For interfaces such as VPNs or other devices that might have multiple "versions" of their settings, you can create configurations. A configuration holds information such as the server you're connecting to and your specific network settings.

A location, on the other hand, has a much broader scope. Locations enable you to create new configurations across all your interfaces and swap them out instantly. Creating a new location is like establishing an entirely new network setup—making instant reconfiguration a snap.

Creating Configurations

To create a configuration, do the following:

1. To create a configuration (if supported by your network interface), first open the System Preferences and click the Network icon.

2. Click the interface for which you want to create a new configuration.

3. Using the Configuration pop-up menu, choose Add Configuration.

4. Enter a name for the configuration.

5. Click Create. You may now configure the network interface as described in the chapter.

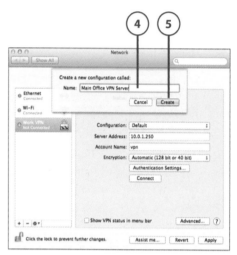

6. Your new settings are stored and accessible under the configuration name you provided so that you can easily switch from one to another. (You can also remove or rename configurations under this menu.)

Adding and Using Locations

Locations are like configurations on steroids. Lots of steroids. Using locations, you can create entirely new sets of network interfaces and options and switch between them easily.

1. Open the System Preferences and click the Network icon.

2. The default location of Automatic is set at the top of the network panel.

3. Choose Edit Locations from the Location drop-down menu.

4. A dialog box that lists any configured locations displays.

5. Click the + button to add an entry for a new location. (Use – to remove locations you no longer want.)

6. Type a name to describe the location, such as "Office Intranet."

7. Click Done.

8. All your network settings are now set to their defaults for the new location. All VPN connections and other interfaces are gone. You are, in effect, starting fresh with configuring your Mac network setup.

9. Configure your network settings as described in this chapter.

10. After you've completed your setup, you can switch between locations using the Location drop-down menu within the System Preferences Network panel. Remember that you can return to your original network settings by choosing the location named "Automatic."

Seeking Automated Network Assistance

The Mavericks operating system provides a few automated tools to help you configure and diagnose your Mac's network settings. Be aware that the automated tools might not be able to fully set up your connection; and if you have complicated network configurations, you might want to manage the settings manually anyway. Let's review what you need to do to use these tools.

Launching Diagnostics

To launch the diagnostics system, follow these steps:

1. Open the System Preferences panel and click the Network icon.

2. Click the Assist Me button at the bottom of the window.

3. Click Diagnostics in the dialog box that displays.

4. Choose the Network interface to run diagnostics on. If you've configured locations, you are first prompted to choose your location.

5. Click Continue.

6. Review the results and follow the onscreen instructions.

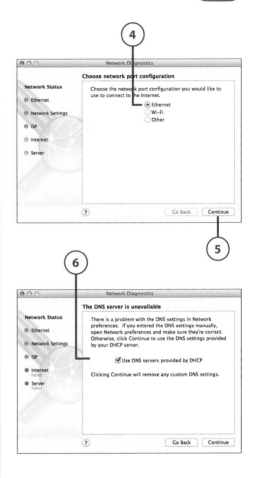

Launching the Setup Assistant

To launch the setup assistant, follow these steps:

1. Open the System Preferences panel and click the Network icon.

2. Click the Assist Me button at the bottom of the window.

3. Click Assistant in the dialog box that appears.

4. Provide a location where you will be using the network connection. This process creates a new location, as described in the previous "Adding and Using Locations" section.

5. Click Continue.

6. Choose the type of connection you are making.

7. Click Continue.

8. Follow the onscreen instructions to let Mavericks attempt to
configure your network settings
for you.

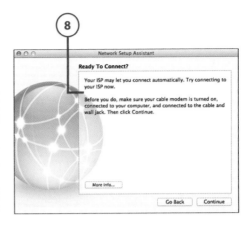

It's Not All Good

DON'T DISCOUNT YOUR ADMIN!

It is impossible for me to stress this enough: Your network administrator or
ISP is your best resource for correcting network problems. Using the assistant tools in Mavericks is not a silver bullet; if you don't have the information required to make a network connection (IP address, and so on), it won't
"just work"!

Establish accounts to popular Internet services.

Explore iCloud features and options.

In this chapter, you learn about iCloud services and unified account management in Mavericks, including:

→ Activating iCloud services
→ What iCloud is and does
→ Interesting iCloud services
→ How to move files to and from iCloud
→ How to manage your myriad of Internet accounts

4

Setting Up iCloud Services and Internet Accounts

One of the coolest features of Mavericks isn't really located on your Mac—it's "in the cloud." The Mavericks iCloud services enable you to keep all of your information in sync in your digital life. Your iPhones, iPads, and Mac—coupled with iCloud—make up the perfect digital workplace and playground.

In this chapter, you find out how to establish and configure iCloud accounts and get to know some of the basics of using iCloud services. You also learn how Mavericks manages all of the accounts that you may use on popular social network sites, email, and online sharing services.

Setting Up iCloud

One of the most convenient features of using multiple Apple devices is the difficult-to-describe iCloud service. iCloud provides data synchronization between your computers and iOS devices (such as synchronizing your web browser bookmarks, passwords, and even credit card information). It also gives you free email, contact storage, beautiful online office applications, and it even provides the ability to connect to your home Macintosh from your work computer. Best of all, all you need to do to use iCloud is establish an account and click a few checkboxes.

Integrated iCloud

I mention iCloud where relevant throughout this book, but keep in mind that Apple is continuously upgrading iCloud services and adding new features. The goal is for your computing life to be more intuitive and seamless without having to worry about what is going on in the background.

Configuring iCloud for the First Time

The first step in using iCloud is configuring your Mac to log into your account. If you have an Apple ID, chances are you already have an iCloud account. If not, the setup process guides you along the way. Note that you only need to follow these steps once—after that, you remain logged in even if you reboot your Mac.

To access your iCloud account, follow these steps:

1. Open the iCloud System Preferences panel. A sign-in window displays.

2. Enter your Apple ID and Password, or click Create Apple ID to generate a new safe ID.

3. Click Sign In to log in to the iCloud service.

4. iCloud prompts to automatically install basic services—contact, calendar, reminders, notes, and bookmark syncing as well as Find My Mac. You can either enable these now, or you can do it later by following the instructions in the "Activating iCloud Services" task.

5. Click Next.

6. You might be prompted for information as some services start. If you're using Find My Mac, for example, you're prompted to allow Location Services. Click Allow to move on.

7. You are shown the list of active iCloud services. Close the System Preferences, or proceed to the next section to learn more about the available services.

Activating iCloud Services

Your iCloud account comes with many free services that work across your OS X systems and iOS (iPhone/iPad) devices. The following list summarizes the available services at the time of this writing:

- **Mail**—When activated, Mail sets up a Mavericks email account associated with your iCloud account. This will be an @icloud.com address that you established when registering for an Apple ID (discussed in Chapter 5, "Accessing Email and the Web").

- **Contacts**—Moves your contacts to iCloud storage, making them accessible and editable on any device that has iCloud configured. (See Chapter 8, "Managing Who, Where, When, and What," for more details.)

- **Calendars**—Sets up shared calendars between all iCloud devices. (See Chapter 8 for more details.)

- **Reminders**—Creates shared lists—everything from shopping lists to to-do lists that are shared between all iCloud devices. (See Chapter 8 for more details.)

- **Notes**—Connects your Mac Notes application to iCloud storage, making all your notes available across all your Macs and iPhone/iPad (see Chapter 8 for more details.)

- **Safari**—Enables syncing of your Safari bookmarks and your reading list across devices as well as providing a list of open Safari tabs on other devices. This makes it possible to start browsing in one location and finish in another. (Read more in Chapter 5.)

- **Keychain**—Enables syncing of secure passwords and credit card information between your devices. This will be used for auto-fill data in Safari. Note that when enabling this feature, you'll need to bounce back and forth between your Mac and iOS devices to ensure that they are all properly authorized to share the data. (Read more in Chapter 5.)

- **Photos** —If you have iPhoto installed on your Mac, Photos automatically makes the photos you take on your iPhone or iPad available on your Mac (and vice versa) and enables you to share albums with anyone. (Discussed later in this chapter in the "Using Photo Sharing" task.)

- **Documents & Data**—This makes it possible to save files to iCloud rather than your local hard drive. Using this feature, you can start editing a document on one machine and finish it up on another. (Discussed later in this chapter in the "Using Documents and Data" task.)

- **Back to My Mac**—When activated, this unique iCloud feature makes your computer visible to any other computer where you have activated Back To My Mac. Using this, you can access your home computer from any other network-connected Mac—no network configuration required. (See Chapter 6, "Sharing Files, Devices, and Services," for details.)

- **Find My Mac**—If your Mac is lost or stolen, Find My Mac attempts to locate it. Using the icloud.com website, you can track your Mac on a map and even lock or erase it. (Discussed later in this chapter in the "Using Find My Mac" task.)

To activate an iCloud service, first make sure you have completed the task "Configuring iCloud for the First Time" and then follow these simple steps:

1. Open the iCloud System Preferences panel.

2. Click the checkboxes in front of the services you want to use. If prompted to provide access to additional system services (Find My Mac requires you to grant access to your location, for instance), click the appropriate response.

3. Close System Preferences when satisfied with your selections.

More Storage Is a Click Away

At the bottom of the service list is a bar showing how much storage you have left. By default, iCloud includes 5GB of storage—but storing documents and data, backups of your iOS devices, and other information can eat the space up quickly. Click the Manage button to buy more storage if needed.

Exploring Unique iCloud Services

It's pretty easy to describe the use of features like Contacts and Safari book-mark syncing, and they fall neatly into place in many of this book's chapters. There are a few "unique" iCloud services that are important to cover, but don't quite fit as cleanly elsewhere. One such service, for example, enables you to find your Mac on a map, should it be lost or stolen. Another provides direct access to your contacts, events, and mail from a web interface no mat-ter where you are. Rather than leave these topics out, they are covered in the following tasks.

Accessing iCloud Applications Online

After you activate iCloud services like Mail, Calendaring, and Remind-ers, you can log into Apple's online iCloud service and use web appli-cations that resemble their Mac counterparts. To access iCloud appli-cations, do the following:

1. Open a current version of a web browser (Safari, Internet Explorer 8+, Firefox, or Chrome) and browse to http://www.icloud.com.

2. Enter your Apple ID and Password.

3. Click the Remember Me checkbox if you'd like to be able to access iCloud from your computer with-out logging in again.

4. Click the arrow to log in.

5. Click the icon of the application you want to launch.

6. Use the web application as you would the desktop version. If your app makes changes to data, those changes will be pushed out to all your iCloud-connected devices.

7. Click the Cloud menu to jump to other applications.

8. Close your browser when finished.

Using Find My Mac

To turn on Find My Mac and make your Mac location available via the iCloud website, follow these steps:

1. If you haven't already, activate Find My Mac using the technique described in "Managing iCloud Services," earlier in this chapter.

2. If prompted, click Allow on the Allow Find My Mac to Use the Location dialog.

3. If you need to find your Mac, go to iCloud.com in a browser on any Internet-connected device and log in. Click Find My iPhone.

4. Click All Devices to show the list of tracked devices.

5. Click the name of your Mac in the list.

6. The Mac's location is highlighted on the map.

7. The web app displays options for sending a message/playing a sound on the computer, locking it, or wiping the contents of the hard drive.

Using Documents and Data

The Documents and Data feature of iCloud is meant to make it easy to work on a document in one location, and then open it again in another.

It's Not All Good

WHERE DID I PUT THAT?!?!

In my opinion, the Mavericks implementation of Documents and Data leaves a bit to be desired. Although this feature sounds like a useful tool, it requires that you have the same application on all the machines that need to edit an application's files.

For example, assume you edit a file on your Mac using an iCloud-enabled word processor and save the document to iCloud. You then go to your desktop, which has a different, but compatible, word processor installed. Surprise! You won't be able to see the file. You can only open iCloud files in the applications that created them.

If you ever need to see *all* your iCloud files, you *will* be able to see them from the "All My Files" favorite item in the Finder sidebar.

Before starting, be sure to activate Documents and Data using the steps described at the end of the "Activating iCloud Services" section, earlier in this chapter.

Saving Your Mac Files to iCloud

1. Edit the file as you normally would in an application of your choice (be aware that not all applications support iCloud at this time).

2. Choose File, Move To from the menu bar.

3. When prompted for a filename, set the "Where" location to iCloud.

4. Click Move to save the file to iCloud.

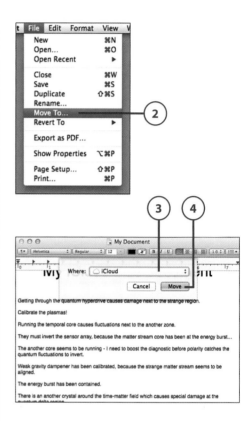

Opening iCloud Files on Your Mac

To open a file that you've saved in iCloud (from any iCloud-connected device), first open the same application you used to create the file, and then follow these steps:

1. Choose File, Open.

2. Make sure iCloud is selected in the dialog.

3. Use the icon and list buttons at the bottom of the dialog to switch between icon and list views.

4. Click the file you want to work with.

5. Click Open. The file opens and you can begin working with it wherever you left off, no matter which device you were using.

When It's in iCloud, It's in iCloud

When you open and edit a file in iCloud, it stays in iCloud. You don't need to worry about moving it from your local computer to iCloud after editing it, or anything of the sort. Just think of iCloud storage like any other disk, except that you have access to it no matter where you are or what iCloud-enabled device you are using.

It's Not All Good

USE THE CORRECT APP!

Documents can only be opened (at this time) in the application that created them. You won't even see the files on another device unless the device is running the app that was used to create it. You also won't see it in the open file dialog of any other iCloud application. In other words, if you want to share files created in Pixelmator (a great photo-editing app) across systems with iCloud, both systems *must* have Pixelmator available for editing the file.

Opening iCloud Files in iCloud

If you save a file to iCloud using Pages, Keynote, or Numbers on your Mac or iOS device, you can open and edit the file with nothing more than your web browser. To do this, first follow the steps in the earlier task "Accessing iCloud Applications Online."

1. Use the iCloud webpage to choose the application whose files you want to open.

2. The application opens, displaying all the files you saved to iCloud from your Mac.

3. Drag and drop new files into the empty area of the web browser to upload them.

4. Double-click a file you want to work with.

5. The file opens and you can begin working with it directly in your browser.

Moving Existing Files to and from iCloud

If you create a document locally (such as on your desktop) and want it to be available everywhere, you need to move it to iCloud. Similarly, if you want to take a document that has been shared via iCloud and move it so only a single copy exists on your Mac, you need to move it locally. To move in either direction, first open the file in your application of choice, and then follow these steps:

1. Click the filename in the window's title bar to open a pop-over window.

2. Click the Where pop-up menu to view the locations where you can send the file.

3. To move a local file to iCloud, choose iCloud or a folder within iCloud.

4. Choose a local destination to move the file to your local machine.

5. Choose Other to pick from any destination on your computer.

6. Click outside the pop-over window to save your changes.

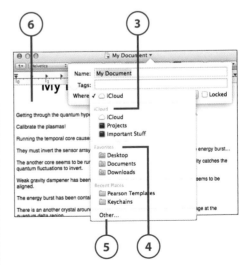

ORGANIZING YOUR iCLOUD

If you find yourself using iCloud as an integral part of your document workflow, you'll notice that it quickly becomes full of files with no organization. Unlike OS X, iCloud won't let you create zillions of nested folders. In fact, it uses a completely different interface for organizing files, but, thankfully, it's one you're probably used to.

When viewing files in the iCloud Open File dialog, you can create whatever file organization you like by dragging the icons around—it works *exactly* like the Launchpad organization covered in Chapter 2, "Making the Most of Your Screen Space." Drag a file onto another file, and a folder/group is automatically created. Drag files out of the folder, and the folder disappears. If you're used to working with Launchpad or iOS, you'll have no problem organizing your iCloud documents.

Using Photo Sharing

Another extremely useful (and fun) feature of iCloud is Photo Sharing. Photo Sharing automatically keeps copies of your most recent 1,000 photos taken using iOS devices and makes sure that your Mac has copies of them all. It also enables you to share collections of photos with anyone you'd like.

Enabling Photo Sharing

To get started, enable and configure Photo Sharing in iCloud. To enable the service, follow these steps:

1. Open the iCloud System Preferences panel.

2. Enable the Photos item.

3. Click the Options button beside the Photos line.

4. Click the My Photo Stream check-box to keep all of your latest photos synced between devices.

5. Enable the Photo Sharing option to share photos with individuals that you select.

6. Click OK.

7. Close the Preferences window.

Viewing Shared Photos

To view your shared photos and photo stream, you need to use iPhoto. If you don't have it installed, you can download it from the App Store.

1. Open iPhoto from the Applications folder or Launchpad.

2. Click the iCloud icon in the left iPhoto navigation pane.

3. Your shared photos are displayed.

4. Double-click an album.

5. The album opens and the pictures display.

Sharing Photos

To share your photos with others, you also use iPhoto.

1. Open iPhoto from the Applications folder or Launchpad.

2. Navigate to a photo collection (Events, Albums, Faces, Places, and so on) or select a group of photos from the Photos section.

3. Click the Share button and choose iCloud.

4. Choose an existing shared album, or click the + icon to create a new shared album.

5. Enter the addresses for people who should be able to access the shared album, the name of the album, and any comments.

6. Check Subscribers Can Post to allow comments from people viewing your photos.

7. Check Public Website to publish a publicly accessible version of your photos.

8. Click Share to begin sharing!

Getting Started with Accounts

For all the fun and information the Internet has brought us, it has also created a mess in terms of managing all the accounts we use to communicate online. If you're like many people, you have multiple email accounts—possibly one through iCloud, one from work, and one at home. You have accounts for chatting with instant messenger. You have accounts for sharing contacts and calendars. In other words, you've got multiple usernames and passwords that need to be configured in different applications, just so you can be connected.

In OS X, Apple has recognized the problem of account overload and worked to consolidate all your online account management in a single centralized preference panel—Internet Accounts. Here you can set up email, instant messenger, Exchange, Calendar, and other account types—without needing to figure out where they're managed in your individual applications.

I show the use of this panel as needed in the relevant chapters, but let's take a very brief look at how you interact with this tool on your Mac.

More iCloud Settings?

When you use the Internet Accounts panel to manage your accounts, you'll notice that it also includes iCloud. The iCloud settings in this panel are identical to what you configured in the iCloud panel shown earlier in this chapter—this is just a different way to access them.

Adding an Account

To add an account for an online service (email, contacts, calendars, Exchange, etc.), follow these steps.

1. Open the Internet Accounts System Preferences panel.

2. Choose an online service provider that you want to configure by clicking its name. Select Add Other Account from the bottom of the list to pick from additional service types.

3. Fill in the requested information in the setup wizard that appears.

4. The completed account is listed in the preference panel with its settings available on the right.

5. Close System Preferences when finished.

Exploration Is Rewarded!

While the Internet Accounts panel is a great place for establishing new accounts and performing high-level configuration, you might still find yourself needing to dig for various esoteric settings (such as specific server addresses, proxies, and other technical tweaks) within your individual Internet applications.

Browse the web and keep track of your favorite articles in Safari.

Create beautiful email in the Mail application.

In this chapter, you learn how to use your Mac for common Internet uses, including:

→ Connecting to email servers
→ Using VIP and Smart Mailboxes
→ Browsing the Web
→ Creating web clippings
→ Using Safari Extensions

Accessing Email and the Web

The Internet (for better or worse) is everywhere we turn. To be effective in our professional (and frequently social) lives, we need best-of-breed Internet tools on our iMac. The good news is that we've got 'em.

In this chapter, you find out how to use some of the unique features of the Mail and Web applications in Mavericks. Even if you're working in a Microsoft-centric environment, you'll find that your Mac's tools are up to the job.

Using Mail

The first thing that many of us do when we have an Internet connection is check our email. Email is now a way to exchange rich media—such as photos, files, and movies—in addition to a way to exchange written messages. The email application, Mail (found in the Applications folder by clicking the Mail icon), is provided with your Mac. With Mail, you can connect to a variety of different mail servers, including Microsoft Exchange, with only a few clicks of your mouse.

Things You Need Before Setting Up an Email Connection

As with the networking information in the last chapter, configuring your email account isn't a matter of guessing. Apple's Mail application can auto-matically set up several popular email services (such as Google and Yahoo!), but if you're connecting to a corporate email server, you should collect as much information as possible from your email system administrator or ISP before proceeding. This includes your email address, password, email server, email server type (POP, IMAP, or Exchange), and SMTP server:

- **Incoming Mail Server**—The server that you connect to when retrieving your email.

- **Incoming Mail Server Type**—The type of server that you're connecting to. Apple's Mail application supports Exchange, IMAP, and POP servers.

- **Outgoing (SMTP) Server**—The server that sends your messages.

- **Authentication**—Typically, a user name and password required to retrieve or send messages.

Adding an Email Account

If you have an email account that Mavericks recognizes, configuration couldn't be easier—you just need your email address, name, and password to make a connection. Mavericks attempts to identify and configure your account. If for some reason it fails, you can continue with an advanced manual configuration (see the next task).

Note that if you've already activated iCloud email, your account is already set up! You don't need to do anything else.

1. Open the Internet Accounts System Preferences Panel.

2. Choose an email service that you want to configure by clicking its name on the right.

3. The Add Account window displays. Type your name (as you want it to appear in outgoing messages), email address, and password for the account.

4. Click Set Up.

5. Mavericks attempts to automatically configure your account. If additional features are determined to be available from the email provider, they are listed in the window. Choose which services you want to use by checking/unchecking the checkboxes.

6. Click Done to finish adding the account.

7. If it's successful, the newly configured email account appears in the account list. If the setup fails, cancel setup and skip ahead to the next section, "Adding an Email Account (Advanced)."

8. Clicking the account name in the list displays the account details on the right.

9. You can click Details to edit the basic account settings if, for example, you want to change your display name or the name of your account.

10. Close System Preferences and begin using your account in Mail.

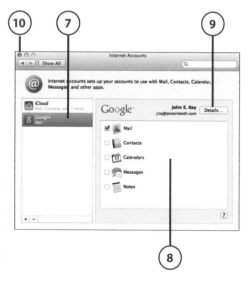

Configuring Advanced Account Settings

Email accounts that aren't immediately recognized by Mavericks require more information to be entered before they can be used. This is the case for some ISP email accounts, corporate, and educational systems. Be sure you have all the information listed previously in the "Things You Need Before Setting Up an Email Connection" section and then start by setting up an account as best you can using the process described in the previous task.

1. Open the Mail application from the Dock or Applications folder.

2. Choose Preferences from the Mail menu.

3. Click the Accounts button within the Mail preferences window.

4. Click the account that you want to configure with advanced settings.

5. Use the Incoming Mail Server fields to set a specific server that will handle your incoming messages.

6. To set an SMTP server, Choose Edit SMTP Server List from the Outgoing Mail Server (SMTP) drop-down menu.

7. Use the +/− buttons to add and remove servers.

8. Configure the server by setting the description and address (Server Name) in the fields below the list.

9. Choose a security certificate, if any, using the TLS drop-down menu.

Troubleshooting Your Connection

To troubleshoot your account settings, from within Mail choose Window, Connection Doctor. Your Mac tests all your email account settings and shows you exactly where any errors are occurring.

10. Click Advanced to access port and authentication settings.

11. Click OK when finished. The server you configured will be accessible from the Outgoing Mail Server (SMTP) menu.

12. Check Use Only This Server if you want to force all messages from this address to go through the chosen SMTP server.

13. Set a TLS certificate for your incoming mail server (if any) using the TLS Certificate.

14. Finally, make sure that the Enable This Account checkbox is selected so you can begin using your account settings.

15. Close the Mail Preferences.

Multiple Email Addresses, One Account

It isn't uncommon for one email account to have multiple addresses associated with it. I might have a single account with addresses, such as *myMac@placeforstuff.com* or *johnray@me.com*, which I want to appear when I send a message. To configure multiple addresses for a single account, open Mail's preferences, click Accounts, and then click the account you want to add an alias to. Enter the alias email addresses, separated by commas, in the Email Address field in the account details. The email addresses are then available in a pop-up menu when you compose a new message.

Finding Your Way Around Mail

After your email account is configured, Mail connects and retrieves your messages. The Mail application workspace is split into three columns, from left to right: mailboxes, a message list, and message content.

On the left, the mailbox list shows different mailboxes (or folders) for categorizing your messages. In Mavericks, Apple has decided to conserve as much space as possible by hiding the mailboxes by default. There's also a quick hide/show mailboxes button to show the mailbox column and links to the important mailboxes (Inbox, Sent, and so on) directly below the toolbar.

When you click a mailbox, the message list refreshes to show all of the email within the mailbox, including a several-line preview of the contents. Any message that you click in the Message list is displayed in the message content area on the right.

Now that you know the basics of finding your way around Mail, take a look at the common tasks you should familiarize yourself with.

Reading Email

Reading messages is typically a matter of finding a message in the message list, clicking it, and reading. Even so, you can improve the experience by taking advantage of several tools built into Mail.

Sorting Mail

You're certainly used to sorting information by clicking column headings, right? In the Mail application, however, the message list doesn't have columns, so you need to follow this approach:

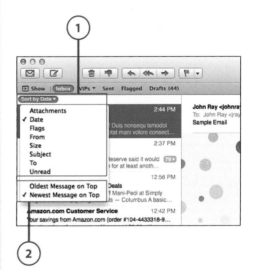

1. Use the Sort By drop-down menu above the message list to choose a message attribute to use as your sorting criteria.

2. Use the same menu to set the order of your sorting preferences.

Viewing Additional Attributes

Much as you can set the mail attributes you want to use for sorting, you can also set the attributes displayed in the message list. Use the View, Message List menu to set which attributes will be visible in the message list items.

Previewing Attachments

In Chapter 1, "Managing Your Desktop," you learned about the Quick Look system for previewing files in the Finder. In Mail, if your message contains an attachment, you can also use the Quick Look system.

1. Choose a message with an attachment—represented by a paperclip in the message list.

2. Position your cursor near the top of an email to show buttons for interacting with the message.

3. Click the Attachment button.

4. Select Quick Look from the menu that appears.

5. A Quick Look window appears, displaying the selected content.

Saving Attachments

You can easily save one or more attachments to your Mac's hard drive, and even add images to iPhoto, directly from Mail.

1. Choose a message with an attachment—represented by a paperclip in the message list.

2. Position your cursor near the top of the message and click the Attachment button.

3. A menu appears, enabling you to Save All, choose an individual file to save, or, if applicable, add the file to iPhoto.

WORKING WITH ATTACHMENTS

If you prefer a more Finder-like approach to dealing with attachments, you can also work with attached files as icons. Scroll through your email and you'll see the attached files represented as icons in the message (usually at the bottom). You can drag these icons to your desktop (or anywhere you'd like to store them). You can also click an icon to immediately open it in a compatible Mavericks application.

Viewing Web Pages within an Email

Have you ever gotten a link to a webpage in email and wanted to view it without having to launch Safari? In Mavericks, you can. To preview a web link directly in Mail, follow
these steps:

1. Position your cursor over the link within the message content, but do not click!

2. A small downward-pointing arrow appears to the right of the link. Click it.

3. A pop-over window appears displaying the web page.

4. Click Open with Safari to open the full page in your web browser, or Add to Reading
List to save the page to your Safari reading list.

Using Data Detectors

The icon that appears at the end of a web link in mail (and the subsequent preview of the page) is an example of a Mavericks "Data Detector" in action. You may notice other icons beside dates, addresses, phone numbers, and so on. Clicking these icons will do similar helpful actions, such as setting appointments, adding information to a contact, or tracking shipments.

Organizing with Email Conversations

Email conversations can grow quite lengthy with back-and-forth replies. To help keep long conversations under control, Mail, by default, collapses your conversations into a single entry in your message list. You can expand the entry to show the individual messages whenever you need to see one.

1. Conversations are denoted by a number within an entry in the message list.

2. Click the message list entry to show all the messages in the conversation within the content area.

3. Messages are numbered at the top to show the order in which they were received.

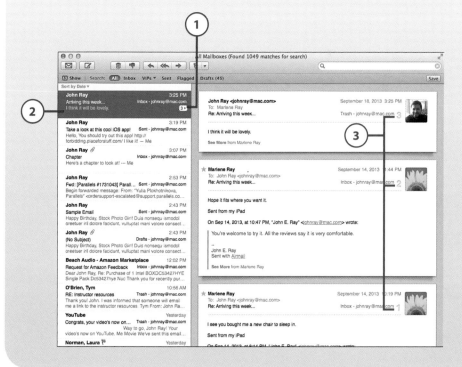

4. To focus on a single message, click the arrow beside the number in the message list to show a list of individual senders and dates.

5. Click the individual name/date to show only that message.

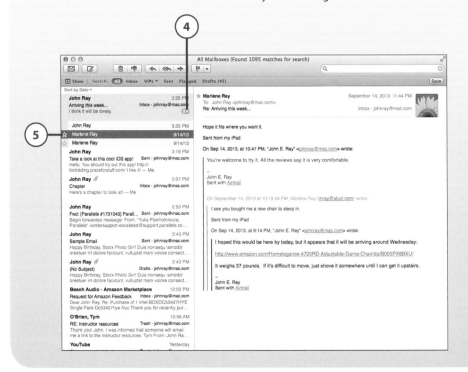

It's Not All Good

SILENCE THE CONVERSATION!

Many people find the conversation view to be disorienting in Mail. If you're one of those people, you can turn it off entirely by choosing Organize by Conversation from Mail's View Menu.

See My Smiling Face!

To see your friends' (and other contacts') photos beside each message summary in the message list, open Mail's preferences (Mail, Preferences from the menu), and within the Viewing section, click the Show Contact Photos in the Message List checkbox.

Managing Spam Filtering

Mail can learn (with some help) which messages in your inbox are spam and then filter similar messages so you don't have to see them. To manage your spam filtering, follow these steps:

1. Choose Mail, Preferences from the menu bar.

2. Click the Junk Mail toolbar icon.

3. Click Enable Junk Mail Filtering to turn on spam filtering. You can disable it by unchecking this box at any time.

4. Choose where Mail should file spam messages. Moving messages to the Junk mailbox is a good choice.

5. To help prevent getting false positives, use the spam exemptions to identify types of messages that you don't consider to be spam.

6. If your ISP offers spam filtering (and you trust it), make sure the Trust Junk Mail Headers in Messages option is set.

7. Close the Mail Preferences.

Classifying Spam

If you receive spam mail, select it and click the Junk icon (thumbs down) in the Mail toolbar. This classifies messages as spam. When new messages recognized as spam come in, they are automatically placed in the Junk folder. If *good* mail is accidentally classified as spam, use the thumbs up icon in the toolbar to tell Mail it made a mistake.

Changing How Often Mail Is Retrieved

You can force Mail to retrieve messages using the Get Mail toolbar button, but to change the frequency with which it forces a check you need to access the preferences.

1. Choose Mail, Preferences from the menu bar.

2. Click the General icon in the preferences toolbar.

3. Use the Check for New Messages pop-up menu to set how frequently Mail looks for new messages.

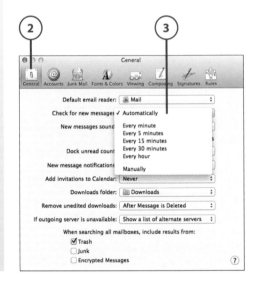

Composing Email

Email today is a bit more than just typing a message—it can include sending photos, files, or even professionally designed invitations and announcements. Mail on your Mac enables you to do all of these things.

Sending Messages with Attachments

Mail can attach virtually any type of file to your messages with ease. Follow these steps to add Windows-compatible attachments to a mail message.

1. Start a new message by clicking the new message icon (pencil and paper) in the Mail toolbar.

2. Click the Attach icon (paperclip) in the New Message window.

3. Choose the files or folders to send from the file chooser dialog. Select multiples by holding down the ⌘ key and clicking.

4. Check the Send Windows-Friendly Attachments checkbox to ensure that anyone (regardless of their platform choice) can open the attachments.

5. Click Choose File to add the attachments.

6. Compose the message as normal and then click the send icon (paper airplane).

Attaching Pictures from iPhoto

To quickly attach photos from iPhoto, click the Photo Browser button to open a small window that shows your iPhoto galleries. Choose your photos and drag them into the message to attach them!

Using Stationery Templates

If you'd like to send an invitation or a fancy greeting, you can make use of prebuilt templates, called "Stationery," that come with the Mail application. Stationery is available whenever you're composing a message:

1. Start a new message by clicking the new message icon (pencil and paper) in the Mail toolbar.

2. Click the Show Stationery icon (paper with dots) in the New Message toolbar.

3. Choose a category of templates on the left side of the Stationery bar.

4. Click the thumbnail of the template you want to apply.

5. Click to edit the text within the template.

6. If the template contains images, replace them by dragging photo files from the Finder onto the template image or use the Photo Browser button to locate an image and drag it in.

7. Click the send icon (paper airplane) when you are finished with the message.

Changing Templates

After you change the content of a template, you can choose another template and your changes will be maintained as much as possible.

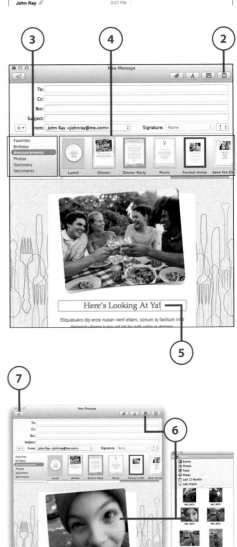

Creating Signatures

When you send a lot of email, you probably get a bit tired of typing the same thing at the end of each message—your name, email, and other contact information. To add this information automatically to the end of each message you write, create a signature.

1. Choose Mail, Preferences from the menu bar.

2. Click the Signatures icon in the preferences toolbar.

3. Choose an account that the signature should be used with, or choose All Signatures to not associate the signature with a specific account.

4. Click + to add a new signature.

5. Type a name for the signature.

6. Enter the text for the signature in the space to the right.

7. Click Always Match My Default Message Font so that the signature always matches the font you're using.

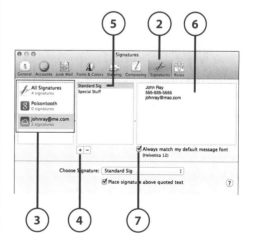

8. If you're adding the signature to an account, use the Choose Signature pop-up menu to choose which signature is automatically added when you write a message. You can also manually choose a signature using the Choose Signature pop-up menu in the message composition window.

9. Click Place Signature Above Quoted text to have Mail position your signature above earlier (quoted) text when replying to messages.

10. Close the Mail Preferences window.

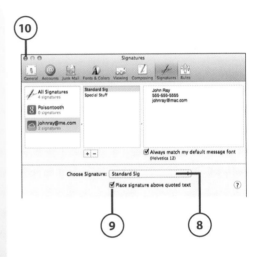

Adding a vCard

To attach your personal information to your signature as a virtual business card, you can drag a card out of your Address Panel (Window, Address Panel) into the signature.

Managing Your Email

Email can be overwhelming, especially if you have several different accounts and dozens of incoming messages each day. To help you cope with the incoming mail, you can create mailboxes in which to file or copy messages. You can also set up smart mailboxes that automatically display messages that match certain criteria.

Creating Mailboxes

To create a new mailbox, follow these steps:

1. Click the + button at the bottom of the Mailbox list.

2. Choose New Mailbox.

3. Using the Location pop-up menu, choose where the mailbox should be stored. You see all of your existing Mailboxes in the menu, as well as On My Mac. Choosing an existing location creates the new mailbox inside of that location.

4. Enter a name for the new mailbox.

5. Click OK.

6. The new mailbox is created and displayed in the Mailbox list.

Make Room for Your Mail

Remember: Because the mailbox display eats up a bunch of room on your screen, Apple has made it simple to hide and show the mailbox column using the Hide/Show disclosure button in the upper-left corner of the Mail window. In addition, you can quickly change between your Inbox, Sent, Drafts, and Flagged folders using the links directly in the Mail toolbar.

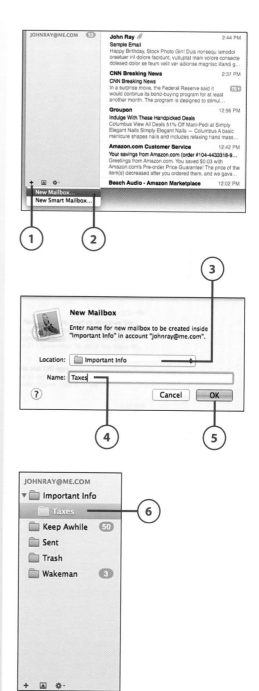

Deleting and Renaming Mailboxes

If you find yourself with extra mailboxes or mailboxes that are no longer serving their original purposes, you can delete or rename them.

1. Select the mailbox you want to change in your mailbox list.

2. Click the Action icon (the gear) at the bottom of the mailbox list.

3. Choose Delete Mailbox or Rename Mailbox as needed. Any messages stored in a mailbox being deleted are also deleted.

Nesting Folders

Even though you chose where to put your mailbox when it was first created, you can move it within your mailbox hierarchy easily. Mailboxes can be moved inside of other mailboxes by clicking and dragging their folder icons into (or out of) another mailbox.

Filing Messages in Mailboxes

Mailboxes are only useful if you file your messages in them. You can copy or move messages one at a time or en masse to a mailbox. You can do this either manually, as described here, or automatically using Smart Mailboxes or Email Rules, discussed in the tasks following this one.

1. Select a message by clicking it in the message list. You can select a contiguous range of messages by holding down Shift and clicking another message, or select several scattered messages by holding down ⌘ and clicking multiple messages.

2. Move the messages to a mailbox by dragging them onto the desired mailbox. To copy—rather than move—the messages, hold down the Option key while you're dragging the messages. The messages are moved (or copied) to the other mailbox.

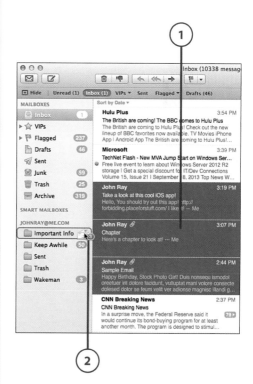

Filing Without Dragging

If you have a large number of mailboxes, or just find the process of dragging to the mailbox list to be cumbersome, you can select the messages and then use Move To or Copy To from the Messages menu to file the email without any dragging required.

Automatic Email Organization with Smart Mailboxes

Much as Smart Folders in the Finder can help you keep track of files that share certain attributes, Smart Mailboxes can do the same for your email. Using information such as the sender, recipient, and even attachment names, you can group messages together in a Smart Mailbox, regardless of what mailbox, or even what email account, they're associated with. Apple includes one Smart Mailbox by default—"Today"—showing all the messages you've received today.

1. To create a new Smart Mailbox, click the + button at the bottom of the Mailbox list and choose New Smart Mailbox.

2. Type a name for the mailbox.

3. Choose whether the mailbox should match any or all conditions.

4. Configure your search criteria. Use the first pop-up menu to choose a message attribute (such as Subject), the second to choose a comparison, and the field (where applicable) to provide the value that you are comparing against.

5. Use the + and – buttons to add or remove additional criteria.

6. To include messages from the Trash mailbox or Sent mailbox, click the appropriate Include Messages checkboxes.

7. Click OK when you're finished configuring the Smart Mailbox.

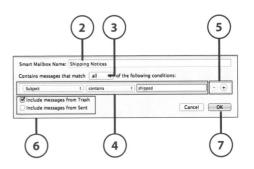

8. The new mailbox is created and displayed in the Smart Mailboxes section within the Mailbox list.

Nesting Smart Mailboxes

Smart Mailboxes can't be arranged hierarchically inside one another as normal mailboxes can. To create a hierarchy of smart mailboxes, you must create a Smart Mailbox Folder (Mailbox, New Smart Mailbox Folder). This special folder will be added to the Smart Mailboxes section and can be used to organize any Smart Mailboxes you create.

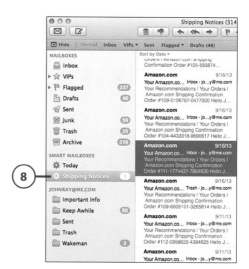

Keeping Track of Your Very Important People with VIP Mailboxes

Mail includes a feature that makes it very simple to track and view all messages from a specific person— the VIP Mailbox. VIP Mailboxes are like smart folders, but with a targeted purpose—showing you all messages from an individual person. To create a VIP mailbox, follow these steps:

1. Choose a message from a sender you want to designate as a VIP.

2. Position your mouse beside the sender's name in the content window and click the star that appears.

3. The sender is added to a new VIP mailbox.

4. Clicking the VIP mailbox shows all messages from the sender.

5. Click the star in the content view again, or select the new VIP mailbox and choose Remove from VIPs from the Action pop-up menu (gear) to remove VIP status (and the corresponding VIP mailbox).

Searching for Messages

Mail makes it easy to quickly search all of your email for particular content, and to turn that search into a Smart Mailbox for future reference.

1. Type the text you are looking for into the search field in the upper-right corner.

2. Using the links below the toolbar, click the mailbox where the search should be performed.

3. Potential search options appear in a drop-down list for matched people, mailboxes, subjects, and message content. Choose what best matches what you want to find.

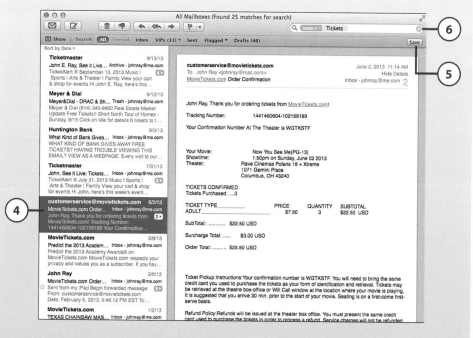

4. The results appear in the message list.

5. Click Save to save the search as a Smart Mailbox. (See steps 2–8 of the "Automatic Email Organization with Smart Mailboxes" task.)

6. Alternatively, click the X button in the search field to clear the search results.

Writing Email Rules

If you'd prefer to have messages filed to actual mailboxes rather than Smart Mailboxes, you can write email rules. Email rules can file messages, highlight messages in the message list, and even forward them to another account. To write a rule, follow these steps:

1. Choose Mail, Preferences from the menu bar.

2. Click the Rules icon in the Preferences toolbar.

3. Click Add Rule.

4. Enter a description for the rule so that you can identify it later.

5. Use the Any pop-up menu to choose where any or all rules must evaluate as "true" in order for the rule's actions to be carried out.

6. Configure the conditions under which the rule executes. The first pop-up menu chooses what is evaluated, the second the comparison to be made, and field is the value that should be used in the comparison.

7. Use + or – to add or remove additional conditions.

8. Configure the actions that are performed when the conditions are met.

9. Use + or – to add or remove actions.

10. Click OK to save the rule.

11. Close the Mail Preferences.

Web Browsing in Safari

Although similar in many ways to other web browsers, Safari offers a few unique features that set it apart. You can open Safari from its icon on the Dock or Launchpad, or in the Applications folder.

Safari has seen dramatic improvements over the past few years. Safari uses a web browsing engine called Webkit that was, although not an Apple product, engineered by mostly Apple developers. This engine is the same engine on many platforms, including WebOS, Android, and others. This means that Safari is quickly becoming a web browsing standard, rather than an exception.

It's Not All Good

BRING YOUR OWN FLASH

If you're browsing with Safari and your webpages seem a bit "bare," it might be because Mavericks doesn't include Adobe Flash by default. To add the Flash plug-in to your browser, visit http://www.adobe.com/products/flashplayer/ in Safari.

Managing Your Bookmarks, Top Sites, and Reading List

In Safari, there are four primary areas where you can store sites for easy access: the bookmark menu, which appears under the bookmarks menu item; the favorites bar, displayed under the URL; the top sites screen, which shows the sites you (or Safari) have identified as being frequently visited; and Bookmark/Reading List pane. The Reading List (denoted by an icon of eyeglasses) holds pages and links that you want to visit at a later time, but aren't planning to keep as a permanent bookmark. You can also add your own bookmark folders to organize things however you see fit.

When Safari first starts, it displays the Top Sites view with Bookmark/Reading List pane active.

It's Not All Good

SEARCHING FOR SEARCH?

The first time you start Safari in Mavericks, you may notice something is missing—the search field. Apple has taken the approach of many other browsers and combined the search with the URL field. To go to a particular URL, type in a URL. To perform a search, type in the search. It can be a bit disconcerting at first, but it works just fine.

Socially Aware Bookmarks

If you set up access to a social networking site via Mavericks (see Chapter 7, "Being Social Online"), your Reading List/Bookmark pane takes on an additional type of information—shared bookmarks. Bookmarks posted via your social networking accounts will automatically be visible in the pane.

Adding a Webpage to Bookmarks, Reading List, or Top Sites

To add a webpage to the reading list, bookmarks, or even top sites, you simply need to know what site you want to bookmark, and then follow these steps:

1. Visit the site you want to book-mark by typing its address into the URL field.

2. Click and hold the + button to the left of the URL.

3. Choose where to file the book-mark (Reading List, Top Sites, Favorites Bar, Bookmarks, or a folder within one of these areas).

Organizing Bookmarks

After you've added a few bookmarks
to the bookmark menu or bookmark
bar, you can re-categorize them
using these steps:

1. Click the button to show the
   Bookmark/Reading List pane.

2. Click the + button at the bottom
   of the pane to add a new folder, if
   desired.

3. Provide a name for the folder by
   clicking and typing within the
   pane.

4. Drag bookmarks from anywhere in the list into the order you want. You can drag them into folders, or even place folders inside other folders.

5. To view the contents of a folder, simply click it and the bookmarks it contains will be displayed.

Organizing Top Sites

As you browse, Safari identifies your "top sites." The Top Sites button switches to display previews and marks sites that have updates with a star. Clicking a site opens it in Safari.

To manage the ordering and display of the top sites in Safari, follow these steps:

1. Click the Top Sites button.

2. Position your cursor near the top left of one of the top sites to show the management controls.

3. Click the X button by a site to remove it.

4. Click the pin button to make sure the site always stays on the screen.

5. Rearrange the sites by clicking and dragging their preview images.

Adding Your Top Sites

You can add to your top sites by dragging items from the URL field, bookmarks pane, and so on—pretty much anywhere you see a URL.

A History Lesson

In Mavericks, Apple has changed where the browsing history is located in Safari. You can access (and search) your browsing history by choosing History, Show History from the menu bar.

Managing Your Reading List

After you add things to your list, you want to read them, right? To manage your list, just follow these steps:

1. Open the Reading List by clicking the Bookmark/Reading List pane icon.

2. Click a Reading List entry to load the page in Safari.

3. While hovering over an entry, click the X icon in the upper-right corner to remove it from the list.

4. Click the Bookmark/Reading List pane icon again to hide the list when you're finished.

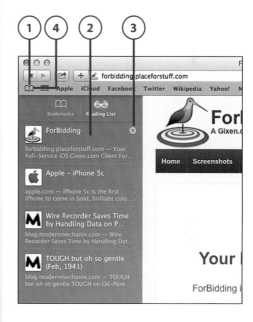

Paneless Reading List Additions

If you get in the habit of using the Reading List, Apple provides some shortcuts to make additions while you're browsing. Shift-click links to add them to the Reading List, or press Shift-⌘-D to add your current page to the list. If you're more of a click-and-drag person, you can drag individual links to the Reading List pane or to the Reading List icon to add them to the list as well.

Advanced Browsing Features

Although "web browsing" as a pastime is only a little more than a decade old, it's a skill that it almost seems that we were born with. Little by little, browser developers have been refining the process to add additional features. Safari is no different.

Using Tabbed Browsing

Originally, web browsers created a new window for each page you visited. In Safari, all these windows can be combined under a single window with tabs representing individual websites within that window. To use tabbed browsing in Safari, follow these steps:

1. Click the + button near the far right of the Safari toolbar.

2. A new tab is added with your default homepage (here www.apple.com).

3. Enter a URL (or choose a bookmark) to browse to a new site in that tab.

4. Use the tabs to quickly switch between webpages. Note that while you're browsing, you can hold down Command as you click links. The links create a new tab in the Safari browser window.

Fine-Tune Your Tabs

To fine-tune your tabbed browsing behavior (or disable it entirely), use the Tabs section of the Safari Preferences. (Choose Safari, Preferences, from the menu bar).

Viewing All Tabs

If you find yourself lost in tabs, not knowing what they all are, you can view all the tabbed web pages at once in a pretty scrolling view. To do this, follow these steps:

1. Perform a pinch gesture (only works with the trackpad, obviously) within a webpage or click the Show All Tabs icon at the far right of the Safari toolbar.

2. The tabs appear in a horizontally scrolling list. Use two fingers to swipe side to side and view, or click the small circles underneath the web page images.

3. Click within a page to go to that page, or reverse your pinch to return to your standard tab view.

Viewing PDFs Online

In Mavericks, Apple has included a helpful PDF viewer that makes reviewing PDF documents a breeze. When you click a PDF link, the viewer opens. To control the viewer, follow these steps:

1. Position the cursor near the bottom center of the browser window to show the PDF controls.

2. Click + or – to zoom in and out.

3. Click the Preview icon to open the PDF in the Mavericks Preview (an Image/PDF viewer) application.

4. Click the Download button to save the PDF to your Downloads folder.

Distraction-Free Reading with Reader

Webpages, unfortunately, are rarely dedicated to getting you just the information you need. They are filled with ads and other distracting content, and frequently require you to click multiple links to get the whole story. To provide a distraction-free reading experience, Apple includes a Reader feature with Safari that strips out all the unnecessary cruft. To use Reader, follow these instructions.

1. When viewing a webpage with a story you want to read, check to see if the Reader button is lit up at the far right of the URL field. Click it.

2. You are now viewing a clean version of the content.

3. Use the A icons at the top of the window to change the font size.

4. Click the Reader button again to close Reader.

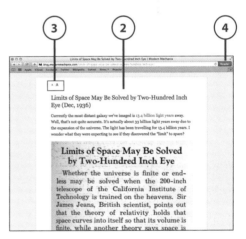

It's Not All Good

DISABLED READER BUTTON? C'EST LA VIE!

The Reader feature of Safari does not work with all articles—only those that it can correctly identify and reformat. If the button shows up as disabled, Reader can't work with the content you're viewing and no amount of reloading or fiddling with settings is going to help.

Continuing Browsing with iCloud Tabs

Ever start reading something on one computer or iOS device and want to pick it up somewhere else? Instead of having to remember to add things to your reading list (or email yourself a bookmark), you can use the iCloud tabs button. This simple feature makes it easy to see what tabs are open on your other devices and quickly open them wherever you are.

1. Click the iCloud button in the toolbar.

2. A pop-over window appears showing all your open tabs, by device.

3. Click an entry to open it in your local browser.

Enable the Safari iCloud Service

This feature requires the Safari service to be active on your iCloud account, as described earlier in this chapter.

Saving and Sharing Account Information

In Mavericks, if you've enabled the Keychain option in iCloud (see Chapter 4, "Setting Up iCloud Services and Internet Accounts"), Safari tracks auto-completion information, stores credit cards, and shares all of the data between all your devices.

1. Browse to a login form on a website where you'd like to log in.

2. Enter your login information.

3. Safari prompts to save your information.

4. Choose to save the information, or not.

Managing AutoFill Data

In addition to the information stored as you browse, Safari can also fill in forms using your Address Book data, or credit card information that you store. To manage all of this data, you need the Safari Preferences:

1. Choose Preferences from the Safari menu.

2. Select Autofill from the toolbar.

3. Check the sources of information you want to use for auto-completing web forms.

4. Click the Edit button to edit that category of information. (Editing the Contacts information opens Address Book).

5. Close the preferences.

Editing AutoFill User Names and Passwords

To edit user names and passwords that you've stored while browsing, complete the steps in "Managing AutoFill Data" and then do the following:

1. Click the Edit button beside User Names and Passwords.

2. Use the search field to locate stored information.

3. Click a stored URL and press delete to remove it.

4. Click Show Passwords for Selected Websites to display passwords in clear text.

5. Click Allow Autofill to store information for sites that request information not be saved.

6. Close the preferences.

Editing AutoFill Credit Cards

While you're checking out in popular online websites, Safari may prompt you to save credit card details. To edit and manage the saved information, complete the steps in "Managing AutoFill Data" and then follow these additional steps:

1. Click the Edit Button beside Credit Cards.

2. Select a card and click Remove to delete it.

3. Click Add to create a new card entry.

4. Fill in the data for each field.

5. Click Done to save the card.

6. Close the preferences.

And All the Rest...

The final type of AutoFill information you can edit is Other forms. This is just other information that Safari stores as you provide data on various web forms. If you click the Edit button for Other forms, you have the ability to browse for web addresses and remove stored data, not edit or view the data.

Sharing with Others

To share the page that you are currently reading with someone else via email or Messages, you can use the Safari Share Sheet. Share Sheets are covered in more detail in Chapter 6, "Sharing Files, Devices, and Services," and 9, "Entertainment on the (Big) Little Screen." For now, follow these steps:

1. Click the Share Sheet icon when browsing a page you like.

2. Choose to share the page via one of the methods displayed.

3. When sharing via email, a new email is created and you can choose whether to share a reader version of the page, the full webpage, a PDF of the page, or just the link!

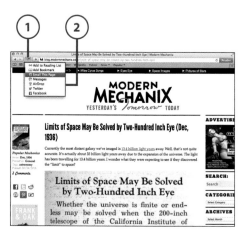

Tweet-Ready Sharing
In Chapter 6 you find out how to add Twitter to the Sharing Sheet, making it simple to quickly tweet the current URL to your followers.

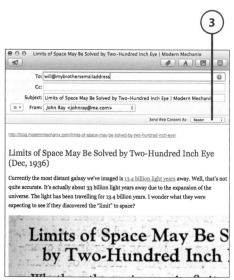

Enabling Private Browsing

If you share a computer with other people, and there's a chance that they might stumble upon something in your web history that you'd prefer they didn't (holiday gift orders, for example), you can enable private browsing.

When private browsing is enabled, no website content is saved to your Mac—it's as if you were never there:

1. Choose Safari, Private Browsing from the menu bar.

2. Click OK when prompted to verify whether private browsing should be enabled.

3. You can now use Safari as you would normally, but your session is private—as indicated in the URL field.

4. Choose Safari, Private Browsing again to disable private browsing.

Protecting Your Mac and Yourself Online

Safari offers several tools to help protect you from fraudulent activity online. To ensure that you have the most secure browsing experience possible, complete the following configuration:

1. Choose Safari, Preferences from the menu.

2. Click the Security toolbar icon.

3. Check the checkbox beside Warn When Visiting a Fraudulent Website.

4. Check the checkbox beside Block Pop-up Windows.

5. Click the Privacy toolbar icon.

6. Be sure that the Block Cookies option is set to From Third Parties and Advertisers.

7. Choose whether Safari should deny all access to your location information, or to prompt you if a website requests it. Note that some online services can provide valuable customized information using your location.

8. Click Ask Websites Not to Track Me to request that your website visits be logged as little as possible. Note that web service providers may not pay attention to this setting.

9. To remove all information stored on your computer by the sites you've visited, click Remove All Website Data. You might want to repeat this from time to time.

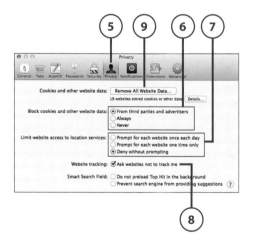

10. Use the Notification Preferences section to manage which websites can post notifications to the Mavericks Notification Center.

11. Close the Safari Preferences.

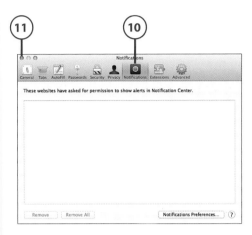

Go With What You Know

As a general rule, you should never download files online unless you trust the source. By default, Safari opens files that it has identified as safe. If you prefer to prevent Safari from opening *any* file it downloads, you can find this option under the General Safari Preferences.

Adding Web Content to the Dashboard

Many of us visit a webpage just to see a tiny piece of content, such as the latest weather report or breaking news. With Safari and the Dashboard, you can create your own widget, called a web clipping, that is accessible directly from your Mac's Dashboard. This gives you instant access to information you like without needing to open Safari. The content even updates automatically as long as you are connected to the Internet.

1. Visit the webpage with the content you want to add to the Dashboard.

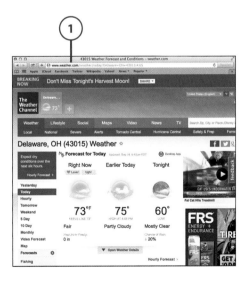

2. Choose File, Open in Dashboard.

3. Position the box on the page so that the content you want to capture is highlighted as best as possible, and then click your mouse.

4. Fine-tune the selected area by dragging it within the Safari window and using the handles on the sides to resize it.

5. Click Add when you are satisfied with the results.

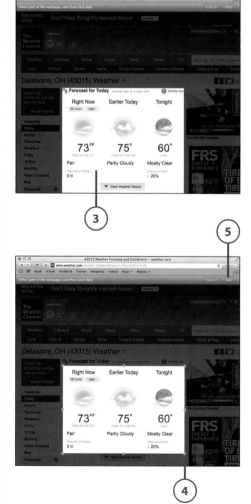

6. The Dashboard opens and the new web clipping widget is displayed.

6

Changing the Clipping Appearance

To customize the web clipping even more, click the i icon in the lower-right corner of the widget in Dashboard. You are given the option of several different borders that can be applied to stylize the clipping.

Extending Safari's Capabilities with Extensions

Safari supports developer-created extensions that can add additional functionality to your browsing experience—such as the ability to quickly access Twitter, eBay, and other services without leaving your current webpage. Safari extensions are supported by the individual developers, so after you install one, you need to refer to the documentation for further support.

Installing an Extension

Installing extensions doesn't require anything more than clicking a link on a website.

1. Choose Safari, Safari Extensions from the menu bar.

1

2. An Apple website opens listing all registered extensions.

3. Use the website to browse to an extension you are interested in, and then click the Install Now button beside the extension.

4. After a few seconds, the extension is installed and activated. Depending on how it works, you might see a new button or area added to the Safari toolbar. Follow the developer's instructions to use the extension.

Managing Extensions

To manage the extensions you've installed—including configuring them, if configuration is necessary—use Safari Preferences. Follow these steps to access your extension preferences:

1. Open the Safari Preferences by choosing Safari, Preferences from the menu bar.

2. Click the Extensions button in the top of the Preferences window.

3. Click an individual extension to view its configuration options.

4. Use the Enable checkbox to enable or disable individual extensions.

5. Click Uninstall to remove the extension entirely.

6. Use the On/Off switch to disable all extensions.

7. Click the Updates button to look for and install updates to any installed extensions.

8. Close the Preferences panel when finished.

Configure file, printer, screen, and Internet sharing in the Sharing System Preference panel.

Point and click to browse available servers on your network.

Connect directly to a wide range of servers using their Internet addresses.

In this chapter, you learn how to use your Mac to share and access resources over a network, including:

→ Sharing files and folders using AirDrop and File Sharing
→ File sharing with Windows computers
→ Setting Share Permissions
→ Using Share Sheets to quickly share files online
→ Sharing and accessing network printers
→ Sharing your screen and viewing remote systems
→ Turning your Mac into an Internet Access Point

Sharing Files, Devices, and Services

Your Mac is a self-contained workstation that packs all the power you need into a highly integrated package—and one that is fully capable of integrating with new or existing networks. Mavericks can share and access a variety of resources with other computers on your network. Files and folders can be shared with other Macs and Windows PCs; printers can be shared with other Macs; even your screen can be made available to other computers on your network.

To make the most use of the information in this chapter, the assumption is that you've already established a network connection and have connected any printers or scanners to either your Mac or another Mavericks-based Macintosh on your network. You might want to refer to Chapter 3, "Connecting Your Mac to a Network," and Chapter 12, "Connecting Devices to Your Mac," for more details on networking and peripherals, respectively.

File Sharing on Your Mac

The most common network activity (beyond email and web surfing) is file sharing. Your Mac comes ready to share files using several popular protocols—AFP (Apple Filing Protocol) and SMB (Simple Message Block) are the most popular. AFP, as the name suggests, is a Mac-to-Mac file sharing protocol, but with Mavericks, Apple has switched to SMB as the preferred protocol. SMB has traditionally been used primarily in Windows environments and offers significant performance improvements over AFP.

In addition to the *protocols* for sharing files, you also have different *methods* for *how* you share them. Traditional file sharing requires that you turn on file sharing, choose what you want to share, tell another person how to connect, and so on. With Mavericks, your Mac includes a zero-configuration version of file sharing called AirDrop. AirDrop enables you to wirelessly share files with other users who are in your vicinity—with no setup required!

Authenticate to Make Changes!

Many of the settings in this chapter require you to authenticate with Mavericks before the settings can be made. If you find yourself in a situation where a setting is grayed out, click the padlock icon in the lower-left corner of the window to authenticate and make the necessary change.

Using AirDrop to Wirelessly Share Files and Folders

AirDrop is a fast and easy file-sharing system that enables you to send files to another Macintosh without any setup—no usernames, no passwords, nothing except a Wi-Fi adapter that is turned on! Unlike traditional file sharing, AirDrop's simplicity does present a few challenges that might make it less than ideal for your particular file-sharing situation. Specifically, AirDrop requires the following:

- All computers sharing files must be using the Lion (or later) operating system.

- All systems must have recent wireless-AC or N Wi-Fi hardware—2011 or later Macs will work fine.

- Your computer will not be able to browse the contents of other systems, only send files.

Sending Files with AirDrop

To use AirDrop, be sure that your Wi-Fi adapter is turned on (see Chapter 3 for details), identify the files that you want to share with another person, and then follow these steps:

1. Open a new Finder window and make sure the Favorites sidebar section is expanded.

2. Click the AirDrop icon to browse for other OS X computers.

3. Other computers are shown using the owner's avatar picture (set in Address Book) as their icon.

4. Drag the files you want to transfer to the icon of another computer.

5. Confirm the transfer by clicking Send when prompted.

6. You will be asked to wait while the remote system confirms the transfer.

7. The files are copied to the remote system. A blue circle around the receiving computer indicates progress.

8. Close the AirDrop window to stop being visible on the network. After you've closed the AirDrop window, you can go your merry way. You don't need to disconnect or change your network settings. You're done!

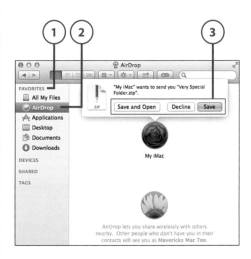

Receiving Files with AirDrop

Receiving files with AirDrop is even easier than sending them. When a nearby Mavericks user wants to send files to your Mac, follow these steps:

1. Open a new Finder window and make sure the Favorites sidebar section is expanded.

2. Click the AirDrop icon to become visible to other AirDrop users.

3. When prompted to receive files, click Save or Save and Open to accept the transfer, or Decline to cancel.

4. The files are transferred to your Downloads folder.

5. Click the X on the download-ing file or folder to cancel the download.

6. Close the AirDrop window to stop being visible on the network. That's it! Your AirDrop session is automatically ended when the window closes.

No AirDrop? Your Mac Might Be Too Old.

AirDrop uses peer-to-peer ad hoc wireless networking, which is only supported in recent Macs (2011 and later). Although this may seem limit-ing, this hardware is what makes it possible to communicate with zero configuration and without using a common Wi-Fi access point.

Using Share Sheets to Send via AirDrop

Share Sheets are a new user inter-face (UI) element and feature in Mavericks. They enable applications to share files and folders from almost anywhere—even file open and save dialog boxes, as you'll see here.

1. Select a file (or open a file) within an application.

2. Look for the Share Sheet button. Click to show the Sharing menu.

3. Select AirDrop from the list of sharing options.

4. A new window appears listing all nearby users with AirDrop open in the Finder.

5. Click the person you want to send the file to.

6. The copy begins as soon as the recipient accepts the transfer. On the receiving end, an AirDrop transfer sent via an application appears identical to one sent directly from the Finder; the process is the same as that discussed earlier.

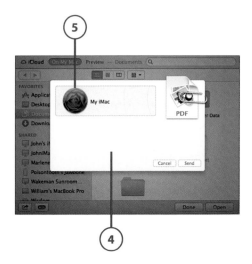

Beyond the 'Drop

Share Sheets are much more powerful than just sharing via AirDrop. We look at a few other sharing scenarios that use this feature later in this chapter.

Configuring Traditional File and Folder Sharing

When AirDrop won't do (you need to browse another computer's files or share with Windows/older Macs), you need to turn to the traditional file sharing features built into OS X. Mavericks provides consolidated controls for sharing files, regardless of what type of computer you want to share them with. You set up file sharing by first enabling sharing for your Mac and then choosing the protocols available for accessing the files. Finally, you decide which folders should be shared and who should see them.

Enabling File Sharing

Before your Mac can make any files or folders available over a network, you must enable File Sharing.

1. In the System Preferences, click the Sharing icon.

2. Click the checkbox in front of the service labeled File Sharing.

3. The details about your sharing configuration are displayed on the right side of the sharing window.

4. Close the Sharing Preferences panel, or continue configuring other sharing options.

Choosing File Sharing Protocols

Files can be shared over AFP (Legacy OS X) or SMB (Mavericks and Windows). If possible, stick to SMB for the best speeds.

To choose which protocols can be used to access the files on your Mac, follow these steps:

1. In System Preferences, click the Sharing icon.

2. Click the File Sharing service label.

3. Click the Options button to display the available sharing protocols.

4. Check or uncheck the protocols that you want to use. If you are only sharing between Mavericks machines, all you need is SMB.

5. If you want to use SMB to share specifically with Windows systems, you must enable each account for access. Within the Windows File Sharing section, check the box in front of each user that should be *allowed* to connect.

6. Enter the password for each account.

7. Click Done.

8. Close the Sharing Preferences, or continue configuring sharing options.

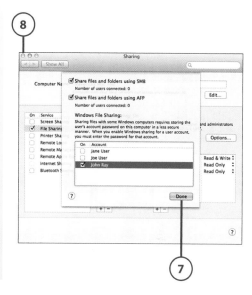

WHAT IS WITH THE ACCOUNT CHECKBOXES AND PASSWORDS FOR WINDOWS FILE SHARING?

To share with Windows clients, the Mavericks SMB implementation requires that user accounts and passwords be stored in a different format than how they are used natively by OS X. By enabling or disabling accounts for Windows File, you are creating the user authentication information that Windows users will need to connect.

Selecting Folders and Permissions

After enabling file sharing and choosing the protocols that are used, your next step is to pick the folders that can be shared. By default, each user's Public folder is shared and accessible by anyone with an account on your computer. (See Chapter 13, "Securing and Protecting Your Mac," for configuring user accounts.)

1. In the System Preferences, click the Sharing icon.

2. Click the File Sharing service label.

3. Click the + button under Shared Folders to share a new folder.

4. Find the folder you want to make available and then click the Add button.

5. Close the System Preferences, or continue configuring sharing options.

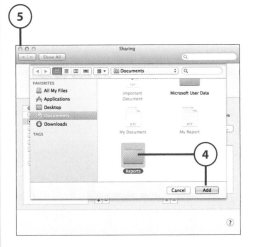

Setting Folder Access Permissions

By default, your user account has full access to anything that you share. The default user group named Staff, and everyone with an account on the computer, have read-only access.

To change who can access a file share, complete the following steps:

1. In the System Preferences window, click the Sharing icon.

2. Click the File Sharing service label.

3. Click the Shared Folder name that you want to modify.

4. Click the + button under the Users list to add a new user (or – to remove access for a selected user).

5. A window for selecting a user displays. Within the Users & Groups category, pick the user or group and click Select.

6. Use the pop-up menu to the right of each user in the Users list to choose what the user can do within the shared folder.

7. Close the System Preferences.

WHAT PERMISSIONS CAN BE APPLIED TO A SHARED FOLDER?

>>>Go Further

Shared folders can have the following permissions set on a per-user or per-group basis:

- **Read & Write**—Grants full access to the folder and files within it. Users can add, edit, and delete items within the folder.

- **Read Only**—Provides access to the files in the folder, but users cannot modify or delete them, nor can they create new files or folders.

- **Write Only (Drop Box)**—Allows users to write to the folder, but not see its contents.

- **No Access**—Available only for the Everyone group; disables access for all user accounts except those explicitly granted access in the permissions.

Accessing Shared Files

Shared files are only useful if you can access them! Your Mac provides two methods of connecting to shared folders: by browsing for them on your local network and by entering a URL to connect directly to the shared resource.

Browsing and Connecting to Network Shares

Browsing and connecting to a local network share is similar to browsing through the folders located on your Mac. To browse for available network shares, do the following:

1. Open a new Finder window and make sure the Shared sidebar section is expanded.

2. Click the computer that is sharing the folders and files that you want to access.

3. If you have not logged into the computer before and saved your password, a list of the publicly accessible file shares is displayed in the Finder window.

4. Click the Connect As button on the upper right of the Finder window.

5. Enter the username and password that you have established for accessing files on the server.

6. Click Remember This Password in My Keychain to enable browsing directly to the file shares in the future.

7. Click Connect.

8. The file share list updates to display all the shares that your user account can access. Double-click the share you want to use.

9. The share is mounted as a disk and can be used as if it were local to your Mac.

One Password to Rule Them All

You may notice when connecting to other Mavericks or Mountain Lion servers that you are given the option of connecting with your Apple ID. This will work if your account has had an Apple ID associated with it on the remote server. This association is made by selecting a user within the Users & Groups System Preferences panel and then clicking the Set button that is next to the Apple ID field.

Browsing Large Networks

If there are many different computers sharing files on your network, you can browse them in a Finder window rather than the Finder sidebar. To open a Finder window that browses your network, choose Go, Network from the menu bar, or click the All... icon within the Shared section of the Finder sidebar.

Connecting to Remote Shares

Sometimes file shares aren't directly browseable because they're hiding their available shares, or they are located on a different network from your Mac. To access remote shares by URL, follow these steps:

1. When you create a new file share on your Mac, Mavericks provides you with a list of URLs that can be used to access that file share (see step 3 of "Enabling File Sharing"). You can use these URLs to directly access a file share rather than browsing.

2. Choose Go, Connect to Server from the Finder menu.

3. Enter the URL for the file share in the Server Address field.

4. Click + if you want to add the server to the list of favorite servers.

5. Click Connect to connect to the server and view the available shares.

Talking the (Windows) Talk

Your Windows friends might give you network shares to connect to in the format *servername**sharename*. You can translate this into a "Mac-friendly" URL by adding the prefix smb: and reversing the direction of the slashes— that is, smb://*servername*/*sharename*.

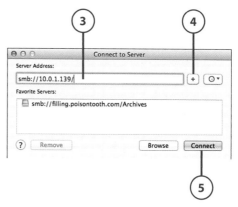

Sharing Files via Share Sheets

Mavericks includes a way of sharing files from almost anywhere via Share Sheets. You can use a Share Sheet menu (indicated by an icon of an arrow pointing out of a rectangle) to quickly send a file through a variety of different means, including AirDrop (discussed earlier in this chapter), Messages, and other online services.

Sharing Files via Messages

A simple example of Share Sheets is using the sheet to share a file via Messages. To do this, either open the file or select it in the Finder, and then follow these instructions:

1. Click the Share Sheet button.

2. Choose Messages from the drop-down menu.

3. A panel appears with the file added as an attachment.

4. Add the user that you want to send the file to.

5. Click Send to send the file and get back to work!

Uploading Files to an Online Service

Using Mavericks, you can now share your files with the world via a number of online services—such as YouTube, Facebook, Vimeo, and Flickr—without even needing to touch a web browser. YouTube is the most popular destination for videos on the Internet, so we'll use that as our example. To upload a video to the online service of your choice, follow these steps:

1. Locate the movie file you want to upload, and double-click to open it in QuickTime Player.

2. Click the Share Sheet to display sharing options and choose the online destination (in this case, YouTube) from the pop-up menu.

3. Enter your username and password when prompted.

4. Choose Remember This Password in My Keychain to streamline the process in the future.

5. Click Sign In to log into the YouTube service.

6. Set a category for the uploaded video file.

7. Enter a title, description, and a set of keywords (called Tags) to describe the video.

8. Use the Access setting to set the video as Personal, if desired. This limits viewing of the video to individuals who you share it with via the YouTube website. Please note that these settings may vary between the various online services supported in Mavericks.

9. Click Next.

10. Review the YouTube Terms of Service, and then click Share.

11. The Movie Export window appears and displays the status of the encoding process.

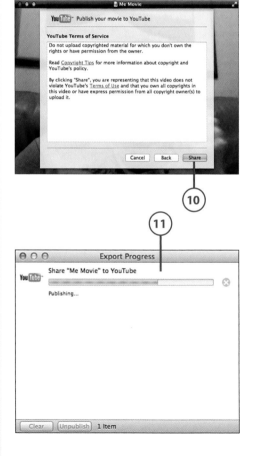

12. When finished, a link to the video is displayed.

13. Close QuickTime Player. Your movie is available online.

Cutting It Down to Size

To trim a video before sharing it, click the Share Sheet button and choose Edit, Trim from the menu bar. You can move the start and end points of your video clip to wherever you'd like and then trim off the extra.

Sharing Printers

Sharing a printer is a convenient way to provide printing services to your Mac without having to connect any physical wires. With Mavericks, printer sharing just takes a few clicks and then your system acts as if it has a physical printer attached.

Enabling Network Printer Sharing

To share a printer, you must first have the printer connected and configured on another Macintosh (see Chapter 12 for details). After the printer is set up and working, follow these steps to make it available over a local network:

1. In the System Preferences window, click the Sharing icon.

2. Click the checkbox in front of the Printer Sharing service.

3. Within the Printers list, click the checkboxes in front of each printer you want to share. The printers are immediately made available to everyone on your network.

4. Close the System Preferences, or continue setting sharing preferences.

Setting Printer Sharing Permissions

Any shared printer is initially available to anyone with a computer connected to your network. To restrict access to specific user accounts on your computer, do the following:

1. In the System Preferences window, click the Sharing icon.

2. Click the label for the Printer Sharing service.

3. Highlight the name of the shared printer that you want to configure.

4. Click the + button to select a user that can print to your printer. (Use – to remove access for a user you added previously.)

5. A window is displayed to select a user. Choose the user or group and click Select.

No Access for Everyone

The Everyone group can't be removed from the Users list. To remove access for Everyone, the group must be toggled to No Access.

6. Toggle the pop-up menu beside the Everyone group to No Access to keep everyone except the listed individuals from being able to access the printer.

7. Close the System Preferences.

Accessing a Network Printer

To access a printer that is being shared by another Mac, first make sure that both computers are on and connected to the same network and then follow these steps:

1. Choose File, Print from the menu bar within an application of your choice.

2. The Printer dialog box appears. Click the Printer drop-down menu to see the options.

3. If you haven't used the shared printer before, select the printer from the Nearby Printers section of the drop-down menu.

4. Mavericks automatically connects your Mac to the printer and configures it.

5. Choose the options for the document you are printing and then click Print. The printer behaves exactly as if it is connected directly to your computer. The next time you print, the printer will be available directly in your main printer list.

Printing to Protected Printers

If you set up specific user accounts that can access the printer, you are prompted for a username and password the first time you print. You can, at that time, choose to save the printer connection information to your keychain, which eliminates the need to authenticate for subsequent use.

Sharing an Optical Drive

If you're using a CD- or DVD-less Mac (which is most of them!) you can use another Macintosh on your network to share a CD or DVD inserted into its drive. This gives you the ability to install software and access files even if you don't have a physical drive connected.

Enabling DVD and CD Sharing

From a Macintosh with CD or DVD drives available, follow these steps to turn on optical drive sharing:

1. In the System Preferences window, click the Sharing icon.

2. Click the checkbox in front of the DVD or CD Sharing service.

3. Click the Ask Me Before Allowing Others to Use My DVD Drive checkbox to prompt you when other people attempt to access your optical drive.

4. Close the System Preferences.

Accessing a Shared Optical Drive

To access a shared optical drive from your DVD-free Mac, do the following:

1. Open a new Finder window and make sure the Devices section in the Finder sidebar is expanded.

2. Click the Remote Disc item in the Devices sidebar area.

3. Double-click the computer that is sharing the DVD you want to use.

4. If the DVD is not immediately visible, click Ask to Use to prompt the host computer that you'd like to use its drive.

5. After access has been granted, the available DVD or CD is listed. Double-click the DVD or CD to begin using it.

Can I Access a Shared Optical Drive Even if My Mac *Has* a DVD Drive?

Yes, but not without a few changes. You need to open the Terminal application (found in the Utilities folder in the Applications folder) and then type in the following two lines to enable optical drive sharing:

```
defaults write com.apple.NetworkBrowser EnableODiskBrowsing -bool true

defaults write com.apple.NetworkBrowser ODSSupported -bool true
```

Reboot your computer after entering these commands.

Sharing Your Mac Screen

Chapter 8, "Managing Who, Where, When, and What," includes instructions on how to share your Macintosh's screen using Messages, but there are many instances where you might want to access another Mac's display without having to start a chat.

Built into Mavericks is a standards-based screen-sharing system. Using screen sharing, you can access your Mac's display from anywhere on your local network or, in some cases, from anywhere in the world. Mavericks even has the ability to share a computer's "screen" even if someone else is using the computer. The screen sharing software can now automatically create a virtual screen that you can see and use while the person sitting in front of the computer continues to see their own desktop!

Enabling Screen Sharing

To configure another Mac so that you can access its screen from your Mac, you initially need direct access to the computer:

1. In the System Preferences window, click the Sharing icon.

2. Click the checkbox in front of the Screen Sharing service.

3. A URL that you can use to connect to your computer is displayed on the right side of the sharing pane.

4. Close the System Preferences, or continue setting sharing preferences.

Setting Screen Sharing Permissions

After screen sharing is enabled, choose who can access the display. Initially, only administrative users can view your screen.

1. In the System Preferences window, click the Sharing icon.

2. Click the Screen Sharing service label.

3. Choose whether All Users on the computer can access its screen, or click Only These Users to restrict access to specific individuals or groups.

4. Use the + button to choose a user or group that should be granted access, or use – to remove a user or group that you had previously added.

5. A window for selecting a user displays. Choose the user or group and click Select.

6. For additional control, click the Computer Settings button.

7. In the dialog box that appears, click Anyone May Request Permission to Control Screen to allow anyone to access the display if the person sitting in front of the computer grants them access.

8. To provide access to your Mac's screen using a standard VNC (Virtual Network Computing) client, click the VNC Viewers May Control Screen with Password checkbox and provide a password that grants access to those users.

9. Click OK.

10. Close the System Preferences.

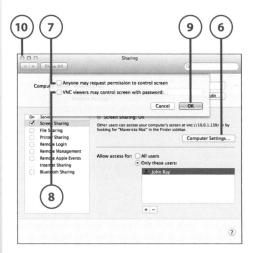

VNC Is Everywhere

There are VNC clients available for Windows, Linux, and even platform-independent Java. If you want to access your Mac's screen from another operating system, check out TightVNC (www.tightvnc.com).

Accessing the Screen of a Local Mac

To access the shared screen of a Mac on your local network, make sure that your Mac is connected to the network and then follow these steps:

1. Open a new Finder window and make sure the Shared sidebar section heading is expanded.

2. Click the computer whose screen you want to access.

3. Click Share Screen in the upper-right corner of the Finder window.

4. Enter your username and password on the remote system, if prompted.

5. Click Remember This Password in My Keychain to store the password and enable password-less connections in the future.

6. Click Connect to begin using the remote display.

7. If another person is using the computer, you can ask to share the display with them, or connect to a new virtual display. Click whichever approach you prefer.

8. The remote display is shown in a window on your Mac.

9. Toggle between controlling and observing with the Control Mode icons in the toolbar.

10. Use the Scaling Mode icon to view the screen fullsize or shrink it to fit your window.

11. Use the Clipboard icon to choose how to transfer your clipboard to and from the remote system, or simply share the clipboard.

12. Drag files to and from the remote system to transfer them to (and from!) your computer.

13. Close the window when you're finished using the remote system.

Capture the Moment

If you'd like to take screenshots of the remote system, you can add a screenshot button to the toolbar by choosing View, Customize Toolbar from the menu bar. You can also take a screenshot directly by choosing Connection, Save Screen Capture As.

Accessing Remote Computers and Non-Macs

If you can't browse to a computer to access its screen, or you need to connect to a non-Macintosh computer, you can do so using almost the same process as you used to connect to a remote file share:

1. When you're sharing a screen on your Mac, Mavericks provides you with a URL that can be used to access your screen, even if you can't browse to it on the network.

2. Choose Go, Connect to Server from the Finder menu bar.

3. Enter the screen-sharing URL in the Server Address field. Alternatively, if you only have an IP address (such as 192.168.1.100), prefix the IP address with vnc:// to create a properly formed URL (for example, vnc://192.168.1.100).

4. Click + if you want to add the server to the list of favorite servers.

5. Click Connect to connect to the remote server's screen.

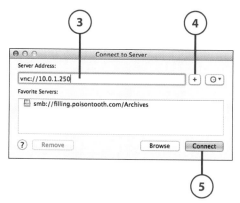

6. Enter a username (and/or password), if prompted, and click Connect.

7. The remote display is shown in a window on your Mac.

VNC for Windows/Linux

To connect to a Windows or Linux computer, you need to first install a VNC server (Virtual Network Computing) on the computer whose display you want to share. TightVNC (www.tightvnc.com) is an entirely free Open Source option that works on both Windows and Linux platforms.

>>>Go Further

THERE ARE A LOT OF PLACES LIKE HOME

The Shared portion of the sidebar shows you the computers on your local network. This is great for accessing things around you, but what about accessing your computer at home or from work? You could use the address of your home computer to access it remotely, but you'd need to remember the address and have your home network configured correctly. Instead, you can simply enable the iCloud service "Back to My Mac" (see Chapter 4, "Setting Up iCloud Services and Internet Accounts," for details). Once enabled, this free service makes all your computers visible to one another wherever you have an Internet connection. You won't be able to tell the difference (network-wise) from being at home or being on a remote (well-connected) island.

Sharing Your Internet Connection

Your Mac is a perfect Internet-sharing platform because it includes both Ethernet and wireless network connections. You can, in a matter of minutes, create a wireless network using just your computer and a cable or DSL modem.

Sharing Your Connection

1. In the System Preferences window, click the Sharing icon.

2. Click the Internet Sharing service label. (Note: The checkbox is initially disabled!)

3. Use the Share Your Connection From drop-down menu to choose how you are connected to the Internet (Ethernet, Airport, iPhone, and so on).

4. Within the To Computers Using list, click the checkboxes in front of each of the interfaces where the connection should be shared.

5. If you're sharing a connection over your Wi-Fi card, a Wi-Fi Options button appears. Click this button to configure how your computer presents itself wirelessly.

6. Set the name of the wireless network you are creating.

7. Leave the channel set to the default.

8. If you want to enable password protection for the network, choose WPA2 Personal from the Security drop-down, and then provide a password.

9. Click OK to save your settings.

10. Click the checkbox in front of the Internet Sharing service.

11. Close the System Preferences.

12. Connect to the new wireless network from other computers as described in Chapter 3. You should set the other computers to configure themselves automatically rather than manually configuring the network (not shown).

Keep a Switch Handy

If you're sharing your connection over Ethernet, you need to connect a switch to your Mac's Ethernet port and then connect the other computer systems/devices to the switch.

Chat with friends and family in Messages.

Connect to Twitter and Facebook.

Post updates and tweets throughout Mavericks.

In this chapter, you learn how to use your Mac to be social online, including:

→ Configuring instant messaging in Messages
→ Conducting video and audio chats
→ Chatting across computers and iOS devices
→ Posting Tweets and Facebook Updates

Being Social with Messages, FaceTime, Twitter, and Facebook

In addition to providing methods of sending and consuming content, the Internet (and Mavericks) gives us new ways to be social. Using the tools built into OS X, you can send instant messages, conduct video chats, send tweets, and keep in touch with FaceBook.

In this chapter, you find out how to use many of the features of Messages, FaceTime, and Mavericks social networking options. These will help you stay on top of current events in your friends' lives and interact with people around the world—without driving up your phone bill.

Instant Messaging with Messages

When email isn't conversational enough, instant messaging can take over. Your Mac comes with a first-rate instant messaging application called Messages (found in the Applications folder). You can use Messages for text messaging, audio conferencing, video conferencing, and even screen sharing. If you have an iCloud, GoogleTalk, Jabber, or AIM (AOL Instant Messenger) account, you're ready to go.

There are two ways to use Messages, although both are integrated (somewhat poorly) into the same interface. First, you can use Apple's unique iMessage protocol to send and receive messages on all your iOS devices and Macs simultaneously. Using this approach, you can start a conversation on Messages on your iPad and then pick it up immediately on your Mac just by starting Maverick's Messages app. Best of all, after you enable an iMessage account, you don't even have to *start* Messages to receive notifications. As long as your Mac is online, you will receive your iMessages.

The second way to use Messages is with a traditional instant messaging account, such as AIM, Yahoo! Messenger, or GoogleTalk. The process is pretty similar, regardless of your approach, and when you've started a messaging session, you'll be using the same interface regardless.

To keep things straight in your mind, remember that if I talk about using an iMessage account or sending an iMessage, I'm referring to Apple's Mac and iOS messaging system. I'll be as specific as possible as I describe the features in Messages.

Adding Accounts to Messages

Apple simplifies the process of configuring Messages by emailing you to create an iMessage account *and* a traditional account the first time you run the app. After that, however, I recommend that you manage your accounts in different locations.

Configuring Your Account During Startup

Unlike other accounts, to configure iMessage within Messages, you need to use the application itself. This is likely to change in the future, but for now, don't expect too much consistency in the interface. The easiest way to configure Messages with an iMessage account is to do so during the first run, like this:

1. Start Messages from the Dock, Launchpad, or Applications folder.

2. Enter the Apple ID (and password) you want to use with the iMessage protocol.

3. Click Sign In.

4. By default, the email address associated with your Apple ID can receive iMessages. Uncheck addresses to remove them. To add other addresses, edit your account settings after this initial setup.

5. Choose whether you want your contacts to view when you read messages sent using the iMessage protocol.

6. Click Done to begin using Messages

Editing Your iMessage Account Settings

To manage an iMessage account after you've first started the Messages application, you need to use the Messages preferences. Follow these steps to manage your settings:

1. Choose Messages, Preferences from the menu bar.

2. Click the Accounts toolbar icon.

3. Select the iMessage account entry.

4. Use the Enable This Account checkbox to enable or disable the account.

5. Uncheck Send Read Receipts if you don't want your contacts to see when you've read their messages.

6. Click Add Email to add a new account that can receive iMessages.

7. Close the preferences when finished.

Adding a Traditional IM Account to Messages

If you want to configure IM after running Messages for the first time, I recommend using the central Internet Accounts preference panel. You need to know your account type, username, and password before continuing.

1. Open the Internet Accounts System Preferences panel.

2. Choose the online service that provides your IM account by clicking its name on the right. If your service only provides IM and not mail or calendaring, click Add Other Account to directly configure an IM account.

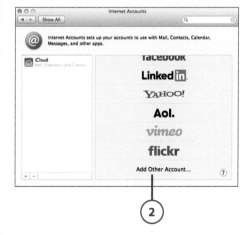

3. If you chose Add Other Account, select Add a Messages Account.

4. Fill in the requested information in the setup wizard that appears.

5. Click Create.

6. Close the System Preferences window.

Multiple IM Accounts? No Problem!

Adding multiple IM accounts to Messages is no problem. The Messages buddy list window combines your buddy lists into a single consolidated list. You can log in and out of the different services using the availability controls for each account (they are stacked on top of each other), as described in the "Logging into (and out of) Your IM Account" task.

Logging into (and out of) Your IM Account

When Messages has an account configured, you're ready to start Messages and begin chatting immediately. No "logging into" iMessage accounts is required; your IM account is automatically logged in when you start the application. To manually log out of or into your IM accounts, you simply need to set your status.

1. Click the status message in the lower-left corner of the Messages window.

2. To keep your status in sync between accounts, make sure Use Same Status for All Accounts is checked.

3. Choose Offline to log out.

4. Choose any other status to log back into your IM account.

5. Choose Invisible to log in but hide your availability from other people.

Adding a Messages Status Menu

To add a Messages status menu to your menu bar, open the Messages Preferences and click Show Status in Menu Bar within the General settings. This gives you the ability to log in and out of your IM accounts when Messages isn't running. Remember, however, that you can't log out of your iMessage account; it is always active unless you explicitly deactivate it in the Messages preferences.

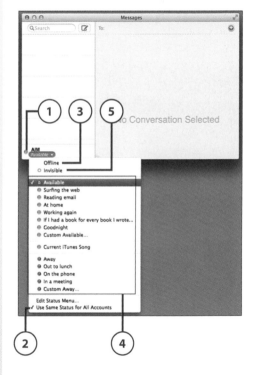

Configuring Your IM Identity

If you're using traditional IM services (AIM, Yahoo!, and so on), you should customize your identity to better represent your online presence. With Messages, it's simple to set custom status messages and pictures to reflect your current mood.

It's Not All Good

IM BUT NOT iMESSAGE

Things get a bit confusing here. These features are not available for iMessage accounts; they apply to traditional instant messaging only. I do hope (and suspect) that Apple will add these features later.

Setting the Messages Picture

Because your Mac has a camera built in, you can swap your IM picture whenever you want. Just smile and click, and instantly your buddies are seeing a new image.

1. Choose Window, Buddies to open the IM buddy list.

2. Click the picture in the upper-right corner of the Messages buddy list.

3. Choose from a Recent picture, iPhoto Faces, iCloud Photostream, Photos linked to your IM account, Default IM pictures, or click Camera to use your Mac's camera.

4. When Camera is selected, click the camera icon to take a new picture.

5. Set cropping and size for the picture by dragging it within the preview window and adjusting the zoom slider.

6. Apply effects, if desired, using the Effects button.

7. Click Done to start using the new picture.

Configuring Custom Status Messages

Your status message can convey your state of mind, ask a question, or present some other information to your buddies. To configure a new status message, follow these steps:

1. Click the status pop-up menu either in your buddy list or in the main messages window.

2. Choose Edit Status Menu.

3. Click + or – under the Available or Away lists to add or remove status messages.

4. Click OK to save your status message settings.

Managing Your IM Buddy List

Sending iMessages to your friends on Macs and iOS devices requires that you know their iMessage address or have it listed in your Contacts application. If you're using an IM account, however, you need to make sure that your buddy list is kept up-to-date with the people you want to chat with.

As you probably know, a buddy list contains all the people you want to chat with (and possibly some you don't). With each buddy is a display of his status (Away, Available, Idle, and so on) and an icon to indicate his chat capability.

Cross-Platform Video Conferencing
Messages can carry out cross-platform A/V chats with Windows users using AIM, Google Talk, or Yahoo!.

Adding Buddies

To initiate an IM chat with someone, you must first add her to your buddy list.

1. Click the + button at the bottom of the buddy list.

2. Choose Add Buddy.

3. If you have a contact card for the person you want to add, click the disclosure arrow in the lower-right corner of the window to display your contacts, and then find and click the person's name.

4. Enter your buddy's screen name (Account Name).

5. Enter a first and last name for your addition, and choose a group, if any are available. Think of groups as a "folder" for your buddy.

6. Click Add.

Adding Groups

As your IM buddy list grows, you might want to consider organizing your buddies into groups, such as friends, family, coworkers, and so on. Adding new groups is similar to adding new buddies.

1. Make sure View, Use Groups is selected in the Messages menu bar.

2. Click the + button at the bottom of the buddy list.

3. Choose Add Group.

4. Enter a name for the new group.

5. Click Add.

6. Drag buddies within the buddy list into the group where you want them to appear.

Recent Buddies

By default, a group called Recent Buddies is added to your buddy list after you start chatting with people. This group contains all the new contacts you've communicated with recently. You can disable this group within the Messages IM account settings.

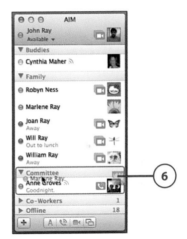

Communicating with IM and iMessages

Messages, through an iMessages account, can communicate with your friends and colleagues using text and file attachments, such as images.

When using IM accounts, Messages supports a number of communications methods, including text, audio, and video. Messages Theater even makes it possible to share visual media from your Mac across a chat session. For example, you might review an upcoming presentation with colleagues to fine-tune the content or present a slideshow of a vacation to friends and family.

Responding to an Incoming Chat via Notification Center

After you've configured Messages and given your iMessages address screen name to your buddies, chances are, you'll start getting a few messages. To respond to an incoming chat request, follow these steps:

1. If you're in another application with no windows open, the Messages icon updates with a count of the messages you have waiting and a notification appears.

2. Click Reply in the notification,

3. Type a reply and press Return.

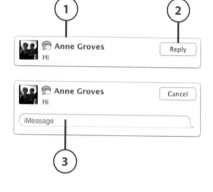

Responding to an Incoming Chat in Messages

Notification Center is useful for quick replies. For a full chat experience, however, you'll want to use Messages itself.

1. Open Messages and make sure the main window is visible. If it isn't, choose Window, Messages from the menu bar.

2. The Messages window shows all your current and new conversations.

3. To accept a conversation request, just click the entry in the list on the left and begin chatting.

4. If you don't know the individual or don't want to hear from him, just hover over his appropriate entry in the conversation list and click the X button that appears.

5. When you're finished chatting, close the Messages window.

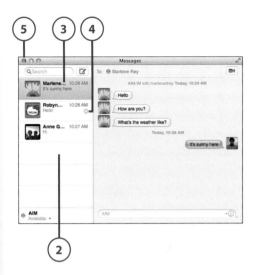

Starting a Chat in Messages

To initiate an IM or iMessage chat with one or more buddies, make sure the Messages window is visible (Window, Messages) and follow these steps:

1. Click the New Chat button.

2. Click the + button to choose from a list of your contacts (useful for iMessaging) or your IM buddy list.

3. Alternatively, begin typing in the To field. Messages autocompletes as you type and shows you the different accounts you can use to communicate with someone. Click the contact (and communications method) you want.

4. Type to your friend, press Return, and wait for a response.

Double-Click to Chat

If you're viewing your buddy list, you can also initiate an IM chat by double-clicking a buddy or clicking his name and then clicking the A (for text chat) button at the bottom of the buddy list.

Consolidate or Separate Messages

Messages automatically consolidates your chats into a single window. To move a chat to a separate window, double-click one of the conversations in the Messages window. It becomes its own standalone chat window.

Starting a Chat via Notification Center

New in Mavericks is the ability to send a message via Notification Center—even if Messages isn't running. To use this nifty feature, follow these steps:

1. Open Notification Center

2. Click the Messages (speech bubble) icon at the top of the Notification Center pane.

3. In the window that appears, type the name of a contact to message. Notification Center will auto-complete the name as you type.

4. Enter your message below the To: line.

5. Click Send to transmit the message.

Starting an IM Audio or IM Video Chat

A/V chats require significantly more bandwidth than text chats. Messages automatically senses the capabilities of your machine and Internet connection, and that of the people involved in your conversations. Messages does not allow chats unless it thinks they will be successful. Using IM, you can chat with up to 3 other people via video and 10 via audio, depending on your connection and assuming that they have microphone- or camera-enabled systems. When chatting with iMessage, you are able to launch a FaceTime conversation with one other individual.

The good news is that, regardless of your system capabilities or those of your chat partners, Messages shows only the relevant options.

1. Begin a chat with the individuals you want to include in an audio or video session.

2. Click the camera icon in the upper-right corner of the chat window.

3. You see the available audio and video chat options listed. Choose one. Note that choosing a FaceTime option (if available) launches the FaceTime application, which we discuss next in this chapter.

4. Your audio/video chat begins. Click the + button to add members to the chat. A four-way video conference is shown here.

5. Toggle mute on the chat by clicking the microphone.

6. When conducting a video chat, click Effects to apply real-time video effects to your onscreen image.

7. Click the double arrows during a video chat to expand the video to full screen.

Be Heard with a Headset

If you find yourself using video or audio chat frequently, you might want to invest in a microphone or headset. To change the Messages microphone and set up a headset, open the Audio/Video section of the Messages preferences.

Sharing Your Files and Screen

In addition to being a great communications tool, Messages can serve as a collaboration platform. If you've ever found yourself in the position of having to talk through a document long distance or troubleshoot technical problems remotely, you'll appreciate the additional functionality built into Messages.

Transferring Files over Messages

Messages provides a convenient mechanism for sending files while chatting. You can send individual files or even entire folders (IM only) just by dragging them into Messages.

1. Find the file or folder that you want to share.

2. To transfer to an online buddy you aren't currently chatting with, drag the file to her name in your buddy list (IM only).

3. To transfer a file within an active chat session, drag the file to the chat window. Files such as images are displayed inline in the chat and can be previewed without opening the file.

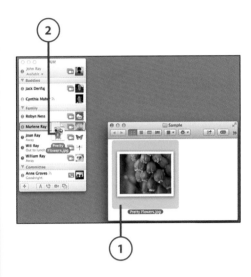

Confirming File Transfers

If someone attempts to transfer a file to you over Messages, you must click the download within the chat window to accept the file. By default, all transferred files are saved in the Downloads directory.

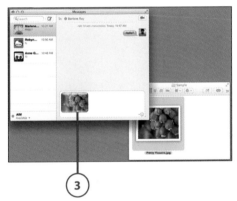

Starting a Screen-Sharing Session (IM only)

A unique Mac-only feature of Messages is the capability to share someone else's screen. Using this tool, you can control the other person's computer as if you were sitting directly in front of it.

1. Begin a chat with the individuals you want to include in a screen-sharing session.

2. Click the camera icon in the upper-right corner of the chat window.

3. Choose whether you want to request access to your buddy's screen or if you want to share your screen.

Remote Support via Messages

When screens are being shared, Messages also starts a simultaneous audio chat, which makes it easy for you to talk through issues with the remote party.

4. After the request is accepted, you (or your buddy) have access to the remote screen. You can interact with the desktop as if you were sitting in front of the computer.

5. Click the miniaturized version of the screen to switch between viewing the local screen and viewing the remote screen.

6. Click the X on the miniature screen to close the session.

Video Calls with FaceTime

Similar to an iMessage account in Messages, FaceTime is an always-running video chat service that bridges your iOS devices and your Macs. FaceTime starts automatically if someone places a FaceTime call, and it simultaneously rings on as many Macs, iPhones, and iPads as you want.

Also as with iMessage, FaceTime requires zero configuration beyond providing an email address that your friends can "call."

Setting Up FaceTime

The first time FaceTime starts, you need to provide it with an Apple ID for registration. After the initial ID is provided, you can associate as many email addresses as you want with a given install. Follow these steps to add FaceTime addresses:

1. Open FaceTime from the Dock, Launchpad, or Applications folder.

2. Enter your Apple ID and password.

3. If you do not have an ID, click Create New Account to walk through an ID creation wizard.

4. Click Sign In.

5. Check (or uncheck) the email addresses associated with your Apple ID that you want to use with FaceTime. You can edit this list in the preferences, discussed later.

6. Click Next.

7. FaceTime logs in, and you're ready for calls.

Placing FaceTime Calls

To place a call with FaceTime, you need to have the address or phone number of a FaceTime-compatible contact in your address book. In other words, make sure your family and friends have an iOS device or a Mac and have configured FaceTime. You also need to be sure you've stored their contact information in the Contacts application. (See Chapter 8, "Managing Who, Where, When, and What," for more information.)

Placing Calls from the Contacts List

When you've got yourself a few equipped friends, follow these steps to call them over FaceTime:

1. Click the Contacts button at the bottom of the FaceTime window.

2. Browse your contacts. When you find the person you want to call, click his name.

3. The contact information for your friend appears.

4. If you want to call the person frequently, click the Add to Favorites button to add a shortcut for future use (you will be prompted for which address or number to add).

5. Click the FaceTime button to try all available contact methods, or click a specific number or email address to contact that device. (Some people, for example, might use only certain email addresses with certain devices).

6. If the call is connected, you are able to see and talk to the other person. Otherwise, skip to step 9.

7. Use the button at the bottom-left corner of the window to mute the call, or use the button at the bottom-right corner to go fullscreen.

8. Click End to hang up when you are finished talking.

9. If the call does not connect, you're given the options of cancelling the call or calling back (redial).

See Your Surroundings

By default, the FaceTime camera takes a portrait image. If you want to see more of your surroundings, you can rotate to landscape mode by choosing Video, Use Landscape (Command+R) from the menu bar.

Placing Calls from the Favorites List

To place a call to someone you've marked as a favorite, complete these steps:

1. Click the Favorites button at the bottom-right corner of the Face-Time window.

2. Click a name in the Favorites list to place a call.

3. Click the arrow at the end of a favorite to open that individual's contact information.

4. The star beside the entry indicates it is used as the FaceTime address for a call from the Favorites list.

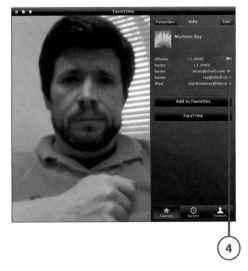

Receiving a FaceTime Call

If you've ever received a call on an iPhone, you'll be right at home receiving FaceTime calls on your Mac:

1. When an incoming call registers, FaceTime displays a notification—no need to start the application.

2. Click Decline to ignore the call.

3. Click Accept to begin talking.

4. Click Remind Me Later to set a reminder to call back.

5. Click Reply with Message to send an instant message to your caller, rather than start a video chat.

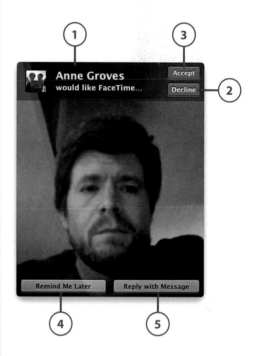

Did I Miss a Call?

If you're wondering whether some-one tried to contact you while you were away, the FaceTime icon shows a count of your missed calls. You can find out details about the missed calls by accessing the call list, our next task.

Accessing Your Call List

FaceTime keeps a list of all incoming and outgoing calls, even if you aren't around your computer when a call comes, so that you can check later to see who called.

1. Click the Recents button at the bottom-right corner of the Face-Time window.

2. Click All to show all incoming and outgoing calls. Missed calls display in red.

3. Click Missed to filter the list to missed incoming calls.

4. Click an entry in one of the lists to place a call.

5. Touch the arrow at the right side of an entry to view that person's address book information and a full call history.

6. Click Clear to remove the call history.

Disabling FaceTime

FaceTime is great, but as with a phone, sometimes you want to just ignore it. If you're having one of those days, you can disable FaceTime on your Mac so that it won't ring if someone tries to call.

1. Choose Turn FaceTime Off (Command+K) from the FaceTime menu.

2. FaceTime is now disabled on your Mac (not shown).

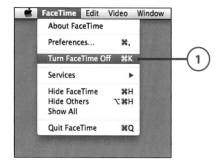

Remember Do Not Disturb!

Turning on Do Not Disturb (see Chapter 1, "Managing Your Desktop") keeps FaceTime from "ringing" your machine. You can effectively use Do Not Disturb to silence FaceTime for short periods of time, if you prefer that approach.

Updating Account Information and FaceTime Addresses

If you've registered several Face-Time accounts and want them all to ring on your Mac, you need to edit the preferences to list all the email addresses you have. To do this, follow these steps:

1. Open the FaceTime Preferences by choosing FaceTime, Preferences from the menu.

2. Click the Apple ID line if you want to change the Apple ID associated with your account.

3. Click Add Another Email to add an alternative email account. If you have not registered that address with Apple, you need to look for an email with a clickable link for verifying your address.

4. Repeat step 3 for as many addresses as you want to use with your FaceTime installation.

5. Click the Caller ID line to display all addresses associated with your FaceTime.

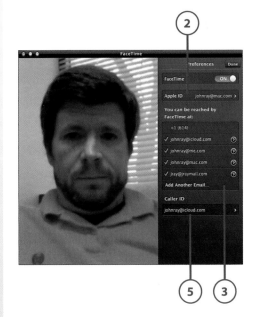

6. Click a line to set that address as your caller ID.

7. Click the Preferences button to return to the main preferences.

8. Click Done to finalize your preferences.

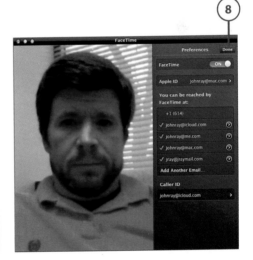

Using the Mavericks Twitter and Facebook Posting Support

Mavericks has baked-in Twitter support to make sending tweets as easy as clicking a button in many of your favorite applications. Facebook users can also get in on the fun by posting to their wall and photo albums in the same way. This section looks at how you can enable Twitter and Facebook support throughout OS X and how to make use of them.

Enabling Twitter

To see the tweeting options in Mavericks, you must first enable Twitter. To do this, follow these steps:

1. Open the Internet Accounts System Preferences panel.

2. Click the Twitter service link on the right.

3. Enter your Twitter username and password.

4. Click Next.

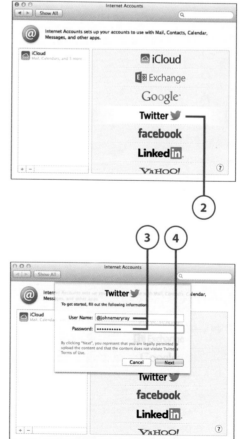

5. Read the service notices and then click Sign In.

6. On the Summary screen, click Update Contacts to pull Twitter usernames and photos into your system-wide Contacts list.

7. Check or uncheck Allow Others to Find Me by Email to enable other Twitter users to find you online using your email address.

8. Close the System Preferences.

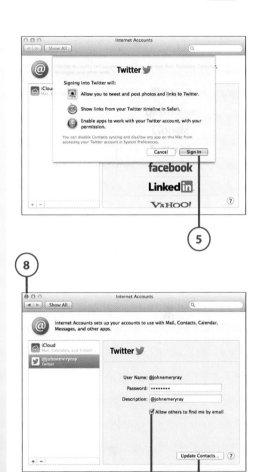

Enabling Facebook

To enable Mavericks to post Facebook updates, follow these steps:

1. Open the Internet Accounts System Preferences panel.

2. Click the Facebook service link on the right.

3. Enter your Facebook username and password.

4. Click Next.

5. Read the Facebook conditions and click Sign In.

6. Click the Contacts checkbox to add Facebook friends to your address book.

7. Click Calendars to tie Facebook calendar into the Calendars application.

8. Click the Get Profile Photos button to pull Facebook photos into your system-wide Contacts list.

9. Close the System Preferences.

Wait, There's More!

If you've opened the Internet Accounts panel, you've probably noticed that there are account options for more than just Twitter and Facebook. LinkedIn, Vimeo, and others are available for you to add. Why aren't they covered here? Because they work identically to Facebook and Twitter. If you can activate one then you can activate them all!

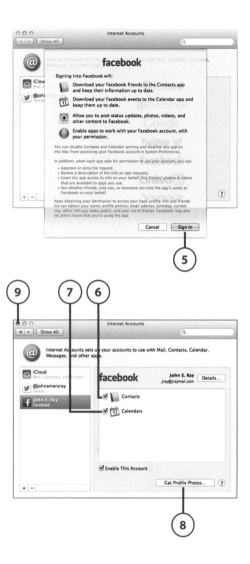

Posting Tweets and Facebook Updates

You can send tweets and post Facebook updates from any application that has been updated to support Mavericks' social networking implementation, such as the Finder or Safari.

Posting From the Finder and Other Apps

For example, suppose you want to post a photo from the Finder. To compose the update, do the following:

1. Select or open an image (if you want to attach an image to the tweet or Facebook update).

2. Click the Share Sheet button.

3. Choose Twitter or Facebook from the drop-down menu. (This example uses Twitter.)

4. A composition window appears with the attachment (if any) in the upper-right corner. Enter your tweet/update here.

5. Click the Add Location button to add your current location to the post.

6. Click Send to send a tweet (or click Post if posting to Facebook.)

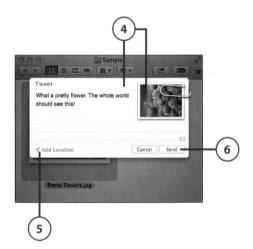

Posting via Notification Center

Mavericks also has the ability to post updates via Notification Center. To use this nifty feature, follow these steps:

1. Open Notification Center.

2. Click the Twitter or Facebook buttons at the top of the pane.

3. In the window that appears, type the message to post.

4. Click Send to send a tweet, or click Post to post to Facebook.

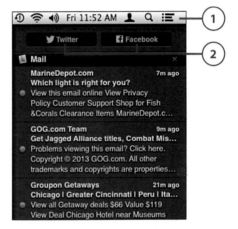

Being Social Is a Two-Way Street

You know how to post to Facebook and Twitter from Mavericks, but that's only part of social networking; you also need to be able to read posts that others send to you. To receive updates from your friends and followers on Facebook and Twitter, configure the Notification Center, as described in Chapter 1. Apple has included Notification Center settings for Twitter and Facebook that let you receive and view updates right on your desktop. Of course, you'll still want a browser handy to access all the features of these popular sites, but OS X has you covered for the basics.

Use Calendar to schedule appointments.

Plan your next vacation with Maps.

Write and sync Notes.

In this chapter, you learn how to use your Mac to manage everything from contacts and meetings to road trips.

→ Adding contacts to Contacts
→ Organizing contacts into groups
→ Finding your way with Maps
→ Creating calendars in Calendar
→ Adding appointments to calendars
→ Scheduling meetings
→ Making lists in Reminders
→ Keeping your thoughts in order with Notes

Managing Who, Where, When, and What

One of the joys of owning a Mac is that it is productive "out of the box." You can integrate with enterprise calendaring and address book systems, plan meetings, even get directions—all using the built-in utilities. Mavericks makes these tools accessible to everyone, regardless of skill level. If you've ever been intimidated by Microsoft Outlook, don't worry—Mavericks will make you just as productive without needing an encyclopedic reference book.

In this chapter, you get the hang of the basics of the Contacts, Maps, Calendar, Reminders, and Notes apps. This suite of tools helps us keep our digital lives in tune with our real lives, and does so in a simple and elegant way.

THE INVISIBLE, EVER-PRESENT, iCLOUD

The apps in this chapter share a unique characteristic that can be a bit confusing to new users—where they store their information. If you've never set up iCloud, Exchange, or a Google account on your computer, you probably aren't connected to any form of network storage. In this case, the data created in each application is stored locally on your Mac.

In practice, however, it's pretty difficult to get through setting up a Mac with Mavericks *without* establishing a free iCloud account. If you've established an iCloud account (see Chapter 4, "Setting Up iCloud Services and Internet Accounts," for details), chances are that the information in the applications discussed in this chapter is synced with an iCloud server. What makes this confusing is that the applications provide very little in terms of visual cues to show that you are using iCloud services for your data. The good news is that it really is transparent, and using iCloud means you can access this information from a web browser wherever you are! If you aren't sure if you're using iCloud, now is a good time to jump back to Chapter 4 so you can ensure you're making the best use of this important suite of Mavericks utilities.

Managing Contacts in Contacts

Many of the applications you use on your Mac send information to, or receive information from, other people. Mavericks offers a central contact database that you can access in Mail, Calendar, Messages, FaceTime, and other programs. Appropriately enough, you manage this database through an application called Contacts (found in the Applications folder).

Contacts acts as a digital Rolodex, pulling together personal and business contacts. With it you can also connect to enterprise directory servers for accessing centralized company personnel listings. The Contacts application is similar to many other Mavericks applications, providing a drill-down view from a group list, to a contact list, and, finally, to contact details.

Search

Sampletons (5 cards)

Contact groups

Contacts

Contact details

New Contact/
Group/Field

Sharing Sheet

Adding Groups

When you first start Contacts, there is a single pseudo-group available: All Contacts. The group displays any contact available in Contacts. To make the most efficient use of Contacts, you should add groups for the different types of contacts you use—businesses, coworkers, family, friends, doctors, and so on. Like Mail, Contacts can use rules to create Smart Groups.

Emailing to a Group

Contacts groups are more than just organizational tools; they also add functionality to applications that support them. After you've defined a group, you can use it in Mail as your message recipient, effectively sending the email to everyone in the group!

Creating a Group

To create a new group, decide what you'd like it to be called, and then follow these steps:

1. Open Contacts from the Dock, Launchpad, or Applications folder.

2. Click and hold the + button at the bottom of the Contacts Window.

3. Choose New Group.

4. A new "untitled group" is added. Type to change the name of the group.

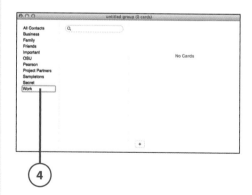

Creating a Smart Group

If you'd like to use search criteria to define your Contacts groups, you're in luck! Contacts supports Smart Groups, capable of pulling contacts together from multiple different groups and even network accounts:

1. Choose File, New Smart Group from the menu bar.

2. Enter a name for the new Smart Group.

3. Use the first pop-up menu from the selection lines to choose a contact attribute.

4. Use the second pop-up menu to set a comparison.

5. Enter the value to use in the comparison in the text field at the end of the selection line.

6. Use the + and – buttons to add or remove additional selection criteria.

7. Click OK when you're satisfied with your group definition.

8. The new group is added and automatically shows the contacts based on the criteria you defined.

Adding Contacts

The bulk of what you'll do with Contacts is entering contacts. When it comes to people, one size contact does not fit all. For your family, you might want to store email addresses, instant messaging screen names, and birthdays. But for business contacts, you might only be interested in an address and a phone number. Contacts adapts to the information that you want to store.

Creating a New Contact

To create a new contact, gather all the information you have available for the person, then do the following:

1. Click the group name that the contact should be added to.

2. Click the + button at the bottom of the window.

3. Choose New Contact from the pop-up menu.

4. A new No Name contact is added, and the empty contact details display. Use the fields in the detail view to enter information for the contact.

5. Click Company to classify the entry as a business rather than a personal contact.

6. Set the context for the card's fields (for example, choose home, work, or cell for a phone number) using the pop-up menu in front of each field.

7. If you'd like to store additional information for the contact, click and hold the + button again, and choose the type of field to add.

8. Click the Done button at the bottom of the contact details to save changes to the contact.

Moving and Editing Contacts

If you find that you've filed your contact in the wrong group, just drag and drop the contact name into another group. You can re-edit contact details at any time by selecting them and clicking the edit button below the details pane.

Setting a Contact Image

Contact images can help you visually identify individuals in your Contacts and are even displayed in Mail or shown on your iOS device if you sync Contacts. To set an image for a contact, complete these steps:

1. Find and select the contact that you want to associate with an image.

2. Double-click the picture within the card details.

3. Click the Camera label to take a new picture, or see step 4 to use an existing picture.

4. Alternatively, use the Defaults, iCloud, and Faces options to select from default OS X images, iCloud PhotoStream photos, or iPhoto Faces.

5. Set cropping and size for the picture by dragging it within the image window and adjusting the zoom slider.

6. Apply effects, if desired, using the Effects button.

7. Click Done to finalize the contact's custom image.

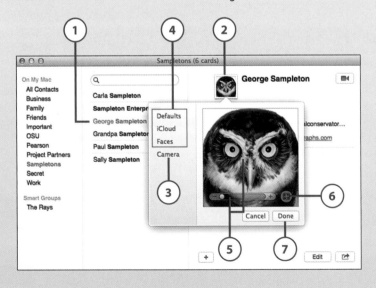

Creating "My" Card

Many system applications and utilities need to identify information about you. To tell Contacts who you are, enter a new contact for yourself, and then follow these steps:

1. Find and select your name in the Contacts.

2. Choose Card, Make This My Card from the menu bar.

The Importance of Me

You need a functional "My" card to fully use Calendar, so be sure to set this if you have any intention of using Calendar.

Editing the Contact Template

If you find that you constantly need to add new fields to contacts, you might want to consider modifying the default contact template. Changing the default gives you a starting place for all future contacts.

1. Choose Contacts, Preferences from the menu bar.

2. Click the Template icon in the Preferences toolbar.

3. Use the Add Field drop-down menu to add additional fields to the contact template.

4. Click the double arrows to open the pop-up menus in front of each field to set the context for fields displayed in the template.

5. Close the Contacts preference window when you're finished.

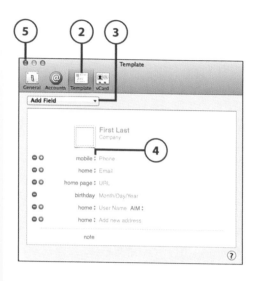

Searching Contacts

When you aren't sure of an exact name, or where you filed a contact, you can quickly search across all your groups and contact data.

1. Click the name of the address group to search.

2. Type into the search field.

3. As you type, the contact list is filtered to show only matching contacts.

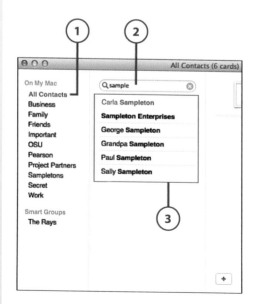

Detecting and Merging Duplicates

Over time you might find that you've created several Contacts entries for a single person. To identify and merge duplicate cards, follow these steps:

1. Choose Card, Look for Duplicates from the menu bar.

2. Contacts analyzes your contacts and presents you with the option to merge identified duplicates.

3. Click Merge to fix the duplicates.

Merging Cards

If you manually identify two or more cards that need to be merged, select the cards, and then choose Card, Merge Selected Cards from the Contacts menu bar.

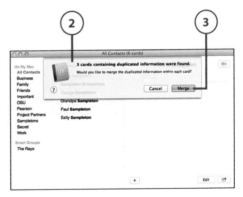

Using iCloud and Server-Based Contacts

Contacts isn't just limited to keeping information on your Mac; it can also synchronize with Google, Yahoo! contacts, and connect to enterprise directory servers such as Exchange, standard LDAP servers, as well as Apple's iCloud service. In fact, if you've already configured iCloud (see Chapter 4), you're probably already storing your contacts "in the cloud."

Connecting to iCloud Contacts Syncing

To connect to iCloud, or verify that your Contacts app is using iCloud to store and sync contacts across your devices, follow these steps.

1. Open the iCloud System Preferences panel.

2. Check the box beside Contacts.

3. Close the System Preferences. Your Contacts application is now connected to iCloud.

Connecting to Other Contact Servers

While iCloud is consumer-friendly, many organizations provide central enterprise contact directories that you can access via Contacts. Contacts supports several standards, including Google and Yahoo! contacts as well as Exchange servers and social networking sites like Facebook and Twitter. Using a central server means that changes and updates are available immediately for everyone who is connected.

To configure server-based contacts, follow these steps:

1. Open the Internet Accounts panel.

2. Choose the service providing contact information from the list on the right. Alternatively, click Add Other Account (at the bottom of the list) to add LDAP, CardDAV, or OS X Server accounts.

3. The account creation window appears. Use the fields in the window to configure your account information.

4. Click Set Up or Continue (the button name depends on your service provider) to walk through the account setup wizard.

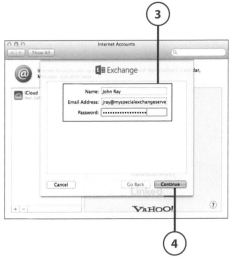

5. If you're setting up a service that provides more than just contacts (such as Exchange), you are prompted to automatically set up corresponding email accounts and calendars.

6. Click Done to configure your Mac to connect to the server.

7. Close the System Preferences.

Settings, Settings, Everywhere!

At the time of this writing, Apple is including the option of defining *some* contact servers directly within the Contacts apps preferences (the same goes for the Calendar app, which we'll cover next). If you happen to stumble upon these, you can use them (it's the same as using the Internet Accounts preference panel), but I'd suggest using the central preferences to be consistent.

8. The new server appears in the Contacts group list. You can click to select groups within it, and from there, create new groups if desired.

Sharing Contacts via Email and Messages

To share a contact via email, messages, or AirDrop, you can use a Mavericks Share Sheet. For detailed information on Share Sheets, refer to Chapter 6, "Sharing Files, Devices, and Services." For now, be aware that the basic process works like this:

1. Navigate to a contact that you want to share.

2. Click the Share Sheet button to show the sharing options.

3. Choose the method of sharing that you'd like to use.

4. Your choice launches the appropriate supporting application and attaches the note for sending.

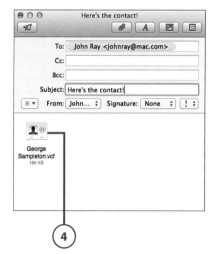

Exporting and Importing vCards

In addition to sharing contacts, you can also export the contact information directly to a vCard. These are small files that store all the information for one or more contact entries. Just highlight the entries in Contacts, and then drag them to your desktop. A vCard file is created with all of the contact data.

To import a vCard, reverse the process. Drag a received vCard into Contacts (or double-click it in the Finder), and it is imported automatically.

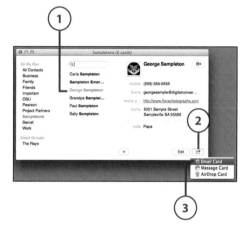

Printing Addresses

When you need to use actual paper for your communications, Contacts provides several useful print options for printing your contacts onto envelopes or labels.

1. Select individual contacts or contact groups to print.

2. Choose File, Print from the menu bar.

3. Click the Hide/Show Details button so that the full print dialog window appears.

4. Use the Style pop-up menu to select an output format (Mailing Labels, Envelopes, and so on).

5. Set any of the additional configuration options for the style you've chosen.

6. Click Print to output the contact information in the selected style.

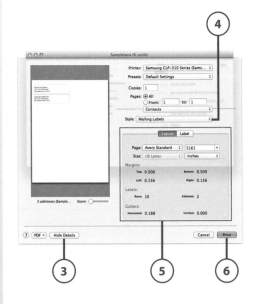

Finding Your Way with Maps

Mavericks continues the tradition of OS X in providing great software for managing your who, when, and what—but it now can help you with the *where*. New in this release of OS X is Maps, a simple, fun, and fast way to access mapping information on your Mac.

Starting and Navigating Maps

To start using Maps, you need an active Internet connection and your Wi-Fi needs to be enabled if you want your system to automatically locate your current position. To get started, follow these steps:

1. Start Maps from the Applications folder, Dock, or Launchpad.

2. After a few seconds, a basic map loads in standard view.

3. You can pan the map by clicking and dragging—or by dragging two fingers on a trackpad.

4. Use the +/– buttons to zoom in and out.

5. Click and drag within the compass to rotate the entire view.

Using Map Views

If you've ever used Google Maps (or any other online mapping service) you'll be right at home with Maps. There are a variety of different views that you can access—right from the Maps toolbar.

Choosing a View Mode

Like your maps flat, like a book? Want to see photography of a given area? How about a combination? Using Maps, you can have all of this, just by clicking a button.

1. Click the Standard button to show a traditional "atlas" style map with roads, points of interest, and so on.

2. Click Satellite to show the area using satellite photography.

3. Click Hybrid to show a combination of the two—photography with overlaid roads and points of interest.

Viewing Maps with 3D Flyover

In addition to the standard map views, you can also look at many large cities in full 3D. To see the map in 3D, follow these instructions:

1. Navigate to a point you want to view in 3D.

2. Click the building button in the toolbar to change the display to 3D.

3. Switch to Satellite or Hybrid modes to view a nearly photo-realistic image of the location.

Tilting Your 3D World

While viewing a map in 3D, you can click and drag up and down in the compass to change the amount of "tilt" with which the map is displayed. You can also hold Option and click and drag anywhere on the map to tilt the view.

It's Not All Good

NO 3D FOR YOU!

If you switch your view to 3D and it looks decidedly "flat," it's because 3D data doesn't yet exist for your location. There's not much to do about this but wait until Apple acquires the right information for your area.

Finding Places

How good would a map be if you couldn't find things on it? Using Apple Maps, you can quickly locate your position, companies, points of interest, people, and so on.

Finding Yourself

Without needing to be a Zen guru, Apple Maps can help you find yourself in the world. Although not as precise as GPS, your Mavericks computer can use Wi-Fi to find its general location (usually within a few blocks). To use this feature, follow these steps:

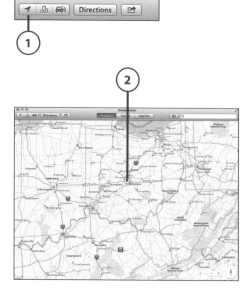

1. While viewing any map, click the arrow icon at the far left of the toolbar.

2. The map zooms in, placing a blue dot on your location.

Closer Please

Don't worry—the map does zoom closer than shown in this example. I manually zoomed out to reduce the amount of competing clutter on the screen.

Finding Contact Entries

Although finding yourself can be handy, finding others is likely more useful. To locate any address (personal or business) stored within the Contacts application, complete the following:

1. Click the Book icon in the Maps toolbar

2. Choose an entry in the Address Book and click it.

3. Click the address for the entry that you want to view.

4. The map zooms in and highlights the chosen address.

Searching the Map

If the place you want to locate isn't in your Address Book—you can just search for it.

1. Type into the search field at the right of the Maps window.

2. As you type, potential matching searches appear below. Choose one, or press return when finished typing.

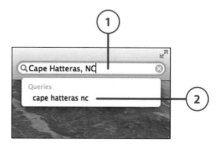

3. The search results are displayed on the right.

4. Click one you want to view.

5. The chosen location is highlighted on the map.

Working with Points of Interest

You've seen how to find places, but how about finding out *about* places? Maps can help you with that as well. You may be surprised at how much Maps can do for you!

Seeing Point of Interest Details

There's more to a location than just a marker on a map. To see more detail for any point on the map, follow these instructions:

1. Find a location on the map that you want to view. Click the i icon.

2. The location window expands to show a photo and additional information.

3. Use the Get Directions button to get turn by turn directions to the location.

4. Click Add Bookmark to add a bookmark to the location (accessible from the Book icon in the Maps toolbar).

5. Click Add to Contacts to add a new contact to your Address Book for the location.

6. Click Report a Problem if there is an error in the listing.

7. Click Reviews to view Yelp reviews of the location (if available).

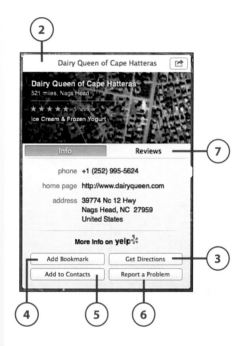

Making Your Own Point of Interest

Sometimes Apple Maps won't have the information that you want. Apple, for example, doesn't know your favorite fishing hole, or in which tree you hid the ransom money. To accommodate your activities, you can create your own points on the map by following these steps:

1. Right-click on the map where you want a point to be located.

2. Choose Drop Pin from the pop-up menu that appears.

3. A new point of interest window appears that you can interact with like any other point.

Sharing a Point of Interest

If you find yourself viewing something on your Mac and want to see it on your iOS device, no problem. You can use Sharing Sheets to share a location via email, or just send it directly to your phone or iPad. To do this, just follow these steps:

1. Locate the point of interest you want to use.

2. Click the Sharing Sheet icon.

3. Choose the method or device that you want to use to share.

Share Your Anywheres, Anytime

You can share what you are looking at in the Map window at any time by using the Sharing Sheet button at the Maps window.

Traveling with Maps

The last trick that Maps has up its sleeve is the ability to view turn by turn directions—and even the traffic that you'll encounter if you follow them. Let's start by looking at directions.

Getting Directions

To get directions from point A to point B, you only need to click. Follow these steps to get where you need to be:

1. Click the Directions button to show the directions panel on the right.

2. Enter an address or location in the Start field (or leave it blank to use your current location).

3. Enter an address or location in the End field

4. Use the person or car icons to choose between walking and driving directions.

5. If multiple paths are shown, click the path you want to take.

6. The turn-by-turn instructions are shown on the right.

7. Click an individual step of the directions to show a close-up of your route—including lane guidance.

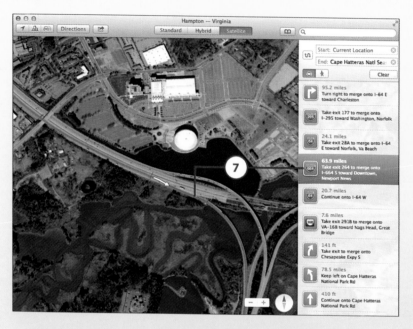

Share the Path!

Remember, using the Sharing Sheet at the top of the Maps window, you can share your location and complete route with your iOS device.

Seeing the Traffic

Apple Maps makes it possible to know what you're getting into, before you even get there. Traffic is available in many metropolitan areas by doing the following:

1. View a location where you want to see the current traffic.

2. Click the car icon in the Maps toolbar to activate traffic.

3. Traffic is shown by dotted lines. The heavier red lines indicate slow traffic.

Working with Schedules in Calendar

Much of our lives, like it or not, revolve around adhering to a schedule. Calendars, in whatever form we use them, keep us informed of upcoming appointments, holidays, birthdays, and anniversaries. Your Mac can serve as your scheduling work center. The Calendar application (found in the Applications folder) is a fast and well-connected way to keep your life in order.

Unlike applications such as Microsoft Outlook, Calendar is an unimposing application that shows you everything you need within a single window.

Calendar's general operation is similar to other Mavericks applications you've used. Clicking the Calendar button displays a list of calendars you have access to. Selecting a calendar in the calendar list displays the content of the calendar to the right. Double-clicking a calendar entry shows the details of the entry. The four buttons at the top (Day, Week, Month, Year) coupled with the View menu control the appearance of the calendars.

Despite its simple styling, Calendar works just as well for managing calendars located on your Mac as it can interacting with Exchange, iCloud, Facebook, Google, and other standards-based enterprise calendaring systems.

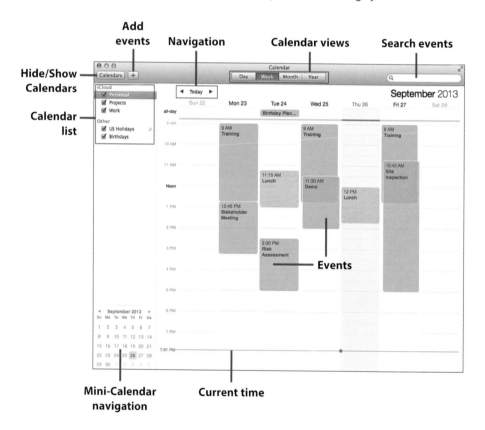

Adding Calendars

The first step in using Calendar is to establish the calendars that you use to store your events. Calendar comes with two calendars already created: Home and Work. If you've established an iCloud account and turned on Calendar syncing, these will be iCloud-based calendars. If not, they'll be stored locally on your Mac. Use these default calendars or create new calendars depending on how you want to categorize your events.

Creating New Calendars

To create a new calendar (locally or on a server), follow these instructions:

1. Open the Calendar application from the Dock, Launchpad, or Applications folder.

2. Click the Calendars button to show the list of calendars (if they are hidden) on your Mac.

3. Click File, New Calendar from the main menu bar. You may have to Choose iCloud (or another calendar provider if you've already set up a calendar account).

4. A new Untitled calendar is added at the bottom of the calendar list. Type to replace Untitled with whatever name you'd like.

5. Verify that the checkbox next to the calendar is selected so that the calendar entries are visible.

Local Versus Network Calendars

The Calendar application can work with calendars located directly on your Mac (local) as well as calendars located on a server, such as iCloud. Depending on how your system is set up, the menus in the Calendar application may change slightly. For example, if you are using calendars hosted on multiple network servers (iCloud and your office's Exchange calendar server, for instance), you'll notice that when you choose to create a new calendar, you are given the option of choosing which server should hold it. Only if no server accounts are visible will the On My Mac (locally) option be available.

Additionally, Calendar supports the notion of local calendar groups (go to File, New Calendar Group) when working with local calendars. Using calendar groups, you can organize clusters of calendars and enable or disable all of them at once. The bad news? As soon as you use iCloud or another network service, this option completely vanishes. Because Apple is obviously weaning us off this feature, we're omitting it from this edition.

Connecting to iCloud and Server-Based Calendars

Server-based calendars are stored on a central network location rather than on your Mac. You can access and modify network calendars on multiple computers. Many businesses use Exchange Server, for example, to provide shared calendars and scheduling. Apple's iCloud service provides free shared calendaring that you can use across your Mac and iOS devices. Another option, Google Calendar, is also free and can be used on virtually any desktop or mobile device.

Connecting to iCloud Calendar Syncing

iCloud is the easiest and fastest way to create shared network calendars on all your devices. To use iCloud to store your calendars, follow these steps:

1. Open the iCloud System Preferences panel.

2. Check the box beside Calendars

3. You might be prompted to merge any existing calendars with your iCloud calendars. Click Merge to move their information to iCloud.

4. Close the System Preferences.

Connecting to Other Calendar Servers

Most server-hosted calendars are associated, in some way, with an email account. To configure a server-based calendar, you probably only need an email account and password. If you know, however, that your calendar is hosted somewhere else, you should collect the server name in addition to your username and password before proceeding. As you'd expect, calendar services are configured through the Mail, Contacts, and Calendars panel, as you've become accustomed.

1. Open the Internet Accounts panel.

2. Choose the service providing the calendar information from the list on the right. Alternatively, click Add Other Account (at the bottom of the list) to manually add a CalDAV account. If you aren't sure, ask your ISP or network administrator.

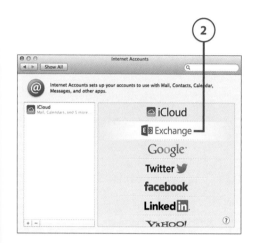

3. The account creation window appears. Use the fields in the window to configure your account information.

4. Click Set Up or Continue (the button name depends on your service provider) to walk through the account setup wizard.

5. If you're setting up a service that provides more than just calendars (such as Exchange, Yahoo!, or Gmail), you are prompted to automatically set up corresponding email accounts and contact servers. Be sure to choose Calendars & Reminders.

6. Click Done.

7. Close the System Preferences when finished.

8. The calendar list displays a new section with any calendars that are located on the server.

Subscribing to a Public Shared Calendar

Another calendar type is a shared calendar. These read-only Internet-published calendars are available for TV show schedules, holidays, sports team game dates, and other useful information. To subscribe to a shared calendar, copy the URL for the calendar and then follow these steps:

1. Choose File, New Calendar Subscription from the Calendar menu bar.

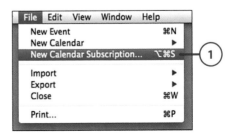

2. Enter the URL for the calendar you are subscribing to.

3. Click Subscribe. If prompted, enter a login name and password to access the calendar, and then click OK to continue.

4. Set a name, color, and storage location for the calendar.

5. If there are any embedded Alerts or Attachments in the calendar (this depends entirely on the person making the calendar available), you may want to strip them out. Click the Remove checkboxes to make sure you get only calendar data and no surprises!

6. To enable the calendar to automatically update, choose an Auto-refresh time.

7. Click OK.

8. Depending on whether you're connected to a network calendar (like iCloud), the shared calendar appears either under your main calendar list or in a section called Other.

It's Your Birthday (or a Holiday)!

By default, Calendar shows two Other calendars, even if you haven't added any. The first is the US Holidays calendar, which displays holidays in the United States. There is a second special calendar added by default—Birthdays—that displays birthdays for the individuals in your Contacts (address book) application.

Viewing Calendars

After you've set up one or more calendars in Calendar, you can view their contents. To view a calendar in the calendar list, follow these steps.

1. Click the checkbox in front of the calendars you want to view.

2. Use the Day, Week, Month, and Year buttons to narrow or expand your calendar view.

3. Use the arrows to move forward or backward by day, week, month, or year, depending on the current view. You can always navigate by month using the arrows by the mini-calendar in the lower-left corner.

4. Click Today to jump to today's date.

Working with Events

What good is a calendar if you don't have the ability to add events? In Calendar, events can be anything you'd like—birthdays, outings, reminders, anything—as long as they are associated with a date. If you'd like to include other people in the event, you can even send out invitations that are compatible with other calendaring systems, such as Exchange.

Creating a New Event

Events can hold a large number of attributes that describe what the events are, when they are, where they are located, and so on. All you need to know to create an event, though, is the date and a name for the event:

1. Navigate to the day on which the event takes place.

2. Switch to Day or Week view.

3. Click and drag from the start time to the end time to create the event. The default event name, New Event, is highlighted automatically.

4. Type a name and location for the event.

5. Click the color square in the upper-right corner of the event information to choose which calendar should hold the event.

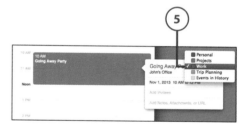

Double-Click to Add

You can add an event in the month view of the calendar by double-clicking a day. This method, however, does not let you define the start and end time of the event initially, so you need to edit it later to add that information.

Using the Quick Event Feature

The Calendar application also supports a simple way of creating events without any calendar navigation at all. Quick Event provides simple, plain-text entry of new events directly from the Calendar toolbar. To use this feature, follow these steps:

1. Click and hold the + icon in the Calendar toolbar.

2. Choose the calendar that should hold the new event.

3. In the Create Quick Event field that appears, type a description of the event, such as "Dinner on November 12th at 6pm," and press return.

4. A new event is added and opened for additional editing.

Editing Event Information

To edit the information for an event that you've created, first find the event on the calendar where you added it, and then follow these steps:

1. Find and double-click the event you want to edit.

2. An event summary window appears.

3. Click any of the available fields to change values such as start or end times, location, notes, and so on.

4. Click off of the event when you are finished editing.

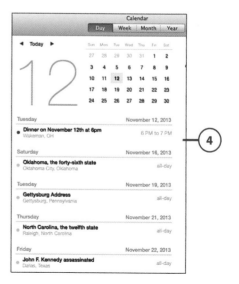

It's Not All Good

WHERE ARE ALL OF MY EVENT ATTRIBUTES?!

When you see the edit event pop-over window, you might ask yourself, "Where in the world are all the fields I need?" Mavericks collapses these into the different sections shown in the pop-over window. For example, if you want to see settings for receiving alerts prior to an event, just click the date—it will expand to show all the date and time related options. Be sure to click around to find all the different fields you can edit for an event.

Browse and Schedule

Need to browse your calendar while editing an event? No problem. To turn the edit event pop-over window into a real draggable window, just click near the top and drag off of the calendar.

Sending Event Invitations

Calendar can work directly with Mail to send invitations for your events. When the invitees respond, their attendance status is updated directly in Calendar. Use the previous task to find and start editing an event, and then follow these steps to send invitations for that event:

1. Click the Add Invitees link.

2. Enter email addresses in the field that appears, just as you would in Mail, pressing return after each one. Add as many as you'd like.

3. Click Send to send the invitations.

4. An icon appears in the upper-right corner of the event to show that invitations have been sent. A question mark indicates that responses haven't been received from all invitees.

Setting Optional Attendees and Resending Invitations

After you've added an invitee to an event, you can click the name in the event summary or edit screen to show a drop-down menu that enables you to flag the person as an optional attendee or to re-send an invitation.

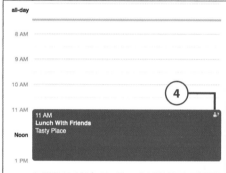

Checking Availability

If supported by your calendar server (such as Exchange), you can view an individual's availability for events by selecting an event and then choosing Window, Availability Panel from the menu bar.

Accepting Invitations

You can easily add to your calendar invitations that you receive. Even though invitations are sent through email, Mavericks' Mail program works with Calendar to automatically transfer the invitations to the Calendar Notifications area where you can act on them.

1

1. When a new invitation arrives, the Calendar application icon updates to show the count of invitations in the Dock.

2. The event is shown with a dotted outline in Calendar to indicate it has not yet been added.

3. Click the Notification button to show the notification panel in Calendar.

4. Use the Maybe, Decline, and Accept buttons to respond to the invitation.

5. Declined invitations are removed from your calendar; accepted and tentative invitations are added.

Changing Your Event Status

If you change your mind about an event, you can edit it in Calendar and change the My Status field to Accept, Maybe, or Decline.

Searching Events

If you're a heavy scheduler, or have dozens of enterprise calendars to manage, sometimes it's useful to be able to quickly search for events, which is a breeze in Calendar.

1. Make sure the checkboxes are selected for the calendars you want to search.

2. Enter your search terms in the Search field.

3. As you type, search options are displayed; pick the best option from the drop-down list.

4. The results of the search are displayed in a pane at the right of the Calendar window. Click an entry to jump to that event.

5. Click the X in the search field to hide the search results.

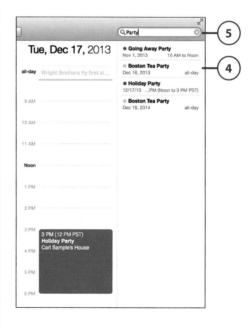

Printing Calendars

Despite our best efforts, sometimes we can't take our Macs (or even our iPads and iPhones) everywhere. When you need your calendar information in paper form, Calendar does an amazing job of printing calendar and itinerary views.

1. Choose File, Print from the Calendar menu bar.

2. Set the view you want to print.

3. Set a time range for the calendar being printed.

4. Click the checkboxes beside each calendar to print.

5. Select which options should be added to the printed page.

6. Click Continue, which takes you to available printing options; after selecting options, you are ready to print.

Remembering with Reminders

Beyond simple events that happen on a given date, day-to-day life often requires that you keep track of multiple to-do lists in your head—from home repairs that need to be done to birthday shopping lists to grocery store visits. Using the Reminders app, you can create your own digital to-do lists and even make them contextually aware of your location—prompting you with reminders that apply only at home or the office.

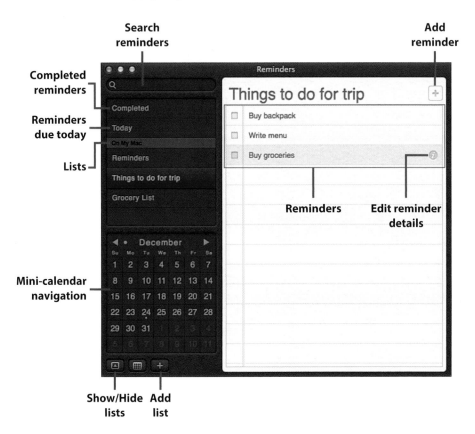

Creating a List

Reminders are organized into Lists of related items. You can have as many lists as you want, but you need to have at least a single list to contain reminders at any given point in time. By default, you start with a single list called Reminders, but you can add as many as you'd like. To create a new reminder list, follow these steps:

1. Open Reminders from the Launchpad or Applications folder.

2. If the Lists aren't visible, click the arrow in the lower-left corner of the window.

3. Click the + button near the bottom of the Reminders window.

4. A new list appears with the name selected. Type a new name and press return. The list is added and ready to be used.

Nothing Is Set in Stone

To rename a list, click its name in the left column in Reminders—it immediately becomes editable. Delete lists by clicking to select them and then pressing your Delete key.

Adding a Reminder

After you've created a list, you'll want to fill it with individual reminders. To create a new reminder within a list, complete the following actions:

1. Click to select the list you want to add a reminder to.

2. Click the + button in the upper-right corner of the Reminders window.

3. The cursor moves to a new line in the reminder list. Type the name for your reminder.

4. Press return to add additional reminders, or click on an empty line to end editing.

Setting Reminder Attributes, Including Location

A reminder can be more than just a title in a list—it can contain a date, a location, a repeating schedule, and more. Set the attributes for a reminder by doing the following:

1. Hover your pointer over a reminder item. An i icon appears near the right side of the reminder.

2. Click the i to show the reminder settings.

3. Use the title field to change the name of the reminder.

4. Click the On a Day checkbox to set a specific date/time for the reminder.

5. Use the date/time field to configure when the reminder is shown and set a repetition schedule.

6. Click the At a Location checkbox to receive the reminder when leaving or arriving at a given location.

7. Use the drop-down list/field to choose a contact's address, or enter a new address to be used in conjunction with the location-aware reminders.

8. Set whether the reminder occurs when arriving or leaving.

9. Set a priority for the reminder using the priority pop-up menu.

10. Use the Note field to set any additional notes related to the reminder.

11. Click Done to save the reminder.

Location Reminders Require Your Location!

The first time you use reminders based on a location, you might be prompted to enable Location services. Click Open Privacy Preferences when prompted, or follow the instructions in Chapter 13, "Securing and Protecting Your Mac."

Completing Reminders

When you're done with a reminder, you'll want to indicate that it is completed. To set the completion status of a reminder, follow these steps:

1. Click the list that contains the reminder you want to complete.

2. Click the checkbox to the left of the reminder.

3. The reminder moves to a Completed list, which you access from the top of the current reminder list (scroll down) or by clicking the Completed heading in the column to the left.

Don't Want to Do It? Just Delete It!

To delete a reminder or a reminder list (rather than having to actually follow through on it), just highlight it and press your Delete key.

Finding Reminders

Because reminders can be created across many different lists and many different dates, it's helpful to be able to quickly search your lists to figure out what you are supposed to be remembering, and when you should be remembering it. Thankfully, Reminders makes it easy to search all your lists and all your reminder dates very quickly.

Viewing Reminders by Date

If you've set dates for reminders, it's easy to see what reminders are associated with what dates (across all your lists) using the built-in mini-calendar in the Reminders application:

1. Show the mini-calendar (if hidden), by clicking the Calendar button in the lower-left corner of the application window. If the button isn't visible, you need to click the disclosure arrow button first.

2. Use the forward and backward arrows to navigate the calendar.

3. Click an individual date to show reminders associated with that day. Double-clicking a date opens it in a new window.

4. Choose View, Go to Today from the menu bar to quickly jump to the current date.

Searching Reminders

To search for reminders across all of
your lists, follow these steps:

1. Click to position your text cursor
   inside the search field, and then
   type a search term.

2. The results are shown, organized
   by list, on the right side of the
   window.

3. Click the X in the search field to
   clear the results.

Using iCloud and Server-Based Reminders

As you might have noticed, reminders are very similar to Calendar entries.
They're so similar, in fact, that they use the same server connections to
manage their information. To learn how to configure Reminders to use an
iCloud account, follow the instructions in "Connecting to iCloud Calendar
Syncing" earlier in this chapter. Similarly, to connect to a different server for
your reminders (Exchange or Google, for instance), follow the instructions in
"Connecting to Other Calendar Servers."

Choosing Servers When Creating a New List

If you are connected to several different servers that each provide Reminder
storage, you can choose which one a new reminder list is created on by clicking
and holding the + icon in the bottom-right corner when you create a new list.

Keeping Track with Notes

Calendars and reminders capture much of our hectic schedules, but life can also be less structured—with new information and ideas coming at us from a dozen different directions. To keep us from losing our idea for "the next big thing," Mavericks includes a simple and effective note-taking application—Notes. Like the other apps in this chapter, Notes is also iCloud/server-connected, meaning that no matter where you take your notes, they'll be seamlessly accessible across all your devices.

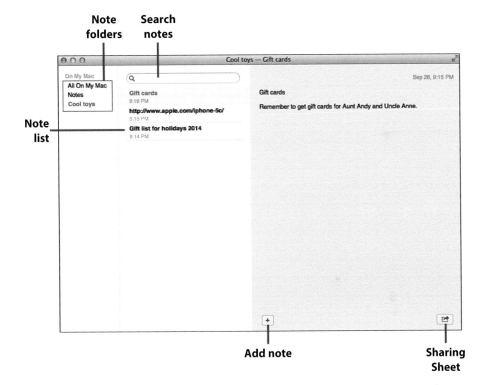

Managing Folders

Thoughts and ideas are rarely truly random. Chances are, you take notes about things you want to do at home, at work, with the kids, and so on. To create a sense of order, you'll want to start your OS X note-taking by setting up some folders for yourself.

Adding Folders

By default, notes are added to a default folder called Notes. To add a new folder of notes, do the following:

1. Open Notes using the icon in the Dock, Launchpad, or Applications folder.

2. Choose File, New Folder from the menu bar, or right-click (Control-click) in the folder list and choose New Folder.

3. A new folder appears with its name selected and editable. Type a new name for the folder and press return to save it.

Delete to Delete

Despite the different appearance, deleting a folder in Notes is the same as deleting a List in Reminders. Click to select its name, and then press the Delete key.

All On My Mac

The "All" folders (All On My Mac, All iCloud) can't be removed. They contain all the notes stored on that device and appear after you have created multiple note folders.

Adding Notes

The most import aspect of using the Notes application is also the easiest—adding notes. To add a new note, follow these steps:

1. Select the folder that should contain the note.

2. Click the "+" icon to the right of the middle column in the application.

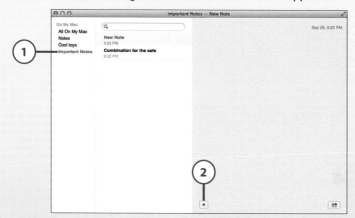

3. A New Note title appears at the top of the list, and the text entry cursor appears in the content area, ready to edit.

4. Type your note as you see fit.

5. The top line of the note automatically becomes the title for the note in the column to the left of the content.

6. If you decide you don't want a note, select it and press the Delete key to remove it (not shown).

Prettify Your Most Mundane Notes

Your notes don't have to be plain text—you can drag or paste in pictures or other media. You can also use the Format menu to apply fonts, add lists, or indent your text.

Moving Notes Between Folders

If you've created notes in one folder that you later want to move to another, this is easily accomplished with a simple drag and drop. Do the following to move notes between folders:

1. Click a note title to select it. Hold the Command key to select multiple notes at a time.

2. Click and drag from the selected note to a folder in the folder list. The notes are immediately transferred to the folder.

Searching and Displaying Notes

Notes can contain quite a bit of information, and after you've amassed a library of hundreds of notes, you might find yourself trying to track down a single tiny bit of information within a note. To search the available notes (in all note folders), just follow these steps:

1. Choose a folder of notes to search or view, or All Notes to access all folders.

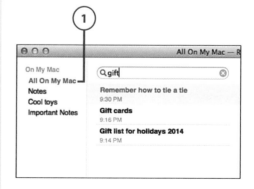

2. Type a search term in the search field to filter the notes being displayed (if desired).

3. The results are shown in the center column of the window.

4. Click a result to show that note's content to the right of the search results.

5. Double-click a note's title to show it in a new window.

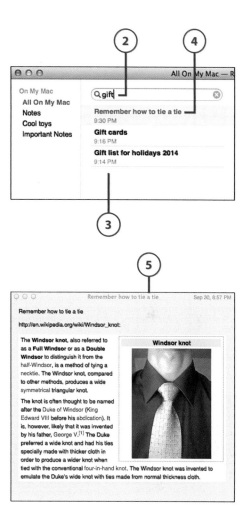

Sharing Notes via Email and Messages

To share a note via email or Messages, you can use a Mavericks Share Sheet. For detailed information on the process, refer to Chapter 6. The basic process works like this:

1. Navigate to a note you want to share.

2. Click the Share Sheet button to show the sharing options.

3. Choose the method of sharing that you'd like to use.

4. Your choice launches the appropriate supporting application and attaches the note for sending.

Using iCloud and Server-Based Notes

Notes, like the other utilities in this chapter, are stored, by default, on an available server account—probably iCloud, if configured. To set up or verify an existing server setup for your notes, you can use the instructions in the next two sections.

Connecting to iCloud Note Syncing

If you've already established an iCloud account, connecting Notes to iCloud is just a matter of clicking the right checkbox. If you do not have an iCloud account, you should review Chapter 4 for information on setting one up.

1. Open the iCloud System Preferences panel.

2. Check the box beside Notes.

3. Close the System Preferences. Your Notes application is now connected to iCloud.

Connecting to Other Note Servers

As you've probably guessed, Exchange servers and Google accounts can also provide shared note storage. To use one of these servers to share notes between your computers or devices, follow these steps:

1. Open the Internet Accounts panel.

2. Choose the service providing Note storage from the list on the right.

3. The account creation window appears. Use the fields in the window to configure your account information.

4. Click Set Up or Continue to proceed.

Choose a Folder to Set Your Server

If you have multiple servers set up, the process of creating a new folder is a bit ambiguous as to what server it will be created on. To force the folder to be created on a specific server, first make sure the Notes folder list is visible and then click a folder name on the server you want to use. Subsequent *new* folders will be created on that server.

5. If you're setting up a service that provides more than just calendars (such as Exchange, Yahoo!, or Gmail), you are prompted to automatically set up corresponding email accounts and contact servers. Be sure to click the checkbox beside Notes.

6. Click Done.

7. Close the System Preferences when finished.

Your Utilities, Everywhere

Wish you had access to the suite of utilities described in this chapter wherever you may be? You do! You can access Calendars, Contacts, Notes, and Reminders using Apple's iCloud web service. Just sign in at http://www.icloud.com/ to use Apple's meticulously crafted and stunningly beautiful web versions of these useful tools.

It's Not All Good

GONE FOR GOOD. EVERYWHERE.

Even though the applications in this chapter are frequently configured to use servers (much like Mail), it doesn't mean that they work with information in the same way as Mail. In email, when you delete a message, it typically gets moved to your email's trash folder—where it can be recovered.

In Calendar, Reminders, and Notes, deleting an event, reminder, or note is permanent. You'll be asked to confirm the deletion, but once it's gone, it's gone.

Additionally, if you delete an iCloud reminder, event, or note using any of the applications in this chapter, it will be removed from all of your devices—virtually simultaneously.

Purchase and read books in iBooks.

Challenge your friends in Game Center.

Enjoy movies, music, and more in iTunes.

In this chapter, you discover how to use digital music and video to turn your Mac into a big-screen entertainment center, including:

→ Buying digital media using iTunes

→ Syncing your iOS device with iTunes

→ Keeping your computers in sync with Home Sharing

→ Purchasing books with the iBooks Store

→ Reading with iBooks

→ Social gaming with Game Center

Entertainment on the (Big) Little Screen

In case you hadn't noticed, your Mac has a gorgeous screen. The LED IPS display provides excellent color reproduction and amazing depth—at HDTV resolutions or higher. Why bother sitting in front of the TV when your Mac does so much more? Using iTunes, you can build a library of thousands of songs, TV shows, and movies.

In addition to iTunes, your Mac also includes software to browse, purchase, and read thousands of the best-selling books. If challenging your friends is more your style, Game Center gives you a full social gaming platform, just a click away.

Creating a Media Library in iTunes

Apple's iTunes enables you to manage and play digital media files, including song tracks you import from CD, content you purchase from the iTunes Store, or podcasts you subscribe to online.

You can also create and sync playlists with your iDevices or share them with other iTunes users on your local network.

Running iTunes for the First Time

The first time you launch iTunes, you won't have anything in your music library. Follow these steps to complete the setup process:

1. Open iTunes from the Dock, Launchpad, or by locating its application icon in the Applications folder.

2. Click Agree after reviewing the iTunes Software License Agreement.

3. The Welcome window, with video tutorials for various tasks, appears. Click Watch Tutorials if you'd like to see video demonstrations of iTunes in action.

4. If you're okay with iTunes sharing information about your library in order to see artist information, album covers, and other niceties, click Agree; otherwise click No Thanks.

5. Click Scan for Media to search your account for any music files you might already have. These are copied to the iTunes folder, inside your Music folder. (This option might not appear if you have a previous version of iTunes already installed.)

6. To immediately start searching the iTunes Store, click the iTunes Store button in the upper-right corner.

Finding Your Way Around iTunes

First, here is a quick tour of the iTunes controls to acquaint you with the basics. The default view in iTunes is the Library view.

1. The Library menu enables you to choose between Music, Movies, TV Shows, and Home Sharing (other computers sharing their iTunes libraries with you).

2. The organization buttons in the center top of the window enable you to choose how your library is displayed (by song, album, artist, genre, and so on). The options change depending on the type of library you have selected.

3. The iTunes Store button jumps you into the iTunes Store. This view takes over the full screen. In this view, you can click a Library button when you are ready to return to your media library.

After choosing a Library and a viewing organization, your screen shifts to one of many different displays of your media library. The interface encourages exploration. The album view for music, for example, has these features:

1. Double-clicking an item (song, album, and so on) begins playback.

2. Clicking an album opens an expanded view of the contents.

3. Positioning your cursor over an item displays a disclosure arrow that opens a menu that enables you to jump between different media organizations, add the item to your playback list, create an iTunes Radio Station, or show the iTunes Store for the artist.

4. Clicking In the Store shows additional items you can purchase related to the chosen media. If iTunes cannot find related content within the store, you do not see this option.

Not In the Store
You can always toggle whether or not iTunes shares information about your library using the Store settings within the iTunes preferences. Be aware that if you choose not to share, certain iTunes features will not be available to you—such as In the Store links that help you locate additional music by your favorite artist.

Along the top of the window are controls for all your playback needs:

1. Move back, forward, play, and pause your media playback.

2. Adjust your speaker volume.

3. Choose a device, such as an Apple TV or Airport Express, to output your sound. If you don't have an Airplay-compatible device, you won't see this icon at all (icon not shown).

4. View the playback progress.

5. Set playback to loop repeatedly.

6. Set playback to shuffle.

7. View the next song that will be played or the songs that already have been played.

8. Search all your media or the iTunes Store.

9. Show iTunes downloads.

10. Switch to a small version of the iTunes player that can sit in the corner of your screen.

Building Your Media Library

Apple offers plenty of content for you on the iTunes store. Everything from music to movies, podcasts, music videos, and TV shows. With just a few clicks, you can go from a Saturday night with nothing to watch to a movie night with the latest blockbuster releases.

Purchasing Digital Media on the iTunes Store

To purchase media from the iTunes Store, follow these steps:

1. Click iTunes Store in the upper-right corner (or use the In the Store link when viewing media) to connect to the iTunes Store.

2. Click Sign In. If Sign In doesn't appear, skip to step 5.

3. Enter your Apple ID and password in the Sign In dialog box.

4. Click Sign In.

Note

You can authorize up to five computers to play songs purchased on a single account. To do this, choose Store, Authorize Computer and enter your Apple ID. (Remember to deauthorize computers that no longer need access, which frees openings for new computers to be added.)

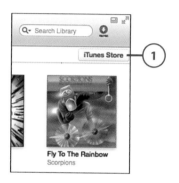

Redeem Your Gift Cards— No Typing Required

If you have an iTunes gift card to redeem, click the button with your Apple ID (visible after signing into the iTunes Store) and then choose Redeem from the menu that appears. On the subsequent screen you can type in your gift card number or click Use Camera to scan the card with your FaceTime HD camera.

5. When you're logged in, your Apple ID appears in place of the Sign In button.

6. Use the links and scrolling content views to browse available media—just as you would a web page.

7. Click the Play button that appears as you move your cursor over a song to play a preview.

8. To make a purchase, click the Price button that appears beside items. In the case of music, you can buy individual songs or albums.

9. When you're asked to confirm that you want to buy the selection, click the Buy button. Your selection is downloaded and added to your library under the Purchased playlist.

10. Click the download button (down arrow) to view all the current downloads taking place.

The Rental Countdown

When you choose to rent a movie, you have 30 days to watch it and 24 hours from the time you start watching it to finish it. Rented movies appear in your library just as other files do.

>>>Go Further

IMPORTING FROM CD

Although Apple has dropped optical drives from virtually all of its shipping Macs, you can still use iTunes to import from a CD. To do this (if you have an optical drive), just insert the CD; iTunes launches and prompts you to import. It's as simple as that.

Additionally, when you import an audio CD, iTunes connects to a music database, identifies your disc, and applies information such as title, artist, and genre to each track. Album artwork might also be available if the album is part of the iTunes Store.

If iTunes doesn't find your CD in the database, you can edit the track information yourself by selecting it and choosing File, Get Info. Select several tracks at a time to update all the shared information and save yourself some typing.

It's Not All Good

BUY HERE, READ ELSEWHERE

One of the types of media available in iTunes is books. You can currently download books, but you need to use the iBooks application to read them. My advice—use iBooks to purchase, download, *and* read your books.

Using Genius Recommendations

Genius Recommendations attempt to predict what new and existing media you might enjoy based on the current items in your library. Follow these steps to enable and peruse Genius Recommendations:

1. Choose Store, Turn on Genius from the menu bar.

2. Click the Turn On Genius button on the screen that appears. (If you're already signed in with your Apple ID, you won't see this or the next step.)

3. Enter your Apple ID and password in the Sign In dialog box and click Continue.

4. Check the box to agree to the terms of service and click Agree.

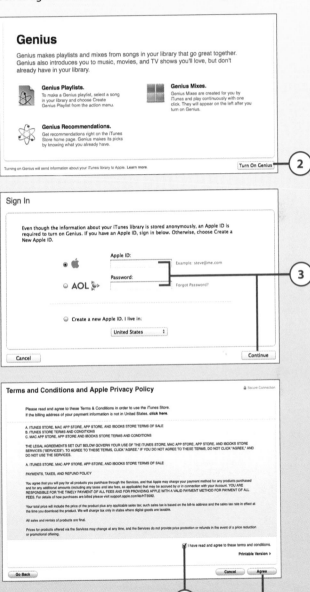

5. A screen announcing Turning On Genius appears while the contents of your library are analyzed and personalized results are prepared. Three stages are displayed while this occurs: gathering information, sending information, and delivering Genius results.

6. Select a song in your library.

7. When viewing In the Store items, new song recommendations are shown on the right.

8. Click the disclosure arrow beside a song or album to view recommendations in your existing library.

9. Choose Start Genius to begin playing a playlist of songs similar to the currently selected song.

10. Pick Create Genius Playlist to create and save a new playlist based on the current song. The new playlist is saved and visible within the Playlists view category.

11. Click Genius Suggestions to list the songs that Genius thinks are similar to the chosen song.

12. Pick from the genius recommendation list to jump to any song.

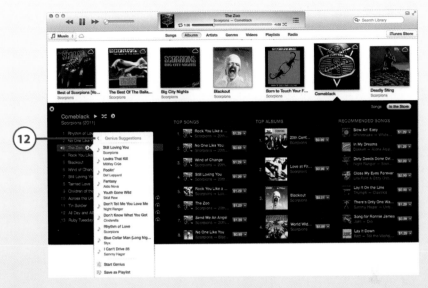

Downloading Podcasts

Podcasts are series of digital files, either audio or video, that you can subscribe to for regular updates. You can locate and subscribe to a variety of podcasts (most of them free) in the iTunes Store by following these steps:

1. Click iTunes Store to open the store.

2. Click the Podcasts button categories list at the top center of the screen.

3. Click an item to see details and a list of available episodes.

4. Click the Subscribe button to download the most recent episode and all future episodes of this podcast. The podcasts are downloaded to your iTunes library.

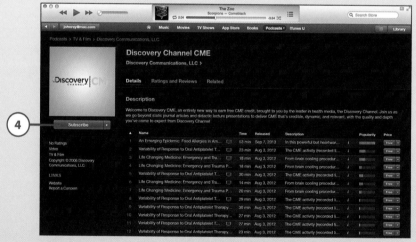

5. Click Subscribe when you're asked to confirm that you want to subscribe.

6. Exit the store and select the Podcasts item in the Library menu.

7. Choose the podcast from the list on the left.

8. Select an episode and click the Play control button to listen.

Oldies But Goodies

Episodes produced prior to your subscription appear when you click the Old Episodes button in the upper-right corner of the Podcast list. Click the cloud icon to download any old episodes not stored on your Mac.

Not Listening? Unsubscribe.

iTunes checks for updates as long as you are subscribed; if you change your mind about following a podcast, select it in the list and click the Unsubscribe button displayed at the top of the list of individual podcasts.

>>>Go Further

FREE EDUCATION WITH iTUNES U

If you're looking for educational materials, iTunes U is the place to go. Here, dozens of schools publish free course material that is yours for the downloading. Audio, video—it's all here, and subjects from business management to programming are available. iTunes U lessons work identically to podcasts, but are downloaded from the iTunes U section of the iTunes Store and are managed in the iTunes U category of your library.

Searching the Library

Your iTunes library can grow large quite quickly with so many sources from which to draw. Fortunately, it's easy to search your library to find just what you're looking for.

Quick Searches

If you know the title of a song or album or the name of an artist, follow these steps to search for it:

1. Click inside the Search box at the upper right of the iTunes window and begin typing a search term. As you type, a pop-over window appears showing potential matches.

2. Choose an item to jump to it within your library.

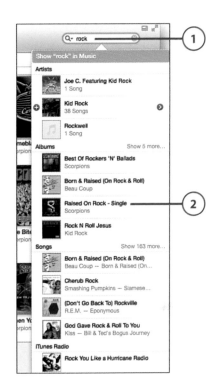

Setting a Search Filter

To filter your search results further, do the following:

1. Click beside the magnifying glass in the search field.

2. Uncheck the Search Entire Library item to search only the type of media you are currently viewing.

3. Choose the filter option you want to apply (Song, Album, Artist, Composer, and so on).

4. Perform the search as described in the section "Quick Searches."

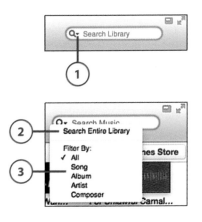

Using Playlists

Playlists help you organize your music and media into themes to suit your mood. You can define your own playlists, set search criteria to automatically cluster certain artists or genres, or have iTunes use the Genius profile it created from your library to generate lists for you.

Creating Playlists

To define a playlist of songs you choose, follow these steps:

1. Within the Music library section, click the Playlists category.

2. Click the plus button at the bottom of the list of playlists on the left. (There are several playlists provided by default.)

3. Choose New Playlist.

4. The screen refreshes with a playlist column on the right and the playlist name highlighted. Enter a name for the new playlist and then press Enter.

5. Browse your music library as you normally would.

6. Drag songs, albums, or artists to the playlist column on the right.

7. When finished adding songs, click Done.

Playlist Organization

If you add so many playlists that you feel the need to put them in folders to keep track of them, choose New Playlist Folder when clicking the same plus button you used to add a playlist.

Defining Smart Playlists

To set criteria that iTunes can use to make a playlist for you, follow these steps:

1. Within the Music library section, click the Playlists category.

2. Click the plus button at the bottom of the list of playlists on the left. (There are several playlists provided by default.)

3. Choose New Smart Playlist.

4. In the Smart Playlist window, set your search criteria. Options include obvious choices, such as artist, album, or rating, as well as more obscure settings, such as bit rate (which relates to sound quality) and skip count (which tells how often you choose not to listen to it). You can also set a limit on the number of songs and allow live updates, which creates a list that changes as your library changes.

5. One option that might not make immediate sense is Match Only Checked Items. This only matches songs that have checkmarks. If you view your library as a list, you can check/uncheck beside each song. This refers to that checkmark.

6. Click OK when you're done setting search criteria. Your Smart Playlist appears under the Playlists.

7. Enter a Name for the new Smart Playlist, and then press Return.

Genius at Work

Refer back to "Using Genius Recommendations" to have iTunes generate a playlist for you based on a song, album, or artist of your choice.

Accessing Playlists

To access, edit, or play back the media in your playlist, follow these steps:

1. Within the Music library section, click the Playlists category.

2. Click the playlist you want to use from the list on the left.

3. Click the View button to switch between song, artist, and album views.

4. Click Add To to modify the playlist (or Edit for Smart Playlists).

5. Click Play/Pause to begin (or stop) playback. Here, Pause is shown.

6. Click Shuffle to randomize the playback order.

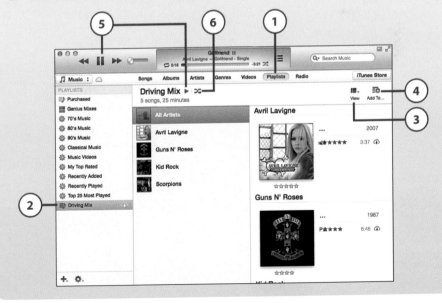

Using the Mini Player

After you've set up your media library and decided on the songs you want to play, chances are you don't want to keep the huge iTunes window around. To use the mini player, follow these steps:

1. Click the Mini Player button in the upper right of the iTunes window.

2. The mini player appears and displays the currently playing song.

3. Move your cursor over the window to show standard playback controls.

4. Click the list icon to show upcoming songs or your playback history.

5. Use the magnifying glass to search for songs directly from the mini player.

6. Click the tiny rectangle on the left to exit the mini player.

Using iTunes Radio

If you find yourself wanting to just listen to good music, iTunes now includes iTunes Radio. iTunes Radio offers both curated and automatically created stations that literally play *anything* you want. Be your own DJ!

We Interrupt This Song…

iTunes Radio is a great service, but it is supported by ads that play between songs. If you want ad-free music, just subscribe to iTunes Match (discussed a bit later in this chapter), and your music won't be interrupted.

Listening to iTunes Radio

To start listening to iTunes radio, you need an active Internet connection. Beyond that, you're just a few clicks away from your favorite artists and songs. Follow these steps to listen to one of the many ready-to-play Featured stations available:

1. Make sure you are in the Music section of your Library.

2. Click the Radio button near the center of the iTunes toolbar.

3. Scroll left and right in the list of Featured stations until you find something you'd like to listen to.

4. Click Play to begin playing iTunes Radio.

5. Click the Star to display options for liking or disliking a song.

6. Click the Fast Forward button to skip to the next song (you can only do this six times in a 60-minute period).

7. Click the Price (displayed to the right of the song information) to purchase the track being played.

Creating Your Own iTunes Radio Station

After you've had a taste of the featured stations, you'll likely want to create your own.

1. Click the + button beside My Stations to create a new station.

2. Use the pop-over display to choose a genre for the station, or type the name of a song or artist to base the station on.

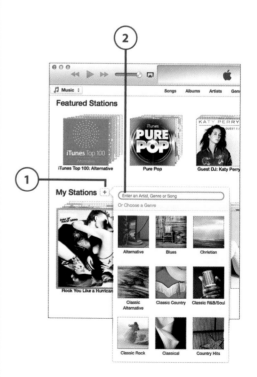

3. Choose the artist or song to use to create the station.

4. Use the Allow Explicit switch to enable or disable songs with explicit lyrics.

5. The new station appears and begins playing. Note that the station also automatically opens for editing, covered in the next task.

More Than Music

iTunes Radio features more than just music! If you'd like to listen to comedy broadcasts, type in the name of your favorite comedian. I recommend Bob Newhart.

Your Radio, Anywhere

Any iTunes Radio station that you create will be available on any Mac or iOS device where you've signed into your iTunes account. It even works with your iPod/iPhone-compatible car audio system!

Fine-Tuning Your iTunes Radio Station

Not only can you build your own station, featuring your favorite song or artist, but you can fine tune the station for your mood. Include multiple artists, exclude songs or artists, even choose to just play hits. Follow these steps to tune your radio station:

1. Click the station you want to edit. The station settings appear below it.

2. Use the Tune slider to choose between Hits, Variety, and song Discovery (finding new music).

3. Use the + button in the Play More Like This section to add additional artists, or songs that you'd like to hear. This process is the same as the initial steps in the preceding task.

4. Use the + button in Never Play This to add artists and songs you never want to hear.

5. Click the X icon in the upper corner of the station information to close the editing screen.

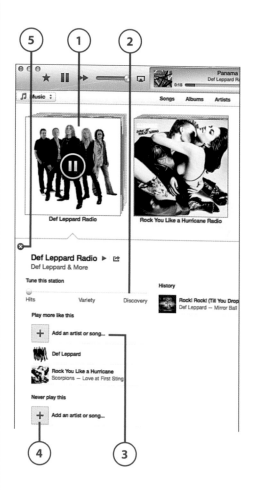

Answering the "What Was That Song?" Question

If you've ever heard a song and wondered what it was, you'll be happy to hear that *can't* happen on iTunes Radio. If you hear something and want to see what it was, follow these steps:

1. Click the list icon beside the playing song information.

2. A pop-over window displays the recently played songs on all your stations.

3. Click the price to purchase any song you've heard.

Station Specifics

To focus on the recent songs on a specific station, click the station to open it and display the recently played songs.

Sharing Your Good Taste

Radio stations are meant to be shared. After you've crafted the perfect station, you can easily share it with your friends by following these steps:

1. Click to open the editing screen for a station.

2. Click the Sharing Sheet icon beside the station name.

3. Choose a method for sending the station to your friend.

Syncing Media Between Devices

iTunes is more than a virtual filing cabinet for storing music and media files. It also syncs with iPods, iPhones, and other computers on your network so you never have to be without those items, even when you're away from your Mac.

Syncing Purchases

By enabling syncing of purchases in iTunes, you ensure that your purchases are downloaded to other copies of iTunes that are signed in with your Apple ID.

Follow these steps to turn on purchase syncing:

1. Open the Preferences from the iTunes menu.

2. Click the Store button at the top of the Preferences window.

3. Click the checkboxes in front of Music and Apps (or any combination of these) to download any purchase made on another Mac (or even your iOS device) to your iTunes library automatically.

4. Click OK to close Preferences.

Syncing Your Media with Your iPod, iPad, or iPhone

iTunes was designed to be used with iPods, iPhones, and iPads, which makes syncing your Library between devices a cinch.

Follow these steps to transfer content from your Mac to your iPod, iPhone, or iPad:

1. Connect your iOS device to your Mac using the supplied USB cable. iTunes detects the device and begins synchronizing. (If it has not been connected before, iTunes guides you through a short registration process.) Click the device button to open information about the connected device.

2. View the Summary screen, which shows the name, capacity, software version, serial number, and any updates available to your device.

3. Choose Sync over Wi-Fi to sync without your USB cable in the future!

Syncing to a New Mac
If your device was previously synced with another Mac, you have the option to Erase and Sync or transfer purchases to your new Mac.

4. To conserve space on your device, open the different Media categories, and, on each, select which items to sync.

5. Click Sync to apply your selection and sync your device. The status of the sync appears at the top of the window. Do not disconnect your device until syncing is completed.

6. When the sync completes, click Eject and unplug your device and cable.

Cable-Free Bliss
After you've enabled Wi-Fi syncing, you can start a sync any time your iPhone, iPad, or iPod is on the same network as your iTunes library. Just open the Settings app on your iOS device and navigate to General, iTunes Wi-Fi Sync.

Everything Everywhere!

If you've chosen to automatically download media purchases to your iOS device, chances are you will rarely even need to sync directly with iTunes because iCloud will keep everything up-to-date on its own!

Even better, with the latest releases of iOS, you don't even need to sync. Just start listening to music or watching your favorite videos and they'll be streamed straight to your device.

Sharing Media Between Home Computers

Home Sharing enables you to browse up to five computers on your local network and import music to your own library. In addition, it enables you to stream media to your iOS device when it is connected to your home network.

1. Using the Library menu, choose Home Sharing. This item only appears when Home Sharing is turned off or iTunes has detected available shared libraries on your network.

2. Sign in with your Apple ID by entering your username and password.

3. Click Turn On Home Sharing.

4. Click Done when the confirmation page appears.

5. Repeat the previous steps for all the other computers in your home, connecting with the same Apple ID.

6. Use the Library menu to choose the shared library you want to peruse.

7. Interact with the songs and media as if they were local to your computer.

Keeping an iCloud Library with iTunes Match

All songs, movies, and TV shows that you purchase through iTunes are available on any of your computers, as long as you're signed into iTunes with your Apple ID. These are referred to as being "stored in iCloud." Although this is fine and dandy, what about all the media you have that you *didn't* purchase through iTunes?

For that, you have Music Match. Music Match keeps your entire iTunes music library in Apple's iCloud service and makes it available to all your devices, including the Apple TV. What's more, it replaces poorer quality recordings you have in your library with the best Apple has to offer.

It's Not All Good

PAY TO PLAY

iTunes Match isn't free. It costs $25 per year and matches up to 25,000 songs that you didn't purchase from iTunes. Any song purchased through iTunes doesn't count toward the total song limit. A big plus to paying for iTunes Match is that you get ad-free iTunes Radio. It's a pretty good deal, all things considered!

Activating iTunes Match

To sign up for iTunes Match, follow these simple steps:

1. Choose Turn On iTunes Match from the Store menu.

2. Click the Subscribe button to join the iTunes Match service, or click Add the Computer (not shown) if you're already a subscriber.

3. Enter your Apple ID and password.

4. Click Subscribe.

Adding Your Existing Library to iCloud with iTunes Match

After signing up for iTunes Match, you can connect your Mac's iTunes library to the service and begin uploading your songs. If you have multiple computers, each can connect and upload its songs individually.

1. Within the Music library, choose Match from the category list at the top center of the screen.

2. Click Add This Computer.

3. Enter your Apple ID and password when prompted.

4. Click Add This Computer.

5. The iTunes Match process runs, analyzing your library and adding your music to iTunes Match in iCloud. You can continue to use iTunes during this process.

Accessing Music in iCloud

After you've activated iTunes Match on a computer or iOS device, all your songs appear—whether they're located in iCloud or stored locally. To access your music, simply follow these steps:

1. Choose Music from the Library menu—there will now be a cloud icon next to the pop-up menu.

2. Browse your library. Songs and albums available for download from iCloud (but not stored locally) are shown with a cloud and a download arrow. Songs that are stored locally have no cloud icon.

3. You can select and play any song or album. As long as you are connected to the network, iTunes Match songs are instantly streamed.

4. Click the cloud/arrow icon to download a local copy of the song.

Music and More

In addition to your music being stored in the cloud, any TV shows and movies are also available through iTunes on machines that are signed in with your Apple ID. Note that this is only for purchased shows and movies—there is no "video matching" within iTunes Match.

>>>Go Further

MEDIA CENTER EXTRAORDINAIRE

Once upon a time, OS X included a media center application called Front Row. Front Row provided a TV-ready interface for browsing and playing your iTunes Media. When Apple discontinued this feature, it left a void that several Open Source projects quickly filled.

The most Mac-like and feature-rich of these projects is Plex (www.plexapp. com). Using Plex, you can create a media center system that plays *any* format of video or audio, looks great on a TV, accesses Internet video, streams to iOS devices, shares with friends, and much more. For free. If you're a media junkie, Plex is definitely the way to go.

Reading Your iBooks

If music, TV, and movies aren't your cup of tea, then perhaps a book will do. Mavericks now supports full integration with Apple's iBooks Store and enables you to shop for new titles and read them on your gorgeous Mac display. The iBooks application is *very* similar to iTunes, so please make sure you're comfortable with shopping for content on iTunes before continuing.

Starting iBooks and Authorizing Your Mac

For many users, your first experience with iBooks came on your iPhone or iPad. That's fine, but it means that you might need to authorize your computer before you can read your previous book purchases. Let's walk through the steps of starting iBooks for the first time and then authorizing your Mac to read previous purchases.

Starting iBooks

Before you can start using iBooks, you need to walk through the setup wizard and login with your Apple ID. Follow these steps to get ready to read:

1. Open iBooks from the Applications folder, Dock, or Launchpad.

2. Click Get Started.

3. Click Sign In to log into the iBooks Store with your Apple ID.

4. Enter your Apple ID and password information.

5. You're taken to your iBooks library.

Authorizing Your Mac

If you've previously purchased books on another device and want to read them on your Mac, you probably need to authorize your computer.

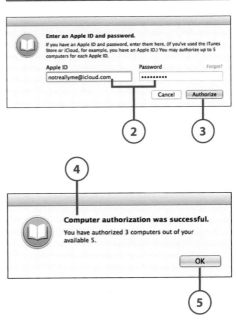

1. Choose Authorize This Computer from the Store menu. (If this is not visible, you are already authorized and can skip this task.)

2. Enter your Apple ID and password.

3. Click Authorize.

4. A confirmation message is displayed.

5. Click OK. Your system is now prepared to read previous purchase.

Purchasing Books

When iBooks is up and running, your next step is adding content. This is identical to the iTunes store, so refer to the previous section for a more detailed walkthrough. To use iBooks to purchase new books, follow these basic steps:

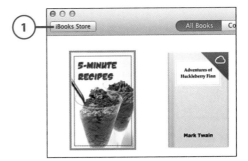

1. If you are viewing the iBooks library (you see either books you already own, or a blank screen), visit the iBooks Store by clicking the iBooks Store button in the upper left.

2. The iBooks window refreshes to show an iTunes-like store.

3. Use the toolbar buttons to choose between Featured content, Top Charts, NYTimes best sellers, and Top Authors.

4. Use the links and pop-up menu on the right-hand side to select between other popular book categories.

5. Search for books using the search field in the upper-right corner.

6. When you arrive at a title that you want, click the Buy Book button.

7. Enter your Apple ID and Password.

8. Click Buy.

9. Click the Arrow icon in the upper-right corner to show your iBook download status.

Kindle Me

Not a fan of the iBook Store? If you're a user of Amazon's Kindle eBook service, you'll find everything you need in a download of the "Kindle" app from the Mac App Store.

Viewing and Arranging Your Library

After you've made a few purchases, you can browse your virtual library—and even arrange your books into Collections. iBooks is perfectly suited to accommodate both prolific readers and the occasional book browser.

Browsing the iBooks Library

To browse the iBooks library (assuming you've made a purchase or two), just follow along:

1. If you are within the iBooks Store, click the Library button to view your book library.

2. Click the All Books button to view all the content in your library.

3. Use the Sort By menu in the upper-right corner to set sorting criteria for the view.

4. Books marked with a cloud icon have not yet been downloaded to your computer. They download automatically when opened.

5. Click the Authors tab to view the books by author, with a list of Authors on the left.

6. Click an author's name to show the books written by that individual.

7. Click Categories to show books by category.

8. Click a category in the list on the left to show only the books in that category.

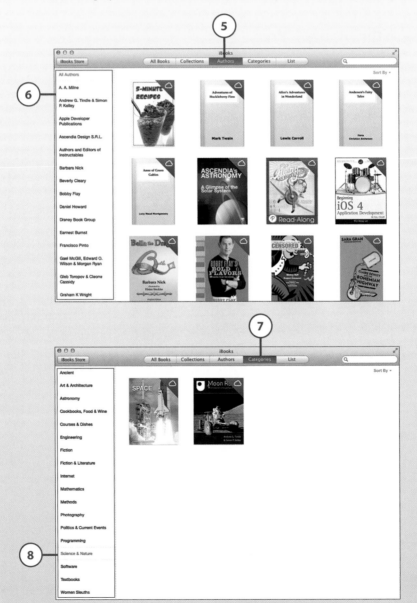

9. Use the List button to quickly view all books in your library and see whether or not they have been downloaded (no cloud icon).

iBooks—It's Not Just for iBooks

You can use iBooks to manage any content in ePub or PDF format. Just drag compatible files into your iBooks library and they'll appear—ready for reading—just as if you had purchased them from the iBooks Store.

Organizing by Collection

In addition to the sections that Apple provides for browsing your library, you can create your own organization with Collections. To view, create, and manage Collections, do the following:

1. Click the Collections tab at the top of the iBooks Window.

2. Click the Purchased collection to see all of your iBooks purchases.

3. Click the Books collection to view all Books, regardless of whether they were purchased or manually added.

4. Click PDFs to view all PDF files that were manually added to iBooks.

5. Click the + button at the bottom of the window to add a new category.

6. Name the category by clicking and typing (Recipe Books is used here).

7. Click and drag books from one of the predefined collections (Purchased, Books, PDFs) into the new collection.

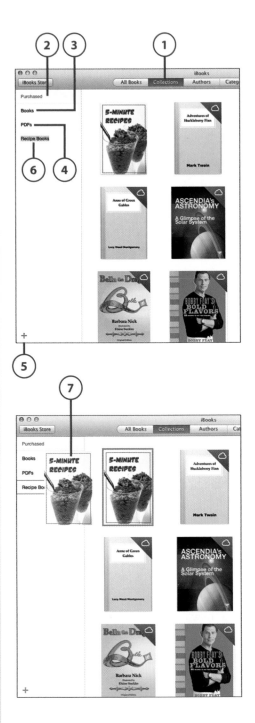

8. Collections help you organize your library as you see fit.

9. To remove a Collection, select it and press delete. The content in the collection is not removed (not shown).

Searching for *Searching For Bobby Fischer*

If you've amassed a huge iBooks collection and no longer know exactly where your favorite book is, you can quickly search your entire library using the search field in the upper-right corner of the iBooks window.

Reading iBooks

Okay, you can buy books, you can organize them, but can you read them? Yes! iBooks does indeed enable you to read books. Not only can you read your books, but you can also make notes and highlights—and even change the color of your virtual paper!

Reading Basics

To get started reading with your favorite book and your favorite computer, first make sure that you've purchased the book and that it appears in the iBooks library. Then follow these steps:

1. Browse (using whatever method you'd like) to the book you'd like to read.

2. Double-click the title. If it hasn't been downloaded yet, iBooks downloads it.

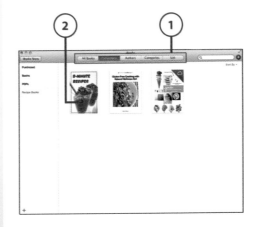

3. A reading window appears.

4. Position your cursor next to the edges of the screen and click the arrows to move from page to page. Alternatively, swipe with two fingers to move between pages.

5. Click and drag at the bottom of the page to quickly move through the book.

6. Click the list icon to show a table of contents for the book. Click any entry to jump to that page.

7. Click the book icon to return to the main iBooks library window.

Using Annotations

Have you ever found something in a book that you wish you could easily refer to in the future? With iBooks, it's simple to create comments and high-lights while you read—and you won't get yelled at for destroying your books!

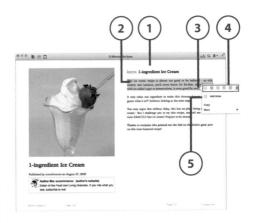

1. Browse to a point in a book that you want to annotate.

2. Highlight the text you are inter-ested in.

3. A pop-up window displays that points to your text.

4. Choose a color (or underline) to highlight the text.

5. Choose Add Note to set a note and highlight the text.

6. A note window appears. Type your message and then click outside the box.

7. View all your notes for a given book by clicking the Notes icon (a square box) in the toolbar.

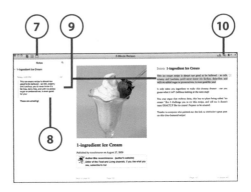

8. The Notes panel lists all notes.

9. Click a note in the list to navigate to that note.

10. Use the magnifying glass icon to search your notes.

The More Menu

When you select text and bring up the annotation pop-up window, you see a More menu. Selecting More gives you the ability to search the Web/Wikipedia for the highlighted text, post it to social network sites, email it, or even hear it read aloud.

Adding Bookmarks

If you'd prefer to just bookmark content within a book (rather than annotating it), you can use the one-click bookmark tool. Follow these steps to bookmark (and return to) any page:

1. Navigate to the page that you want to bookmark.

2. Click the ribbon icon to toggle a bookmark on and off.

3. Click the down arrow beside the ribbon icon to show the bookmarks that have been set.

4. Select a bookmark to jump to that page.

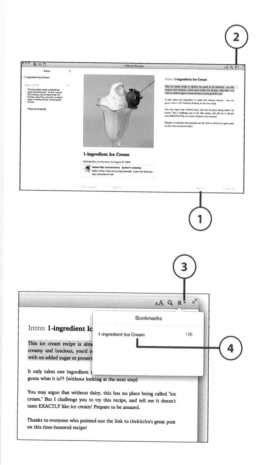

Fine-Tuning Your Display

If the default text size and screen color don't make for a comfortable reading environment, Apple has provided some settings to customize the display. To change your book's appearance while reading, follow these steps:

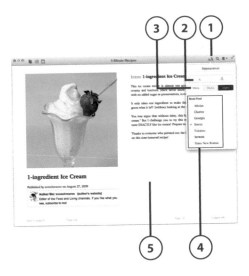

1-ingredient Ice Cream

1. Click the AA icon in the toolbar while reading.

2. Use the buttons at the top to shrink or enlarge the text.

3. Use the White, Sepia, and Night buttons to set the color of the text and background.

4. Choose a font from the Book font list to set the type style for your book.

5. Click outside the menu to continue reading.

Getting Your Game on with Game Center

If your idea of fun is speeding through exotic locations and talking trash to your friends, Game Center may be your preferred entertainment option. Mavericks features Game Center, a social gaming system similar to Xbox Live and the Playstation Network. With Game Center, you can create lists of friends, compare games and game achievements, discover new games, and launch games that you have installed on your Mac. What's more, Game Center is fully integrated with iOS, so you can keep track of your friends (and frenemies) wherever you are.

Cross-Device Play—Sometimes

You might have heard that the OS X version of Game Center enables you to play games on your Mac against friends on their iPhones and iPads. It's true that this feature is available, but it's on a per-game basis for the developers to enable—it doesn't just start working if you have the same games installed on different devices.

Signing into Game Center

The first step to using Game Center is signing in. This requires an Apple ID, so it's a good idea to have one before starting. If you don't have one, however, it can guide you through the setup.

1. Open Game Center from the Launchpad or Applications folder.

2. Click Create Apple ID to get a new Apple ID, if needed.

3. Enter your Apple ID and Password in the provided fields.

4. Click Sign In. If this is your first time using Game Center, complete steps 5–8.

5. Enter a Nickname on the screen that appears.

6. Click the Public Profile if you want others to be able to search and find you within Game Center.

7. Click Use Contacts for Friend Suggestions if you want Game Center to use your Contact list to try to find new friends.

8. Click Continue.

Navigating the Me Screen

After logging into Game Center, you are taken to a screen that describes your account status and provides some additional features.

1. A summary of the games you have installed (across all your devices), points you have accumulated, and friends is shown in banners near the center of the screen.

2. Click the field under the banners to set your current status, or what is displayed to your friends in their Game Center.

3. Click Change Photo (or your photo) to take a new picture of yourself.

4. Click your account name to log out if you share your computer account with other people.

Managing Friends and Friend Requests

After getting into Game Center, it's a good idea to start adding and managing friends—otherwise, you'll be lonely. Let's review the process for sending friend requests, reviewing friend recommendations, and responding to requests that have been sent to you.

Sending a Friend Request

How do you get a new friend? By sending a request. To send a friend request to someone you know, follow these steps:

1. Click the Friends button at the top of the Game Center window.

2. Click the Add Friends button on the left side of the window.

3. A friend request dialog box appears. Enter the email address for the person you want to add.

4. Type a message to your potential friend, or use the default.

5. Click Send. A request is sent to your friend, who can respond on her Mac or iOS device.

Responding to a Friend Request

When a friend request comes in, you can respond wherever you are by clicking a link in email. You can also respond directly in Game Center.

1. The Requests button updates with the number of pending requests beside the name. (The Game Center icon also shows this count.) Click the Requests button.

2. Choose the friend request you want to view.

3. Click Ignore to ignore the request, or click Accept to make the person your friend.

4. If you clicked Accept, the person is added to your Friends list (not shown).

Getting Friend Recommendations

Not sure who you should add as a friend? Game Center can give you recommendations based on your contacts and the games you have installed. To see the recommendations, follow these steps:

1. Click the Friends button.

2. Click Show All under the Friend Recommendations box at the top left of the window.

3. The left side of the window changes to a list of recommendations.

4. Choose an individual from the list to view his information on the right.

5. Click Send Friend Request to send a friend request to the individual.

Sizing Up Your Friends

After you have established a few friends, you probably want to see how your gaming skills compare to theirs. Game Center enables you to drill down to view a number of different stats about your friends and their games. To see a few, follow these steps:

1. Click the Friends button.

2. Choose how your friends are sorted using the buttons at the top of the Friends list.

3. Filter your list down to a specific friend using the Search field, if desired.

4. Click an entry in the list to select a friend.

5. A summary of your friend's game-playing activity is shown on the right.

6. Click a game to drill down to more information.

7. The window refreshes to show the achievements that you and your friends have earned, as well as a summary of your overall scoring. (Note that I haven't earned any achievements in this screenshot.)

Lost? Just Go Back

It's easy to drill down to a great detail of information in Game Center. If you ever feel lost, you can use the forward and back arrows in the upper-left corner; they work just like the arrows in a web browser.

Browsing by Game

In the previous step, you located a friend and used her as the starting point for browsing to a game and showing a comparison of activity. You can also take a more game-centric approach.

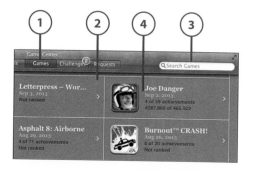

1. Click the Games button at the top of Game Center.

2. The window refreshes to list all your games across all devices. (New game recommendations appear at the top but are not visible here.)

3. Search for individual games using the Search Games field.

4. Click a game to view information about it.

5. Use the Achievements button (the default) to show your personal achievements in the game.

6. Click Leaderboards to show how you compare against players worldwide.

7. Use the Players button to display any friends who have recently played the game.

8. Click the Tell a Friend button to email your friend and convince her to download the game.

Making and Taking a Challenge

Within Game Center, you can challenge your friends to beat your achievements or game scores. For some games, you can even challenge them to a live match.

To send (or receive) a challenge, follow these steps:

1. Navigate to the game you want to challenge your friend in.

2. Click the achievement (or a score from the leaderboards) that you want to base the challenge around.

3. In the pop-over window, click Challenge Friends.

4. Pick the friends you want to challenge.

5. Click Next.

6. Enter a message (if desired) to go with the challenge.

7. Click Send. Your challenge will now be sent, and you'll be notified if your friends meet (or beat!) your results.

8. Click the Challenges button at the top of the Game Center window to view any Challenges your friends have sent you in return.

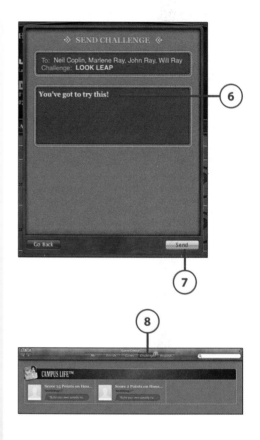

Download and install new apps using the Mac App Store.

Keep Mavericks up-to-date with automatic software updates.

In this chapter, you learn how to install applications on your Mac and keep Mavericks up-to-date, including:

→ Browsing the Mac App Store
→ Downloading and managing App Store applications
→ Downloading and installing non–App Store software
→ Working with OS X software distribution formats
→ Configuring software updates and auto downloads

Installing and Managing Software on Your Mac

Up to this point in the book, you've been looking at software that came as part of Mavericks. That's a bit limiting, don't you think? There is a wide world of software waiting to enhance your computing experience—including upgrades to Mavericks itself.

Through the use of the Mac App Store and its built-in update mechanism, you can install new applications, keep them up-to-date, and keep your Mac running smoothly and securely. When that isn't enough, you can turn to thousands of other non-App Store apps that run natively on your Mac.

Mac App Store

Applications make a Mac a Mac. As intangible as it is, a certain "something" about using a Mac application is rarely replicated on a Windows computer.

When you've become accustomed to the day-to-day operation of your Mac, you'll likely want to begin installing third-party software. The easiest place to do this is through the Mac App Store. Like the popular App Store for iOS devices, the Mac App Store is a one-stop shop for thousands of apps that you can install with point-and-click ease.

Logging into the App Store

To use the Mac App Store, you need a registered Apple ID—the same account you used to access iCloud in Chapter 4, "Setting Up iCloud Services and Internet Accounts," will work just fine. If you don't have an ID, you can create one directly in the App Store. To log into the store, follow these steps:

1. Open the App Store application from the Dock, Launchpad, or Applications folder.

2. The App Store window opens.

3. Click Sign In from the Quick Links on the right side of the page.

4. Provide your Apple ID and password in the form that appears.

5. Click Sign In.

Creating an ID

If you do not have an ID, click Create Apple ID and follow the onscreen prompts.

6. Your Login Status and links to your account information are shown in the Quick Links section.

Browsing for Apps

Part of the joy of using the App Store is that browsing is simple and fun—and, like iTunes and iBooks, it works in the same manner as a web browser. As you encounter links (such as See All), click them to view more information. You can browse within a variety of categories that cover the gamut of what you can do on your Mac:

1. Follow steps 1–6 of the previous task, "Logging into the App Store."

2. Click the Featured icon to browse apps tagged by Apple as New and Noteworthy or Hot.

3. Click Top Charts to see the apps that are currently selling the best or being downloaded the most.

4. Click Categories to browse by the different types of apps (games, business, developer, and so on).

5. When you see an app you are interested in, click the icon or name.

6. A full page of information, including reviews, opens.

7. Use the Forward and Back buttons to move back and forth between pages, just like a web browser.

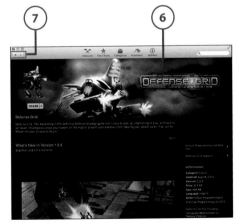

Quick Links for Faster Browsing

The featured page actually contains more than the new/hot apps. In the column on the right side of the page, you can quickly jump to specific app categories to see Top Paid apps, Top Free apps, and more without leaving the page.

Searching for Apps

Sometimes you might know the app you want but do not know where it is located. In these cases, you can simply search the App Store:

1. Follow steps 1–6 of the earlier task, "Logging into the App Store."

2. Type a search term or terms into the field in the upper-right corner. You can use application names, categories (news, for instance), and even author/publisher names.

3. As you type, a list of possible searches appears. Click one if you want to use it; otherwise, press Return to use the search term you've typed.

4. The Search results are displayed.

5. Use the Sort By menu to choose how the results are sorted within the window.

6. Click App Icons or Names to view more information.

Purchasing an App

When you've decided to purchase an app, the process couldn't be simpler. Follow these instructions to download an app and install it on your Mac:

1. Browse or search for an app, as described in the previous tasks, "Browsing for Apps" and "Searching for Apps."

2. From within the search/browse results or the larger application information page, click the App Price button.

3. The Price button changes to read Buy App. If the app is free, it reads Install App. Click the Buy App (or Install App) button.

4. Provide your App Store Apple ID and password, if prompted, and then click Sign In.

5. The application immediately downloads to your Applications folder and is visible in Launchpad.

Remember It on Payday!

The right side of the Price button for an app has a downward-pointing arrow. This is actually a separate button that opens a pop-up menu. Use this menu to copy a link to the app or to send an email message to someone (maybe yourself) about the app.

>>>Go Further

SPARKLING NEW APPS

New apps you purchase through the App Store take on an animated "shimmering" appearance in Launchpad, helping you see where they've been added.

I Don't Want It—Make It Go Away!

If the App Store makes it so easy to install things, it certainly makes it easy to delete them, right? Yes and no. The App Store is used for installing, but Launchpad is used to uninstall the apps. Learn about Launchpad in Chapter 2.

Reinstalling Apps and Installing Purchases on Other Macs

One of the best things about buying applications through the App Store is that you can install them on other Macs you own. No licensing hassles—just download and go. You can also reinstall apps that you may have deleted in the past but want to start using again.

To download an app you've purchased but that isn't installed, follow steps 1–6 of the "Logging into the App Store" task and then complete these steps:

1. Click the Purchases icon at the top of the App Store window.

2. The Purchases list is displayed, along with a button/label showing the status of each app.

3. Apps labeled as Installed are currently installed and up-to-date.

4. Click the Install button to install (or reinstall) an app that you already own.

5. Click the Update button to update a piece of software that is currently installed.

Auto-Install Your Apps!

Mavericks prompts you to turn on automatic downloading of Apps that you download on other machines. If you activate this feature, any software you download on one Mac will automatically be downloaded on any other Mac that is logged into the Mac App Store with your account. You can also control this via the App Store preference pane, which you learn about later in this chapter.

Hiding Apps You No Longer Want

I've downloaded a lot of apps; you probably will, too. Unfortunately, these won't all be apps you want to keep updating (or even remember that you purchased). To hide an app from the update list, follow these steps after logging into the App Store.

1. Click the Purchased icon at the top of the App Store window.

2. Hover your cursor over the item you want to hide.

3. Click the X button that appears to hide your purchase.

Find What's Missing

To show the items that you've hidden, choose the Account quick link from the right side of the Mac App Store after following the instructions in the section "Logging into the App Store." Use the View Hidden Purchases button to show the hidden apps.

Installing Non–App Store Applications

The App Store is great, but it doesn't mean that it defines the limits of what you can do on your Mac. There are certain restrictions in place on the App Store that make some pieces of software impossible to distribute through that site. There are also thousands of developers who want to sell and market their applications through their own websites.

By default, Mavericks enables you to install and run any software you want—but this can be disabled by an administrator. Read the section "Limiting Application Execution," in Chapter 13, "Securing and Protecting Your Mac," to learn how to adjust the controls to enable (or disable) software installations on your Mac.

Installing software from non–App Store sources is frequently a matter of browsing the Web in Safari, clicking a download link, and copying the application to your Applications folder.

Getting the Lowdown on the Download

Recall that Mavericks has a Downloads folder that is available in your Dock. Software archives that you download in Safari or most other Mac applications are stored in this location.

Unarchiving Zip Files

A decade ago, almost all Mac applications were distributed in a compressed archive format called SIT (StuffIt). Today the Mac has adopted a standard used on Windows and other platforms called zip files. A zip file can contain one or more compressed files.

To unarchive a zip file and access the contents, follow these steps:

1. Find the file that you want to unarchive.

2. Double-click the file. Unarchiving can be virtually instantaneous or can take several seconds, depending on the archive size.

3. The contents of the archive are made available in the same folder where the zip file was located.

Just StuffIt

If you find that you need to deal with a StuffIt file, you can download StuffIt from http://www.stuffit.com. Despite the decreasing use of the format, it has been actively maintained over the years.

Accessing Disk Images

Sometimes applications are distributed on a disk image, or DMG file. When mounted on your system, DMGs act like a virtual disk drive. Files in a DMG must be copied off the disk image by way of an installer or a simple drag-and-drop process.

To mount and access the contents of a disk image, follow this process:

1. Find the Disk Image you want to access.

2. Double-click the DMG file. The disk image mounts and appears as a disk in the Finder.

3. Access the files in the disk as you would any other storage device.

4. To eject the disk image, click the Eject icon beside the mounted disk in the Finder sidebar or drag it to the trash.

Adium (http://adium.im/)—We all have friends (frenemies?) who use chat services other than what Messages supports. Adium supports more than a dozen different instant messaging protocols, including MSN, Yahoo!, and Facebook.

AppCleaner (http://freemacsoft.net/appcleaner/)—This finds the files associated with an application and removes them from your system. Mavericks lacks a global uninstaller that works across *all* apps, so one of the first things you should install is an uninstaller such as AppCleaner.

Curio (http://www.zengobi.com/products/curio/)—This is an amazingly flexible project management and brainstorming software. No matter your line of work, Curio can be a valuable partner in exploring new ideas and creating plans.

Coda (http://www.panic.com/coda/)—This integrated web application development environment fits perfectly on your Mac's screen. If you're ready to graduate from Apple's iWeb software, Coda is a great next step.

CrossOver (http://www.codeweavers.com/products/cxmac/)—Run Windows applications (including Outlook!) and games within Mavericks without the overhead of a virtual machine. CrossOver enables you to run many Windows applications directly from your Mac.

Dropbox (http://www.dropbox.com/)—Get 2GB of free online storage that you can sync across OS X, Windows, and Mavericks platforms. This service offers the capability to track multiple versions of files wherever you are.

Hazel (http://www.noodlesoft.com/hazel.php)—Hazel offers automated file organization for your desktop. It can automatically discard incomplete uploads, empty your trash when it gets too full, and help keep your system nice and clean.

Microsoft Remote Desktop (http://www.microsoft.com/mac/)—If you need to use a Windows desktop, you can do so from the comfort of your Mac. Download Microsoft's Remote Desktop to remotely access your Windows system as if you were sitting directly in front of it.

Crashplan (http://www.crashplan.com/)—If you need true offsite continuous backups, Crashplan fits the bill. Crashplan works in the background to upload any files you choose (or your entire filesystem) to a remote storage location for quick disaster recovery.

Dolly Drive (http://www.dollydrive.com/)—Like the idea of Time Machine, but don't want to leave a drive connected? Dolly Drive brings Time Machine to the cloud. $5 a month gets you 50GB of backup space that works with Time Machine over your Internet connection, wherever you are.

1Password (http://agilewebsolutions.com/products/1Password)—Manage your password and other sensitive information, like the keychain, but in a much more functional and usable way. 1Password can autofill web pages and also syncs across computers and with the iPhone.

VirtualBox (https://www.virtualbox.org)—This is full Windows emulation, entirely for free! You'll need a copy of Windows to install, but that's all. VirtualBox is an open source project that can quickly turn your Mac into a full Windows system without having to reboot.

Keeping Your Applications and Operating System Up-To-Date

Keeping your operating system and applications up-to-date is important both from the standpoint of maintaining your system security and providing the best possible user experience.

With Mavericks, you can activate an automatic update process that periodically checks and prompts you with available updates. You can even set all your Macs to automatically download applications that you've purchased through the App Store—ensuring a seamless computing experience moving from system to system.

How Will I Be Notified of an Update?

All Mavericks software update notifications appear in the Notification Center. Using the controls on the notification, you can postpone its install or have it applied immediately. To learn more about the Notification Center, refer to Chapter 1, "Managing Your Desktop."

Configuring Software Updates and Auto Downloads

To configure how Mac handles software updates and new downloads from Apple, follow these steps:

1. Open the App Store System Preferences panel.

2. Select the Automatically Check for Updates check box to have your system periodically look for new software downloads.

3. Check Download Newly Available Updates in Background to have your system download the update packages while it is idle so that they are available to install when you are ready.

4. Click Install App Updates to keep all your App Store purchases automatically updated.

5. Choose Install System Data Files and Security Updates to keep many of the critical OS files automatically updated without any interaction required.

6. If you'd like all your App Store purchases to be downloaded automatically to your Mac, check Automatically Download Apps Purchased on Other Macs.

7. Close the System Preferences.

Manually Applying Software Updates

If you're like many people (myself included), you want the latest and greatest without waiting. With the Mac App Store, you can manually update your system as soon as updates become available: Mavericks manages your applications and system updates in a single location.

To check and install application and OS updates, do the following:

1. The App Store icon displays a counter badge listing the number of updates available to you. Update notifications also appear in the Notification Center.

2. Open the App Store.

3. Click the Updates button in the App Store toolbar.

4. All your available app updates are listed.

5. Click the Update All button to update all software at once.

6. Click an individual Update button to update just a single app.

7. Update progress appears in the App Store window, but you don't have to wait to continue using your computer. The updates are automatically installed in the background.

MICROMANAGE YOUR UPDATE SCHEDULE

>>>Go Further

To force your updates to occur at a specific time, click the right-side of the Update All button. This displays a drop-down menu that enables you to choose when (in an hour, tomorrow, and so on) updates should be applied.

Software Update? Your Assistance May Be Required!

Depending on the type of update, you might be asked to give your password and accept any applicable software license agreements before an update is installed. You might also be required to quit running applications or even reboot your Mac for low-level OS updates.

Optimize your Mac's built-in hardware in System Preferences.

In this chapter, you find out how to make your Mac hardware work at its best for your particular needs, including:

→ Balancing performance and battery efficiency
→ Fine-tuning the keyboard settings
→ Adjusting trackpad and mouse gestures
→ Setting sound input and output
→ Configuring display resolution and color
→ Recording audio and video

Making the Most of Your Mac Hardware

When you purchased your Mac, you bought more than just a "computer"—you bought a power system, monitor, keyboard, trackpad (and maybe a mouse), video camera, microphone, and speakers! On a traditional desktop system, these might all be separate components, but on your Mac, they're part of a tightly integrated package.

To help personalize your Mac, you can adjust many of the settings available for these hardware devices, such as enabling trackpad gestures, setting a system boot and shutdown schedule, setting your microphone up for dictation, and much more. Mavericks even includes a few out-of-the-box tricks such as video, audio, and screen recording that let you take advantage of the built-in FaceTime HD camera without needing any additional software.

Going Green with Energy Saver

A decade ago, computers were appliances—much like microwaves. When you wanted something, you booted them up, performed your task, and shut them down. Today, computers that are actually turned *off* are harder and harder to find. Our expectation is that we can walk up to a computer, access it instantly, and move on.

Your Mac makes this scenario possible, and possible in an energy efficient way. You can always put your computer to sleep or shut it down from the Apple menu, but you can also have it take care of energy-saving tasks for you.

Configuring Display, Computer, and Hard Disk Sleep

To help improve energy efficiency, Mavericks includes the Energy Saver System Preferences panel.

1. Open the System Preferences window and click the Energy Saver icon.

2. Drag the sliders, Computer Sleep and Display Sleep, to set the period of inactivity after which your Mac puts itself or its display into sleep mode.

3. Select Put Hard Disks to Sleep When Possible to spin down your hard drive when it's not in use. This helps save power but sacrifices some speed. If you have a machine with a solid state drive, this option is not available.

4. If you'd like to let your computer wake up if you attempt to access it over a network, click Wake for Network Access.

5. To set the system to sleep when you push the power button in back, click Allow Power Button to Put the Computer to Sleep.

6. If you want your system to boot back up after a power failure, click Start Up Automatically After a Power Failure.

7. If available, select Enable Power Nap to have your Mac wake occasionally for backups and network updates while sleeping.

8. Close the System Preferences.

Creating a Sleep/Wake Schedule

If you have a daily schedule and want your Mac to follow it, you can configure wake-up and sleep/shutdown times. Follow these steps to set a power schedule for your system.

1. Open the System Preferences window and click the Energy Saver icon.

2. Click the Schedule button at the bottom of the window.

3. To have your computer start up on a schedule, click the checkbox beside Start Up or Wake.

4. Use the Every Day pop-up menu to set when (weekdays, weekends, and so on) the startup should occur.

5. Set the time for the computer to start up.

6. To configure your computer to go to sleep, shutdown, or restart, click the checkbox in front of the Sleep pop-up menu.

7. Use the Sleep pop-up menu to choose whether your Mac should sleep, shutdown, or restart.

8. Configure the day and time for the shutdown to occur, just as you did with the start options in steps 4 and 5.

9. Click OK.

10. Close the System Preferences.

Updating Keyboard and Dictation Settings

Having trouble getting used to your keyboard? Never fear! Using the built-in keyboard settings, you can adjust the keyboard repeat rate, key delay, and even set system-wide shortcuts for trackpad and mouse-free operation.

If you prefer to talk rather than type, Mavericks includes built-in dictation, accessed from anywhere with a single keystroke.

Setting Keyboard Repeat Rate

To choose how frequently the keys on your keyboard repeat, and how long it takes to start repeating, follow these simple steps:

1. Open the System Preferences window and click the Keyboard icon.

2. Click the Keyboard button at the top of the panel.

3. Use the Key Repeat slider to set how quickly letters appear when you hold down a key on your keyboard. Move the slider all the way to the left to turn off repeating.

4. Move the Delay Until Repeat slider to choose how long you must hold down a key before it starts repeating.

5. Close the System Preferences.

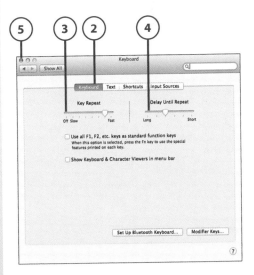

Using Function Keys

You've probably noticed that the top row of keys on your Apple keyboard have special functions, such as dimming the display, changing the volume, and so on. These keys, however, are also function keys that your applications might need. To set the keys to always work as function keys without having to hold down the fn key, click the Use all F1, F2, etc. Keys as Standard Function Keys checkbox.

Creating Keyboard Shortcuts

There are times you might find yourself working with your Mac and thinking, "Geez, I wish I could just push a key for that rather than having to mouse around." Using keyboard shortcuts, you can create key commands for almost anything. There are two types of shortcuts supported in Mavericks—traditional shortcuts where you must press a key combination, and text shortcuts where you type a certain string and it is substituted with another. We will start with the latter.

Enabling Text Shortcuts and Spelling Correction

To set a shortcut for frequently typed text, follow these steps.

1. Open the System Preferences and click the Keyboard icon.

2. Click the Text button at the top of the panel.

3. Check Correct Spelling Automatically to enable auto-correct across all your applications.

4. Check the Use Smart Quotes and Dashes checkbox to enable straight quotes to automatically be replaced by their curly equivalents.

5. Click the + button at the bottom of the list on the left to create a text replacement shortcut.

6. Use the left column field to enter the shortcut text you want to type ("brb," for example).

7. Use the right column to enter the full text it should be replaced with ("Be right back").

8. Use the – button to remove any shortcuts you are no longer using.

9. Close the System Preferences.

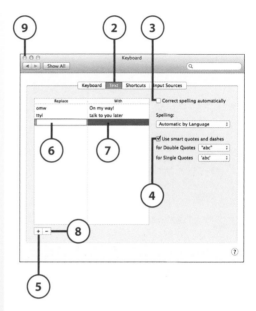

Setting Shortcuts for Existing Mavericks Actions

To set the shortcut for an existing system feature, follow these steps:

1. Open the System Preferences window and click the Keyboard icon.

2. Click the Shortcuts button.

3. Choose one of the Mavericks system features from the left pane.

4. Scroll through the list of available actions in the right pane.

5. Click the checkbox in front of an action to enable it.

6. Double-click to the far right of an action name to edit its shortcut field.

7. Press the keys that you want to assign to the shortcut.

8. Close the System Preferences after making all of your changes.

Setting Shortcuts for Arbitrary Applications

To configure a shortcut that works with an arbitrary application, not a built-in feature, do the following:

1. Open the System Preferences window and click the Keyboard icon.

2. Click the Shortcuts button.

3. Click the App Shortcuts entry in the list on the left side of the window.

4. Click the + button at the bottom of the shortcut list.

5. In the dialog box that opens, use the Application pop-up menu to choose an application to which you want to assign a shortcut.

6. Enter into the Menu Title field the exact wording of the menu item that you want the keyboard short-cut to invoke.

7. Click into the Keyboard Shortcut field and then press the keys you want to set as the shortcut.

8. Click Add when you're satisfied with your settings.

9. Close the System Preferences.

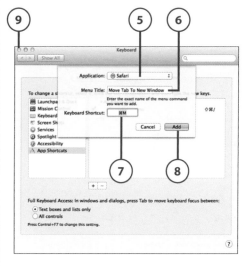

Activating Dictation

If you find that your Mac's keyboard is tiring your fingers, you may want to switch to using the Mavericks dictation feature. This enables you to input text *anywhere* using your voice. The only requirement is that you work in a noise-controlled environment (or have a high-quality headset). In Mavericks, you have the option of voice recognition being performed by Apple's cloud servers or locally on your machine.

Enabling Dictation

To enable dictation support and configure how it is triggered, follow these steps:

1. Open the System Preferences window, and click the Dictation & Speech icon.

2. Click the Dictation button at the top of the panel.

3. Click the On radio button to turn on dictation support.

4. Click Use Enhanced Dictation to enable local (non-iCloud) dictation support. You need about 785MB of free space for Mavericks to download additional software.

5. Click the label below the microphone image to set your preferred input mic.

6. Use the Shortcut drop-down menu to configure what key combination will start dictation.

7. Set the language you will be speaking using the Language drop-down menu.

8. Close the System Preferences when finished.

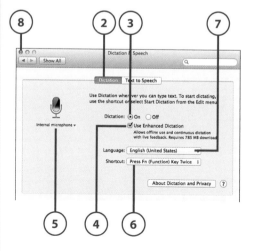

Your Mac Can Talk Back

Your Mac can talk back to you using a variety of different voices. To configure speech feedback, click the Text to Speech button at the top of the Dictation & Speech preference panel. This will let you test and choose your favorite speech synthesizer and the rate of speech.

Using Dictation

To use dictation, you must have it enabled (see the preceding task) and have an active Internet connection. If you meet those qualifications, just complete these steps to type with your voice:

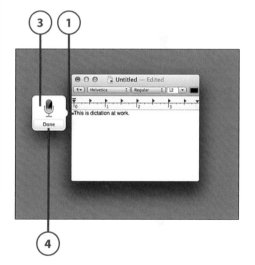

1. Position your cursor where you want to dictate.

2. Press the key combination you configured when enabling dictation (not shown).

3. The dictation microphone appears. Begin speaking now—be sure to speak the name of the punctuation symbols you want to insert, such as "period," "comma," and so on.

4. Press any key or click Done to end dictation. After a short pause, the spoken text is inserted into the document.

Changing Trackpad and Mouse Options

Whether you're a mouser or a trackpad devotee, Apple's hardware offers precision input in a multitouch package. Although these devices are intuitive for beginners, they can be customized to provide advanced features within Mavericks. Using the Trackpad and Mouse preferences, you can fine-tune the operation of your input device and set up different multifinger gestures in popular applications.

Perfect Pairing

If you've just purchased a new input device and need to connect it, skip ahead to Chapter 12, "Connecting Devices to Your Mac," for details on Bluetooth pairing.

Setting the Trackpad Speed

To choose how quickly your track-pad follows your input, follow these steps:

1. Open the System Preferences window and click the Trackpad icon.

2. Click the Point & Click button at the top of the window.

3. Choose how quickly the cursor moves by dragging the Tracking Speed slider.

4. Close the System Preferences.

Controlling Trackpad Gestures

Apple trackpads can take advantage of a wide range of different two-, three-, and even four-finger motions to control your applications.

1. Open the System Preferences window and click the Trackpad icon.

2. Use the Point & Click settings to configure click and drag options.

3. Use the Scroll & Zoom settings section to control scrolling, rotation, and pinching gestures.

4. The More Gestures settings control advanced features, such as whether swiping to the left or right moves forward or backward in Safari and how Mission Control is activated.

5. Many settings contain a drop-down menu to fine-tune the gesture.

6. As you mouse over a particular setting, a video demonstrating the action appears in the right side of the window.

7. Close the System Preferences.

Configuring the Magic Mouse Speed

The Apple Magic Mouse is a multi-touch trackpad and mouse in one. Although it doesn't support nearly as many gestures as the trackpad, it's still a capable device. To configure the Magic Mouse tracking speed, follow these steps:

1. Open the System Preferences window and click the Mouse icon.

2. Click the Point & Click button at the top of the window.

3. Choose how quickly the cursor moves by dragging the Tracking Speed slider.

4. Close the System Preferences.

Configuring Magic Mouse Gestures

To set up the different single and two-finger gestures supported on the Magic Mouse, complete the following:

1. Open the System Preferences window and click the Mouse icon.

2. Use the Point & Click settings to configure click, scrolling, and zooming.

3. The More Gestures settings control advanced features, such as whether swiping to the left or right moves forward or backward in Safari and how Mission Control is activated.

4. Some settings contain a drop-down menu to fine-tune the gesture.

5. As you mouse over a particular setting, a video demonstrating the action appears in the right side of the window.

6. Close the System Preferences.

If you have to choose...

Choose the trackpad. Even if you are a life-long mouser, you'll find that Apple's trackpad gesture support integrates perfectly into Mavericks and makes performing common tasks similar to using an iPad.

Adjusting Your Display

Your Mac's display is your window into your computer, so it's important that you configure your display to best suit your needs. For detailed CAD or drawing, you might want to use the full resolution. Games or late-night typing might call for a larger (lower resolution) option. Using the Display settings, you can control the image so that it is right for the task at hand.

Setting Display Resolution

The display resolution is the number of pixels that are viewable on the screen at any time. Lower the resolution for a larger image—or raise it, for smaller details. To control the screen resolution on your system, follow these steps:

1. Open the System Preferences window and click the Displays icon.

2. Click the Display button at the top of the panel.

3. Click the Scaled radio button. Alternatively, the default radio button (Best for Built-In Display) chooses the best option for your system.

4. Scroll through the list of available resolutions (smaller numbers result in a larger, less crisp onscreen image).

5. Click a resolution to switch immediately.

6. Close the System Preferences.

What Are Mirroring Options?

When setting your display resolution, you'll notice a checkbox for showing Mirroring Options in your menu bar. This is for working with external displays that can mirror your Mac's screen. You can read more about this feature in Chapter 12.

Controlling Display Brightness

Display brightness is a personal setting; some individuals like muted, dimmed displays and others like colors offered by full-brightness settings. To set the brightness of your display, follow these steps:

1. Open the System Preferences window and click the Displays icon.

2. Click the Display button at the top of the panel.

3. Drag the Brightness slider left or right to dim or brighten the display.

4. Click Automatically Adjust Brightness to have your screen dim or brighten depending on the room's ambient lighting.

5. Close the System Preferences.

Adjusting Brightness from Your Keyboard

You can also adjust display brightness using the dim/bright keys (shared with F1 and F2) on your keyboard.

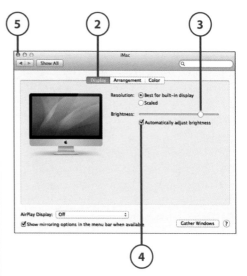

Choosing a Color Profile

Color profiles help keep colors consistent between computers with different monitors. By choosing a color profile that is calibrated for your display, you're ensured that colors you see on one machine match a similarly calibrated display on another machine. To choose a calibration profile, follow these steps:

1. Open the System Preferences window and click the Displays icon.

2. Click the Color button at the top of the panel.

3. Click the preferred profile in the Display Profile list. The changes are immediately applied.

4. Close the System Preferences.

Where Do These Profiles Come From?

You can add profiles to your system by installing software or by running the calibration procedure, which creates your own personalized color profile.

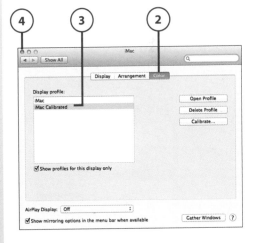

Calibrating the Display

If you'd like to calibrate your display manually, Mavericks provides a wizard-like interface for choosing the best display settings for your Mac.

1. Open the System Preferences window and click the Displays icon.

2. Click the Color button at the top of the panel.

3. Click Calibrate.

4. The Display Calibrator Assistant starts.

5. Click the Expert Mode checkbox to get the best results.

6. Click Continue to proceed through the assistant.

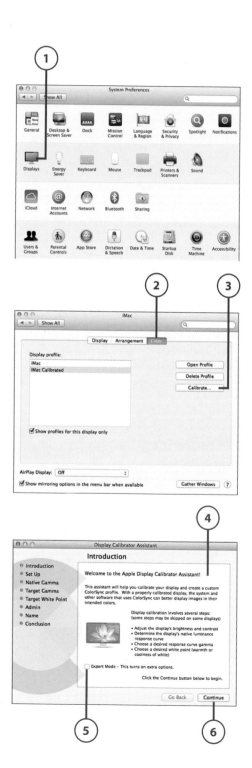

7. Follow the onscreen instructions to test the output of your display and click Continue to move on to the next screen.

8. When finished, enter a name for the new calibrated profile.

9. Click Continue to save the profile.

10. The new profile is added to the color profile list.

11. Close the System Preferences.

Setting Sound Input and Output

Sound has never been an afterthought on Macintosh systems, and yours is no different. Your system is equipped with a stereo sound system, headphone jack, microphone jack (shared with the headphone jack in recent models), and even digital audio out. You can configure these input and output options to reflect your listening needs.

Setting the Output Volume

Volume, as you might expect, is one control that is needed system-wide. To control the output volume of your system, follow these steps:

1. Click the speaker icon in the menu bar.

2. Drag the slider up to increase the volume, or slide it down to decrease the volume.

3. Drag the slider all the way to the bottom to mute all output sounds.

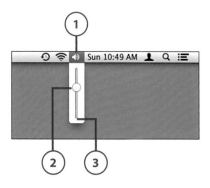

Keyboard Volume Controls

You can also use the special controls located on the F9, F10, and F11 keys to mute, decrease, and increase the system volume.

Adding the Volume Control to the Menu Bar

If sound control is not visible in your menu bar, it has been manually removed. You can re-add it to the menu using the Show Volume in the Menu Bar option in the Sound System Preferences panel.

Configuring Alert Sounds

Your Mac generates alert sounds when it needs to get your attention. To configure the sounds, and how loud they play, follow these steps:

1. Open the System Preferences window and click the Sound icon.

2. Click the Sound Effects button at the top of the panel.

3. Scroll through the alert sound list to see all of the available alert sounds.

4. Click a sound to select it as your alert sound and hear a preview.

5. Choose which sound output device (usually your internal speakers) should play the alert sound.

6. Use the alert volume slider to adjust the volume of alerts that your system plays. This is independent of the system output volume.

7. Check Play User Interface Sound Effects to play sounds when special events occur—such as emptying the trash.

8. Close the System Preferences when finished configuring the sound effects.

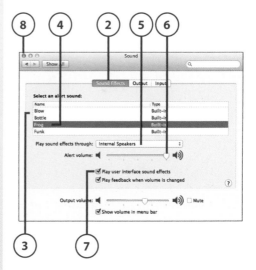

Choosing and Adjusting an Output Device

To configure your sound output options with a bit more flexibility than just changing the volume, you need to adjust the output settings for the device that is being used for playback—typically your speaker.

1. Open the System Preferences window and click the Sound icon.

2. Click the Output button at the top of the panel.

3. Choose the output device to configure (probably your speakers).

4. Use the Balance setting to adjust audio to the left or right speaker.

5. Set or mute the Output Volume.

6. Close the System Preferences when finished.

HOW DO I USE HEADPHONES OR DIGITAL AUDIO?

When headphones are plugged into your Mac, the sound output settings alter to reflect the change. All sound is directed to the headphones rather than the internal speakers.

Your Mac also sports a home-theater-worthy digital optical output, disguised as the headphone jack. To use the digital output, you need a mini TOSLINK adapter, which provides a standard TOSLINK plug for connecting to stereo equipment. These cables from Amazon.com easily get the job done: www.amazon.com/6ft-Toslink-Mini-Cable/dp/B000FMXKC8.

Picking and Calibrating an Input Device

In addition to sound output, you can also input sound on your Mac using either the built-in microphone or the line-in jack on the back. To configure your input device, follow these steps:

1. Open the System Preferences window and click the Sound icon.

2. Click the Input button at the top of the panel.

3. Choose the device to use for input.

4. Use the Input Volume slider to adjust the gain on the micro-phone—this is how much amplifi-cation is applied to the signal.

5. Click the Use Ambient Noise Reduction checkbox if you're working in an environment with background noise.

6. Speak at the level you want your computer to record. The Input level graph should register near the middle when you use a nor-mal speaking level. If it doesn't, readjust the input volume slider.

7. Close the System Preferences.

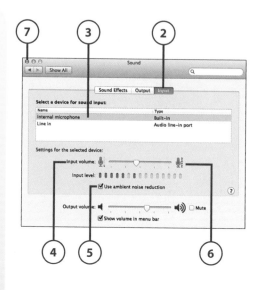

Quick Sound Input/Output Access

If you work frequently with audio and need quick access to your input and output device settings, you can skip the Sound preference panel entirely. Just hold down Option when clicking the speaker icon in your menu bar and, instead of showing you the volume, it will let you pick between all your input and output devices.

Keeping the Input Volume Under Control

It might be tempting to turn the input volume up as high as it goes so that the microphone detects even little noises. Keep in mind, however, that the higher the input volume for wanted sounds, the higher the volume for unwanted sounds as well!

Recording Audio and Video

It has always been possible to record audio and video "out of the box" with a new Macintosh, but not without jumping through a bunch of seemingly unnecessary hoops or trudging through unwieldy software. With Mavericks, Apple has made it easy to take advantage of your Mac's built-in capabilities to record audio, video, and even screen actions.

Recording Audio

To create and save a new audio recording, first make sure that you've configured your sound input settings correctly (including ambient noise reduction, if needed) then follow these steps:

1. Open the QuickTime Player application (find it in the Launchpad or the Applications folder).

2. Choose File, New Audio Recording.

3. Use the drop-down menu on the right of the Audio Recording window to choose an input source, recording quality, and destination.

4. If you want to hear audio through the speakers as it is recorded, drag the volume slider to the right.

5. Click the Record button to begin recording.

6. Click the Stop button to stop recording.

7. Use the playback controls to listen to your creation.

8. Choose File, Export to save the audio, if desired.

Recording with the FaceTime HD Video Camera

Although FaceTime enables you to see video of yourself on your computer, it doesn't give you the option to record. If you want to take a recording of what the built-in camera sees, follow these steps:

1. Open the QuickTime Player application (find it in the Launchpad or the Applications folder).

2. Choose File, New Movie Recording.

3. Use the drop-down menu on the right side of the recording controls to choose a camera (if you have more than one), input microphone, recording quality, and destination.

4. If you want to hear audio through the speakers as it is recorded, drag the volume slider to the right.

5. Click the double arrows to expand the video to full screen.

6. Click the Record button to begin recording.

7. Click the Stop button to stop recording.

8. Use the playback controls to view the video you've recorded.

9. Choose File, Export to save the movie, if desired. (The available options vary depending on the quality of your camera.)

Lights, Camera, Screen Actions

In addition to audio and video, you can record whatever is happening on your screen. QuickTime Player offers a New Screen Recording option under the File menu that does exactly what you'd think.

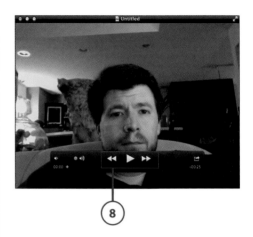

8

Video and Photo Fun!

If you want to record and share videos and photos, or you want to just play around with your Mac's HD camera, try Photo Booth—located in the Mavericks Dock (or Launchpad or the Applications folder). Photo Booth provides a simple interface for taking pictures and video, applying effects, and sharing the results.

9

**Connect your Mac
to external displays
and peripherals using
System Preferences.**

In this chapter, you find out how to connect devices to your Mac and immediately expand your system's capabilities, including:

→ Adding a keyboard and mouse
→ Pairing Bluetooth devices
→ Connecting and configuring external displays
→ Sending video and audio to an Apple TV
→ Adding and using printers
→ Accessing and using popular scanners

Connecting Devices to Your Mac

The Mac comes with everything you need to get started using the system, but that doesn't mean that you can't expand it. Your Mac can interface with many different devices—frequently without requiring any additional software to be installed.

In this chapter we look at the different types of peripherals that work with your Mac out-of-the-box.

Connecting USB Input Devices

The Mac can connect to a variety of devices using the standard USB (Universal Serial Bus) ports located on the back. This section walks you through connecting a generic keyboard and mouse. Keep in mind, though, that there are *hundreds* of different input devices.

You should always refer to the documentation that came with your device. If the manual doesn't mention the Macintosh (such as for a Windows-specific keyboard), try plugging in the device to see what happens!

USB Device Compatibility

The USB standard includes a variety of different profiles that define how a device can be used (input, audio output/input, and so on). These standards are supported on both Macintosh and Windows platforms. Just because a device does not specifically say it supports the Mac, doesn't mean that it won't work anyway.

Configuring a USB Keyboard

Your Mac comes with a perfectly usable keyboard, but if you have a favorite *wired* keyboard, you can plug it in and start using it almost immediately. To use a standard USB keyboard with your Mac, follow these steps:

1. Plug the keyboard into a free port on your Mac (not pictured).

2. If the keyboard is an Apple or Mac-specific keyboard, it is recognized and immediately usable (not pictured).

3. If you are using a generic USB keyboard, the Keyboard Setup Assistant launches and you are asked to identify the keyboard. Click Continue.

4. Walk through the steps presented by the setup assistant, pressing the keyboard keys when requested. If the assistant can't identify the keyboard, you are asked to manually identify it.

5. Click Done at the conclusion of the setup assistant. The keyboard setup is complete and ready to be used.

Manually Configuring the Keyboard Type

If the setup assistant does not start automatically when you plug in a USB keyboard, you can start it by opening the System Preferences window and clicking the Keyboard icon. In the Keyboard panel, click Change Keyboard Type.

Configuring a USB Mouse

The Apple mouse is nice, but some of us like options! Want to use a shiny USB mouse with a zillion buttons? No problem. Like keyboards, USB mice plug right in and start working in a matter of seconds.

1. Open the System Preferences and click the Mouse icon.

2. Plug a USB mouse into your Mac (not pictured).

3. After a few seconds the Mouse panel updates to show the available options for your device.

4. Uncheck Scroll Direction: Natural if you prefer a scroll wheel that behaves in a traditional manner (down to go up, and vice versa).

5. Adjust the Tracking Speed, Scrolling Speed (if the mouse includes a scroll wheel), and Double-Click Speed by dragging the sliders left or right.

6. Choose which button acts as the primary button.

7. Close the System Preferences panel when you've finished your configuration.

Using Bluetooth Devices

The Mac's built-in Bluetooth enables it to wirelessly connect to a variety of peripheral devices, including keyboards, mice, headsets, and so on. As with USB peripherals, your first step toward installing a device is to read the manufacturer's instructions and install any drivers that it came with.

After installing the software that came with the peripheral, you use the Apple Bluetooth System Preferences panel to choose and *pair* your device.

>>>Go Further

WHAT IS PAIRING?

When you're working with Bluetooth peripherals, you'll notice many references to pairing. Pairing is the process of making two devices (your Mac and the peripheral) aware of one another so they can communicate.

In order to pair with your computer, your device needs to be in pairing mode, which should be described in the device's manual.

Pairing a Bluetooth Mouse or Trackpad

To pair a Bluetooth device with your Mac, you follow the same basic steps, regardless of the type of peripheral. This task's screenshots show an Apple Magic Trackpad being paired with the Mac.

1. Open the Bluetooth System Preferences panel.

2. Make sure that your Mac's Bluetooth system is On.

3. Devices that are paired with your Mac are shown at the top of the list on the left, and new devices are shown at the bottom.

4. Click Pair to pair a new mouse or trackpad with your Mac.

5. After a few seconds, the device is paired and available.

6. Click the X beside a device in the list to remove the pairing at any time.

7. Close the System Preferences when finished.

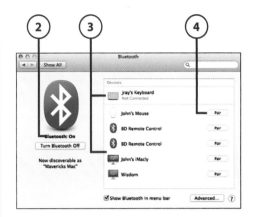

Setting Up Bluetooth Devices from Almost Anywhere

You might notice that there is a Set Up Bluetooth [Keyboard, Mouse, Trackpad] option within the keyboard, mouse, and trackpad system preference panels. You can use these as shortcuts to immediately start searching for a Bluetooth device of that type. The Bluetooth System Preferences panel, however, is the central point for pairing all devices.

8. Your new device is listed in the Bluetooth System Preferences panel (not shown).

9. Use the corresponding (Mouse/ Trackpad) Preferences panel to configure your device.

Monitoring Your Battery

When you're using an Apple Bluetooth device or keyboard, the corresponding preference panels display battery status for the devices. You can also monitor battery status by adding the Bluetooth status to your menu bar by selecting Show Bluetooth Status in Menu Bar in the Bluetooth System Preferences panel.

Pairing a Bluetooth Keyboard

Some Bluetooth devices, such as keyboards, require an additional step while pairing: the entry of a passkey on the device you are pairing with. To pair a keyboard with your system, follow these steps:

1. Follow steps 1–5 of the "Pairing a Bluetooth Mouse or Trackpad" task, selecting the keyboard device from the list of detected devices, then clicking Pair.

2. The setup process prompts you to enter a passkey on your device. Type the characters exactly as displayed on screen, including pressing Return, if shown.

3. If the passkey was successfully entered, the device is configured and paired.

4. Open the Keyboard Preferences panel and configure the device as described in Chapter 11's section "Updating Keyboard and Dictation Settings."

Dealing with Troublesome Passcodes

If, for some reason, you enter the passkey and get an error, look for a Passcode Options button in the lower-left corner of window during setup. Clicking this button *might* allow you to bypass the passkey or choose one that is easier to enter on your device.

Connecting a Bluetooth Headset

Wireless headphones and headsets can help untether us from our computers when conferencing or listening to music. Your Mac with Mavericks supports high-quality audio over Bluetooth connections, and setup is a cinch:

1. Follow steps 1–5 of the "Pairing a Bluetooth Mouse or Trackpad" task, selecting the headset device from the list of detected devices, then clicking Continue.

2. The headset is added to your system. You might need to cycle the power on and off the headset before it will work, however.

3. To set the headset for audio input or output, use the Sound System Preferences panel, as described in the Chapter 11 section, "Setting Sound Input and Output."

Adding and Using the Bluetooth Status Menu

Apple Bluetooth devices report their status directly to your computer, giving you a heads up on battery issues and other status problems. To use the Bluetooth status menu, follow these steps.

1. Open the System Preferences window and click the Bluetooth icon.

2. Click the Show Bluetooth in Menu Bar checkbox.

3. Close the System Preferences.

4. The Bluetooth menu is added to your display.

5. Each paired device has an entry in the menu for quick control of its features and display of battery levels (Apple devices only).

Using External Displays and Projectors

Even the smallest Macintosh screens are larger than the biggest monitors we had a decade ago, yet somehow we manage to fill them. As I'm sure you've encountered, there are times when using an external monitor or a projector is helpful. As long as you have the right cables, running an external monitor is plug-and-play—no rebooting required.

What Kind of External Displays Can I Run?

All modern Macs have Thunderbolt or a Mini DisplayPort video output, which can be adapted to VGA or DVI output with a plug-in dongle from Apple. Earlier models used a miniDVI port, which, similarly, could be output to VGA or DVI monitors with the appropriate adapter.

Extending Your Desktop to Another Monitor

To use another monitor to extend your desktop, follow these steps:

1. Plug the monitor into your Mac using the appropriate adapter cable (not shown).

2. The monitor is initialized and displays your desktop at the highest resolution (not shown).

3. Open the Displays System Preferences panel.

4. A unique window is shown on each connected monitor, enabling you to customize its characteristics.

5. Close the System Preferences.

Setting Monitor Arrangements

After a monitor has been connected to your system, you can choose how it is arranged in relationship to your Mac display and whether or not it displays the menu bar.

1. Open the Displays System Preferences Panel.

2. Click the Arrangement button at the top of the window.

3. Drag the visual representation of the monitors so that it best represents your physical setup (that is, external monitor on the left, right, above, and so on).

4. If you want, change your primary display by dragging the small white line representing the menu bar from one display to the other.

5. Close the System Preferences.

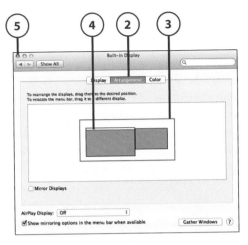

MANAGING MULTIPLE MONITORS

>>>Go Further

When the Displays System Preferences panel is opened with two or more monitors connected, a unique copy of the preference panel is shown on each monitor, representing that monitor's settings.

Within each window, you can adjust the color and resolution of your external display using the same approach described in Chapter 11's section, "Adjusting the Display." You can also use the Gather Windows button to pull all open application windows onto that display.

Adding the Display Mirroring Menu to Your Menu Bar

If you frequently want to mirror your display (rather than extend your desktop), or display content on an Apple TV, you can either use the Displays System Preferences panel or add a global "mirroring" menu to the menu bar.

1. Open the Displays System Preferences panel.

2. Click the Show Mirroring Options in Menu Bar When Available checkbox.

3. Close the System Preferences.

4. The menu item appears when external displays (or Apple TVs) are available to use.

Using Mirrored Displays

When you plug another display into your Mac, it is initialized and activated as an extension to your desktop at the highest resolution it supports. If you'd prefer to mirror the content between your displays, do the following:

1. Click the display mirroring menu item in your menu bar.

2. Choose Turn On Display Mirroring.

3. Your screen might go blank or flash for a moment (not shown).

4. Choose the resolution(s) you want to use from the mirroring menu.

5. Choose Turn Off Display Mirroring from the menu to switch back to using two separate displays.

Note

If the external display is set as your primary monitor or cannot be adjusted to match your internal LCD, your Mac might instead change the resolution on its display to match the external monitor. This change reverts when you turn off mirrored video.

Connecting to an Apple TV (or Other Device) with AirPlay

Taking display connections to the next level, Mavericks makes it simple to wirelessly share your display with an Apple TV (2nd or 3rd generation). Couple an Apple TV with a monitor or a projector, and you have a wireless presentation system for classrooms, businesses, or just at-home fun.

AirPlay works in one of four modes: mirroring, desktop extension, video/image sharing, and audio playback. Before reading any further, make sure you've added the display mirroring menu to your display (if it isn't there already) using the steps in the preceding section, "Adding the Display Mirroring Menu to Your Menu Bar."

Although the Apple TV is the only AirPlay device that currently supports video, there are many speaker systems, amplifiers, and other devices (including Apple's own AirPort Express) that can receive audio over AirPlay.

Old Mac? You Might Be Out of Luck!

Mavericks is only capable of mirroring and extending your display if you have recent Mac hardware. If you don't see the mirroring menu (and you have an Apple TV), your Mac is likely too old to use Mavericks AirPlay features. That said, I strongly encourage you to check out AirParrot—a commercial piece of software that offers all the AirPlay features of Mavericks (and more) on *any* Mac (http://airparrot.com).

Mirroring Your Display to an Apple TV

To display your Mac monitor on an Apple TV, both devices must be turned on and connected to the same network. When things are powered up, follow these steps to mirror your display:

1. Click the display mirroring menu in the menu bar.

2. All available Apple TV devices are shown. Choose the one you want to mirror to.

3. After a few seconds, your Mac desktop is visible on the display connected to the Apple TV via AirPlay (not shown).

4. To disconnect from AirPlay, choose Disconnect AirPlay Display from the mirroring menu.

Mirror, Mirror on the Preference Panel

You can also choose an AppleTV to mirror to directly from the Displays System Preferences panel. If an AppleTV is detected, a mirroring pop-up menu is added to the preferences.

Setting the AirPlay Apple TV Resolution

For the best mirroring performance, your Mac display should match the resolution of the display connected to the Apple TV—otherwise, your desktop will be enlarged and might look blurry. To adjust the resolution of the mirrored display, use these options.

1. Click the display mirroring menu in the menu bar.

2. Choose Match Desktop Size To: Built-in Display to scale the Apple TV image to match your Mac's display.

3. Choose Match Desktop Size To: AirPlay Device to change your Mac resolution to match the resolution of the display connected to your Apple TV (this is the preferred approach).

Extending Your Desktop to an Apple TV

In addition to mirroring, Mavericks actually enables your Mac to use an Apple TV as an entirely new monitor—extending your desktop as if you had plugged a new display directly into your computer!

1. Click the display mirroring menu in the menu bar.

2. All available Apple TV devices are shown. Choose the one you want to use as another monitor.

3. Choose Use AirPlay Display To: Extend Desktop.

4. The Apple TV is added as an external display and can be configured using the Displays preference panel like any other display.

5. To disconnect from AirPlay, choose Disconnect AirPlay Display from the mirroring menu.

Sharing Multimedia to an Apple TV

In addition to acting as a monitor for your Mac, your Apple TV can also play video, audio, and other multimedia content (such as slideshows), if supported by your software. While viewing video, audio, or other multimedia content, look for an AirPlay icon, then, complete the following:

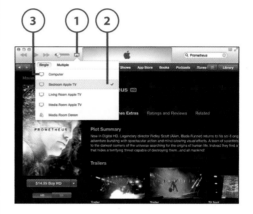

1. Click the icon to display and choose from any available Apple TV.

2. After choosing an Apple TV, the content that was playing on your Mac is automatically transferred to the Apple TV.

3. Choose Computer to return the display to your local Mac.

Sending System Audio to an Apple TV

Any application that outputs audio to your default system audio device can be sent transparently, via AirPlay, to an Apple TV. To send your system audio to an Apple TV connected to a sound system, follow these steps:

1. Open the Sound System Preferences panel.

2. Click the Output button at the top of the panel.

3. Choose the AirPlay device you want to use for audio.

4. Adjust audio and work with the device just like you would with your normal Mac speakers.

5. Close the System Preferences.

Connecting and Using a Printer

Out of the box, Mavericks supports a range of popular printers just by plugging them in. Occasionally, however, you might need to install a driver before you can successfully print. As with any peripheral that you want to use, be sure to read and follow the manufacturer's instructions before proceeding.

Adding a Printer

Your Mac can connect to printers either over a network or via a USB direct connection. Regardless of the approach, configuration is straightforward.

Setting Up a USB Printer

To connect to a printer via a USB connection, set up the printer as directed by the manufacturer, then follow these steps:

1. Connect the USB plug from the printer to your Mac and turn on the printer (not shown).

2. If the Printer is auto-detected, it might prompt you to download software. Click Install and wait for the installation to complete.

3. Open the System Preferences window and click the Printers & Scanners icon.

4. In many cases, the printer is detected and configured automatically and is immediately available for use. If this is the case, it is displayed in the Printers list, and you may close the Print & Scan System Preferences panel.

5. If the printer is not detected, click the + button below the Printer list and choose Add Printer or Scanner from the pop-up menu.

6. A window is shown displaying all of the available printers detected by your Mac. Choose the printer from the list.

7. Your Mac searches for the software necessary to use the printer and displays the chosen printer name in the Use drop-down menu.

8. If the correct printer name is shown in the menu, jump to step 12.

9. If the correct printer name is not displayed in the Use drop-down menu, choose Select Software from the menu.

Setting Up a Network or Airport Printer

To add a network printer, follow the steps described in the Chapter 6 section, "Accessing a Network Printer."

Airport-connected printers, even though they might not technically be network printers, are configured identically to networked printers. The Airport makes them available over Bonjour, a configuration-free networking technology developed by Apple.

10. A window appears that shows all the printers supported in Mavericks. Click your printer within the list.

11. Click OK.

12. Click Add to finish adding the printer. If there are options (such as a duplexer) that your Mac can't detect, it might prompt you to configure printer-specific features.

13. Close System Preferences and begin using your printer.

The Printing Process

The options available when printing can vary depending on the application that you're printing from, but once you're used to the process you'll be able to find your way around any software's printing options.

Printing to a Printer

To output to one of your configured printers, complete the following steps in the application of your choice:

1. Choose File, Print from your application's menu bar.

2. Click the Show Details button to display all the available options, if needed.

Where Is the Page Setup Option?

Apple has been working to streamline the printing process. In many applications, the Page Setup functionality has been combined with the standard Print function.

3. Select the printer you want to print to.

4. Set the number of copies and page range options.

5. Set the paper size and orientation, if desired.

6. Use the advanced printing options pop-up menu to choose specific printing options for your printer or options related to the application you're using.

7. Review the results of your settings in the preview area on the left side of the window.

8. Use the controls below the Preview to step through the pages in the document.

9. Any printer warning messages are shown below the preview.

10. Use the Presets menu to save your settings if you want to recall them in the future.

11. Click Print to output to the printer.

Printing to PDF

In addition to printing to a printer, you can print a document to a PDF, or open it directly as a PDF in Preview. To print to a PDF, click PDF and choose Save as PDF in the Print dialog box. To open the document as a PDF in preview, choose Open PDF in Preview.

Connecting and Using a Scanner

Although it's not a heavily advertised feature of Mavericks, the operating system can detect and drive a range of scanners without any additional drivers or software. This means that you can connect a scanner to your Mac and almost immediately begin scanning images.

Adding a Scanner

To connect a USB scanner to your Mac, complete any initial setup instructions provided in the hardware manual and then follow these steps:

1. Plug the scanner into your Mac and turn it on (not shown).

2. Open the System Preferences and click the Printers & Scanners icon.

3. The scanner, if supported, appears in the Scanners listing on the left side of the panel.

4. Choose the application you want to start when the Scan button is pressed on the scanner. I recommend Preview because it is a convenient application for working with images.

5. Close the System Preferences.

Scanning in Preview

Preview (in the Applications folder, click Preview) serves as the image hub on your Mac. It views images and PDFs, and allows annotations, cropping, image rotation, and more. With Mavericks, it can also act as your scanning software. To scan an image directly into Preview, do the following:

1. Open Preview, or press the scan button on the scanner if Preview is set as the default scanning application.

2. Choose Import from Scanner from the File menu.

3. The basic scanning window appears. If you want to choose your scanning area or set the resolution, click Show Details and skip to step 8.

4. Use the pop-up menu in the lower-left corner to choose the size of the document you're scanning.

5. Choose Detect Separate Items from the pop-up menu to automatically scan individual photos, pictures, and so on into separate images within a single scan.

6. Click Scan. Preview performs a detailed scan, and then opens the result in a new window, where you can save it if desired.

Scanning Options

Originally, the Image Capture utility (found in the Applications folder) handled scanning in OS X. Mavericks has expanded that capability to Preview, but Image Capture is still available if you'd like to give it a try.

7. Repeat step 6 as needed for all of your images (not shown).

8. In detailed scanning mode, full controls for the scanner are shown on the right side of the window. Choose the scan's resolution, size, orientation, and color depth.

9. Configure the format for scanned images.

10. Adjust any image filters and clean-up features you want to apply to the scan.

11. Click Overview to perform a low-resolution scan of your documents and display it in the preview area on the left.

12. Adjust the bounding rectangle to fit your document. If you've chosen to detect separate items, you will see multiple bounding rectangles.

13. Click Scan to begin scanning.

14. The result opens in a new window, where you can save it if desired.

Add and manage user accounts.

Create full system backups using Time Machine.

Apply parental controls to users.

Use Keychain Access to manage sensitive information.

In this chapter, you learn the steps that you can take to secure your Mac and its data, including:

→ Creating user accounts
→ Applying parental controls
→ Keeping passwords in Keychain
→ Encrypting your account data
→ Activating the Mavericks firewall
→ Backing up your files and information
→ Using Time Machine to restore backups
→ Accessing previous files with Versions

Securing and Protecting Your Mac

Security on a computer is important—increasingly we store our lives on our computers. We save our memories, our music and video, and our important documents. Having a computer stolen (or losing the contents of your hard drive) can be more traumatic than losing a credit card. Practicing appropriate account, application, and information security can ensure that even if the worst happens, your data remains private.

In addition to protecting your information from theft and unauthorized access, you should take steps to ensure the data's availability—in other words, you should ensure that your files are available when you need them. By backing up your computer, you can be sure that even in the event your computer is stolen or its hard drive crashes, your work is protected.

Working with Users and Groups

The Mavericks operating system can accommodate multiple users—family members, friends, co-workers, and even guests. By creating and using different accounts, you can limit access to files. In addition, you can combine individual users into groups that have access controls.

Creating User Accounts

When creating a user account, you can control what the users can do by assigning them an account type. There are five account types in Mavericks:

Administrator—An account with full control over the computer and its settings

Standard—An account that can install software and work with the files within the individual account

Managed with Parental Controls—A standard user account that includes parental controls to limit account and application access

Sharing Only—An account that can only be used to access shared files, but not to log into the system

Guest—A preconfigured account that allows the user to log in and use the computer but that automatically resets to a clean state upon logout

By default, your account is an administrative account, but you should create additional user accounts based on what the users need to do.

Unlock Your Preferences

Before making changes to many of the system preferences, you may first need to click the Lock icon in the lower-left corner of the preference panel and supply your username and password. This extra step is frequently required to help prevent unwanted changes to your Mac.

Adding Accounts

To add any type of account to the system, follow these steps:

1. Open the System Preferences window and click the Users & Groups icon.

2. Click the + button below the user list to add a new user.

3. The account creation window appears. Use the New Account pop-up menu to choose the account type you want to create.

4. Enter the full name of the user you're adding.

5. Type the account name for the user. This is the username the person uses to access all Mavericks services.

6. Type a new password for the account into the Password and Verify fields.

7. If desired, provide a hint for the password. The hint is displayed after three unsuccessful login attempts.

8. Click Create User.

9. Close the System Preferences.

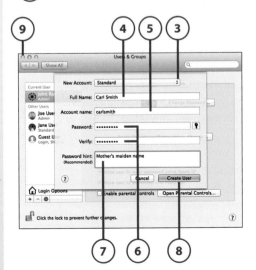

Enabling the Guest Account

The Guest account provides a simple means of giving anyone access to the computer for a short period of time. To enable the Guest account, follow these steps:

1. Open the System Preferences window and click the User & Groups icon.

2. Click the Guest User item within the account list.

3. Check the Allow Guests to Log in to This Computer checkbox.

4. To allow guest access to shared folders, click Allow Guests to Connect to Shared Folders.

5. Close the System Preferences.

Applying Parental Controls

If you've created a managed account with Parental Controls, or have enabled the Guest account, you can configure which applications a user can run, when the user can run the programs, and what parts of the Internet the user can access.

1. Open the System Preferences window and click the Parental Controls icon.

2. Choose the Account you want to configure.

3. Click Enable Parental Controls.

4. Click the Apps button to choose which applications the user can use, what privileges are available in the Finder, what age range of apps can be accessed in the App Store, and whether the Dock can be modified.

5. Use the Web button to restrict access to websites.

Managed Versus Standard

If you've created a Standard account type, you can convert it to a Managed account with Parental Controls by selecting it in the Parental Control list and then clicking the Enable Parental Controls button.

6. Select the People button to limit the individuals the user can email, message, or game with.

7. Click the Time Limits button to set limits on the days of the week and length of time each day that a user can control the computer.

8. Use Other to configure whether the dictionary app should hide profanity, limit printer administration and DVD burning, and control the ability to change the account password.

9. Close the System Preferences.

Creating Groups

For individuals who should have the same kind of access rights (such as your co-workers), you can group them together. You can then use that group in other parts of Mavericks (such as setting file permissions) to refer to all of the accounts at one time.

1. Open the System Preferences window and click the Users & Groups icon.

2. Click the + button below the account list to add a new account.

3. The account creation window appears. Use the New Account pop-up menu to choose Group.

4. Enter a name for the group.

5. Click Create Group.

6. The group appears in the account list. Make sure it is selected.

7. Click the checkboxes in front of each user who should be a member of the group.

8. Close the System Preferences.

Configuring General Account Security

To better protect user accounts from potential security problems, Mavericks has a range of security settings in one place. To configure the best possible security for your account, follow these steps:

1. Open the System Preferences window and click the Security & Privacy icon.

2. Click the General button at the top of the panel.

3. Check the Require Password checkbox and set the pop-up menu to Immediately so that a password is required to wake your computer after the screen saver kicks in.

4. If desired, set a message to display when the screen is locked.

5. Check Disable Automatic Login to disable access to your Mac without a valid username and password.

6. Click the Advanced button.

7. Check Log Out after 60 Minutes of Inactivity. You might want to adjust the time to a shorter period. After this option is set, you are automatically logged out of your Mac if you don't use it for the designated amount of time.

8. Choose to require an administrator password to access locked preferences.

9. Click OK.

10. Close the System Preferences.

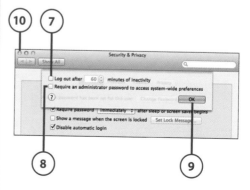

Assigning File Permissions for Users and Groups

After you've created users and groups, you can begin protecting files and folders so that certain users can access them but others can't:

1. Select a file or folder in the Finder.

2. Choose Get Info from the File menu.

3. Open the Sharing & Permissions section of the information window.

4. Click the + button to add a user or group to the permission list.

5. Choose a user or group from the window that opens.

6. Click Select.

Sample Folder

7. Use the pop-up menu in the Privilege column to the right of the user or group to set whether the user can read only, read and write, or write only.

8. To remove access for a user or group, select it and click –.

9. Close the Info window.

Choose Your Permissions

In addition to these permissions, you can set permissions for network shares. The sharing permissions (see Chapter 6, "Sharing Files, Devices, and Services") define who can access a folder over the network. The file permissions, however, can also limit access to the files and folders within a share, or who can see the files and folders when they're logged directly into your computer.

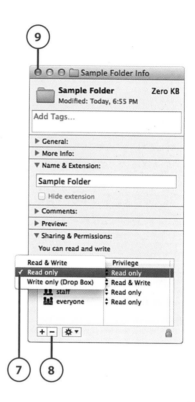

Tracking Passwords with Keychain Access

When you use Safari, connect to file shares, or use other secure services, you're frequently prompted to Save to Keychain. When you save your passwords, you're storing them in a special system-wide database that manages secure information—called the keychain.

Unknown to many, you can use the Keychain Access utility (found in the Applications/Utilities folder or in the Utilities Launchpad group) to view and modify records in your keychain. You can even use Keychain Access to store arbitrary data (such as notes, passwords, and so on) that you'd like to have encrypted. Keychain values can only be accessed when the keychain is unlocked.

There are multiple different keychain databases you can access or create. By default, passwords and account information are stored in a keychain named Login, which is automatically unlocked when you log into your account.

Viewing Keychain Items

You can access your Login keychain entries at any time. To view an item that has been stored in your keychain, follow along with these steps:

1. Open the Keychain Access application from the Applications/ Utilities folder or Launchpad.

2. Choose the keychain you want to view (Login is where most items are located).

3. Select the category of data you want to view.

4. Double-click the keychain entry to open a window displaying the details.

5. Click Show Password to authenticate and display the keychain password in clear text.

6. Close the keychain entry window.

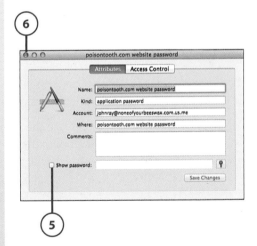

Adding Data to the Keychain

There are two types of information you can manually store in a keychain—secure notes and password items. Notes can be arbitrary text, and password items are generally a username, password, and a name for the item you're adding.

Collect the information you want to add and then follow these steps:

1. Open the Keychain Access application.

2. Choose the Keychain you want to add data to.

3. Select the Passwords or Secure Notes categories to set which type of information you are storing.

4. Click the + button at the bottom of the Keychain Access window.

5. Enter your note or account information in the form that appears.

6. Click Add.

7. The new entry appears in the Keychain.

Using the Password Assistant

When adding a new password, you might notice a key icon by the password field. Clicking the key launches a password assistant that creates a secure password for you. The key icon and password assistant are found throughout the Mavericks interface where passwords are required.

Creating a New Keychain

The login keychain stores almost everything related to accounts you've configured in Mavericks, but because it is designed to be automatically unlocked at login, you might want to create another keychain that is only unlocked when you want it to be. To do so, follow these steps:

1. Open the Keychain Access application and choose File, New Keychain from the menu.

2. Enter a name for the keychain and then click Create.

3. You are prompted for a password to secure the new keychain. Enter a secure password in the New Password and Verify fields.

4. Click OK.

5. The new keychain is displayed in the keychain list and you can store any data you'd like in it.

6. Continue adding items or choose File, Quit Keychain Access to exit (not shown).

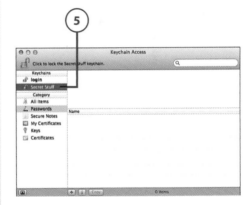

Adding a Keychain Menu Item

To quickly unlock and lock keychains, you can add a keychain item to your menu bar:

1. Open the Keychain Access application and choose Keychain Access, Preferences from the menu.

2. Click the General button at the top of the window.

3. Click Show Keychain Status in Menu Bar.

4. Close the Preferences.

5. The Keychain Lock menu item is added, giving easy access to unlocking and locking your keychains.

Encrypting Your Mavericks Disk

One of the best ways to secure sensitive information is through encryption. The Keychain Utility provides an encryption feature for small pieces of data, but not for your documents. To fully encrypt all data on your Mac, you can make use of FileVault disk-level encryption.

Activating FileVault

To turn on FileVault encryption for your Mac, complete the following steps:

1. Open the System Preferences window and click the Security & Privacy icon.

2. Click the FileVault button at the top of the panel.

3. Click Turn On FileVault.

4. Click Enable User and supply each user's password for those who should be able to unlock the protected disk. By default, the person activating FileVault will have access.

5. Record the recovery key displayed. You'll use it in the event you forget your password.

6. Click Continue.

7. Choose to store the recovery key with Apple (or not). This provides a safety net in case you lose the key and can't access your system.

8. Provide three questions and answers that Apple will use to verify your identity if you need to recover the key.

9. Click Continue.

10. Click Restart to begin encrypting the disk.

Effortless Encryption

FileVault encryption is completely transparent. Your entire disk is encrypted and made available to you when you log in. If another user tries to access files in your account, or even removes the drive from your computer to try to access its contents, they won't be able to.

Limiting Application Execution

With Mavericks, you can limit your computer's ability to run applications from sources other than the App Store or from developers who have registered an ID with Apple. Why would you want to do this? Because software from unknown sources can be hazardous to your system's health!

By default, Mavericks enables you to install and use applications from the App Store and apps published separately from properly registered developers. To change this to better suit your sense of well-being, follow these steps:

1. Open the System Preferences window and click the Security & Privacy icon.

2. Click the General button at the top of the panel.

3. Use the radio buttons at the bottom of the window to choose which application you want to be allowed on your system.

4. Close the System Preferences.

Everyone Is Affected!

The application limits that you set here apply to the entire system, so software that was previously installed and functional might stop working for everyone if you make changes.

Many power users will want to set the limit to allow applications downloaded from anywhere because this provides the greatest flexibility. Most of us, however, will be satisfied (and best protected) using the Mac App Store and Identified Developers setting.

Adding Network Security with the Built-In Firewall

Many applications you run open themselves to connections from the outside world—opening you, in turn, to Internet attacks. The purpose of a firewall is to block these connections before your computer accepts them. Mavericks offers an easy-to-configure firewall that lets you choose what network services your Mac exposes to the world.

Activating the Mavericks Firewall

To turn on the Mavericks firewall, follow these steps:

1. Open the System Preferences window and click the Security & Privacy icon.

2. Click the Firewall button at the top of the panel.

3. Click Turn On Firewall.

4. The circle beside the Firewall: Off label turns green and the label changes to Firewall: On to indicate that the firewall is active.

5. Close the System Preferences, or continue configuring Incoming Services.

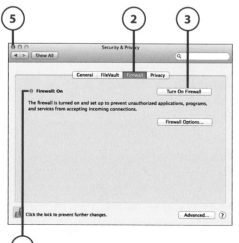

Configuring Incoming Services

After your firewall is active, you need to choose which connections to allow and which to block. To define how the firewall reacts to incoming requests, use this process:

1. Open the System Preferences window and click the Security & Privacy icon.

2. Click the Firewall button at the top of the Panel.

3. Click Firewall Options.

4. To block all incoming connections, click the Block All Incoming Connections checkbox.

5. Use the pop-up menu beside each of your running applications to choose whether it should allow or block incoming connections.

6. Add or remove applications from the list using the + and – buttons.

7. If you want applications that have been signed (where the publisher is a known and registered entity) to automatically accept connections, click the Automatically Allow Signed Software to Receive Incoming Connections checkbox.

8. Enable stealth mode if you'd like your computer to appear offline to most network device scans.

9. Click OK to save your configuration.

10. Close the Security & Privacy Preferences panel.

Advantages of a Signature

An application being signed does not make it more or less susceptible to network attack. It does, however, give you a degree of certainty that the application is not a Trojan horse or spyware.

Hiding Location Information and Application Data

If you have an iOS device, you're probably accustomed to it asking you if it can share your location with an application. In Mavericks, the OS X operating system can also determine your approximate location and share that information as well. It can also collect information on your application usage and send it to Apple for use in "improving its products." If you'd prefer not to make this information available, follow these steps:

1. Open the System Preferences and click the Security & Privacy icon.

2. Click the Privacy button at the top of the panel.

3. Select a category of information to protect, such as your location, your contacts (address book), and information about your application usage.

4. Use the controls associated with each type of data to enable or disable access to it.

5. Close the System Preferences.

Sharing Isn't Always Bad

Before disabling all these services, be aware that sending information to Apple can be critical for them to correct bugs in Mavericks—applications that use your location or contacts will prompt you before they do so, so they can't use location information without permission.

Backing Up Important Information

An often-overlooked part of security is information availability—in other words, ensuring that information is available when it is needed. If your hard drive fails, your data is unavailable, and items of value can be lost.

Backups are the best way to keep your system ready if disaster strikes. Apple provides an extremely simple backup mechanism in the form of Time Machine, a transparent solution built into Mavericks.

Quick Backups

You can create ad-hoc backups in Mavericks by inserting a writeable DVD or CD into your drive and then copying the files you want to protect onto the optical media (which is just like when you add them to a disk).

Using Time Machine

The Time Machine feature in Mavericks is a backup solution that is painless to use, covers your entire system, and can restore files from multiple different points in time. Even better, configuration for Time Machine is actually easier than traditional backup solutions like Apple Backup!

>>>Go Further

TIME CAPSULE BACKUPS

To use Time Machine, you need a hard drive or network share to use as your backup volume. You can use any external drive, but it should have at least twice the capacity of your internal hard drive. An easy solution is to use an Apple Time Capsule wireless access point (www.apple.com/timecapsule/).

Before continuing, you should make sure that you can mount your Time Machine volume (either locally or over the network) on your Mac. (Chapters 8, "Managing Who, Where, When, and What," and 15, "Upgrading Your Mac," can help here.)

Activating Time Machine

After mounting your Time Machine backup volume on your Mac, follow these steps to configure Time Machine to begin backing up your system:

1. Open the System Preferences window and click the Time Machine icon.

2. Click the ON/OFF switch to turn Time Machine On.

3. Choose an available disk from the list that appears.

4. Click Use Disk. (If using a network volume, enter your username and password, then click Connect.)

5. The Time Machine backups are scheduled and begin after a few seconds.

6. Close the System Preferences.

Customizing the Time Machine Backups

To further customize your Time Machine backup, including files that you want skipped, complete these steps:

1. Open the System Preferences window and click the Time Machine icon.

2. Click Options.

3. Use the + and − to add or remove individual files, folders, and volumes to the Time Machine exclusion list. These items are skipped during the backup.

4. Click Notify After Old Backups Are Deleted to receive warnings as old information is removed to make space for new data.

5. Click Save.

6. Close the System Preferences.

Adding a Time Machine Menu Item

To monitor your Time Machine backups and quickly launch a Time Machine restore, you can add a menu item to your menu bar:

1. Open the System Preferences window and click the Time Machine icon.

2. Check Show Time Machine in Menu Bar.

3. The menu item is added to your menu bar. When the menu item icon is animated, a backup is running.

4. Click the Time Machine menu item to start and stop backups and enter the Time Machine restore process.

Recovering Data

Recovering data from a Time Machine backup is one of the more unique experiences you can have in Mavericks. Follow these steps to enter the Time Machine and recover files from the past:

1. Open the Time Machine using the application (Applications/Time Machine) or Time Machine menu item.

2. Navigate to a location on your disk that holds (or held) the file or folder you want to restore. For example, if you deleted an application and want to restore it, open the Applications folder.

3. Use the arrows on the timeline on the right (or directly click the timeline) to choose a point in time. The window updates to show the state of the filesystem at the chosen time.

4. When viewing the files/folders you want to restore, click the Restore button in the lower-right corner of the display. The files are restored to match the snapshot.

5. Click Cancel to exit.

Find the Missing Files

Spotlight searches are active in Time Machine. Use Spotlight to help identify files to restore.

Restoring a Machine from Scratch

If your Mac suffers a complete hard drive failure, you can use your Time Machine backup to recover everything on your system. Make sure you have a bootable disk or can boot from the recovery partition (Command+R); see Chapter 14, "Troubleshooting Your System," for details.

1. Boot from your media or the Mavericks recovery partition, and then click Restore from Time Machine Backup.

2. Click Continue.

3. When the Restore Your System window appears, click Continue.

4. Choose your Time Machine disk from the list that appears.

5. Select the backup and backup date that you want to restore, and follow the onscreen steps to complete the restoration (not shown).

Mavericks's Recovery Feature

If your hard drive is still functional, you can boot off the Mavericks recovery partition that is automatically created when you install the operating system. To do this, simply hold down Command+R while turning on or restarting your computer. Even if your drive has failed, many Mac models made in 2010 and later can boot using the Internet and Apple's remote servers. Command+R first tries to boot from a local recovery partition; if that fails, it then tries using the Internet recovery method. The recovery feature gives you access to disk repair and formatting tools, Time Machine restores, and even a full reinstall of the operating system.

Using File Versions

Mavericks also includes a Time Machine-like feature called Versions. Unlike Time Machine, however, Versions keeps revisions of your files' contents. As you make changes, Mavericks automatically saves the changes so that you can browse your editing history over time.

Manually Saving a Version

The Mavericks versioning system is built to automatically save versions of your files as you edit—no manual saving is required. If you'd like to explicitly tell the system to save a version, you can, by following these steps:

1. Make the desired changes to your document.

2. Choose File, Save.

3. A new version is added to the document's version history (not shown).

Unlock to Change

If you find a document that can't be changed, it is likely locked. You can unlock documents by getting info (File, Get Info) in the Finder and unchecking the Locked box in the General information section.

Restoring a File Version

Accessing the version history of a document is very similar to using Time Machine. To view and access the version history of a file, do the following:

1. Within the document that has history you want to access, choose File, Revert To, Browse All Versions from the menu bar.

2. The Version screen is displayed.

3. The current document is located on the left.

4. Use the timeline on the right to browse through different versions of your file.

5. The previous versions of the file are displayed on the right.

6. You can copy and paste text from the document on the right into the document on the left, but you cannot make changes to the previous versions.

7. To completely restore a previous version of the file, view the version you want to restore on the right, and then click the Restore button.

8. Click the Done button to exit the file version history.

Think You Need Glasses? Just Click.

To get a closer look at the document windows on the right and left of the Versions display, just click on the document. It will zoom in to show you detail.

It's Not All Good

DON'T RELY ON VERSIONS WITHOUT TESTING!

It is up to the individual developer to add Versions support to their apps, so verify that it works in your application before relying on it. If your app doesn't support Versions, you can still use Time Machine to recall earlier copies of its documents.

Use iCloud for Off-Site Storage

To move critical files to iCloud, you can click a document's name in the title bar when editing and then use the Where drop-down menu to choose iCloud. The file immediately moves to cloud storage. Using iCloud ensures that all your iCloud-connected devices (with a matching application) have access to the file as well. Learn more about iCloud in Chapter 4, "Setting Up iCloud Services and Internet Accounts."

Identify and quit applications that have become nonresponsive.

Identify support options customized for your Mac.

View CPU, Memory, Disk, and Network usage in Activity Monitor.

In this chapter, you learn how to recover and correct common errors that you might encounter when using your system, including:

→ Force-quitting applications

→ Removing application preferences

→ Booting in Safe Mode

→ Controlling background processes

→ Changing login and startup items

→ Fixing disk permissions

→ Repairing disk errors

→ Generating a system profile for diagnostics

→ Finding your support options

14

Troubleshooting Your System

The Mac is a great piece of hardware combined with a great operating system. Even so, things can still go wrong; applications can crash or "stop working" and strange errors might crop up over time. If you find that your computer isn't behaving as you expect, you have a handful of Mavericks tools available for identifying or correcting the problem.

Keep in mind that not every problem is a user-serviceable issue. Although I have yet to experience a catastrophe on my Mac, they do happen. Keep the information about your purchase and warranty in a memorable location so that it's handy in the rare case that your system becomes totally nonfunctional.

Dealing with Troublesome Software

The most common problem with the Mac is a frozen or "stuck" application. When this happens, the software becomes unresponsive and the cursor most often turns into the "spinning beach ball of death."

To deal with the problem, first consult any troubleshooting information provided by the software publisher. After you've exhausted any official support sources, you can try the following troubleshooting steps.

Force-Quitting Applications

Correcting most application problems is a matter of forcing the application to quit and then restarting it. To force-quit any application, follow these steps:

1. Press the Command, Option, and Escape keys simultaneously on your keyboard.

2. The Force Quit Applications window appears, listing all of the running applications.

3. Choose the application to terminate by clicking its name. If the system has detected that the application is hung, it is displayed in red.

4. Click Force Quit or Relaunch (if restarting the Finder).

Quick Force Quit

You can also force-quit applications from the Dock by holding down Option while right-clicking the Dock icon (or clicking and holding on the icon). The normal "Quit" option changes to Force Quit, which gives you an easy way to terminate the program.

5. You might receive a prompt to send diagnostic information to Apple to report the crash.

6. You can ignore this message and press Command+Q to exit, click OK to send the report to Apple for review, or click Reopen to send the report and restart the application.

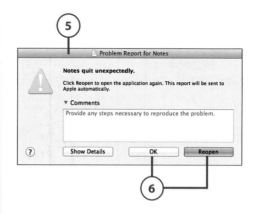

Testing with the Guest Account

If an application continues to crash after it has been restarted, there might be a problem with the application's support or preference files. Before doing any destructive system surgery, follow these steps to verify the problem:

1. Enable the Guest account as described in Chapter 13, "Securing and Protecting Your Mac."

2. Use the Apple menu to log out of your Account.

3. Log into the Guest account.

4. Attempt to run the application that was crashing. If the application runs normally, your main account likely has corrupted files. If the application continues to crash, re-install the most up-to-date version using the installer provided by the software publisher. You might want to disable the Guest account when you are finished testing (not shown).

Speed Up Troubleshooting with Fast User Switching

You can also use Fast User Switching to quickly switch between your account and the Guest account without needing to log out. Add a fast user switching menu to your menu bar by opening the Users & Groups System Preferences panel, clicking Login Options, and then choosing Show Fast User Switching Menu.

Removing Corrupted Application Files

If a crashing application runs correctly under another account, you almost certainly have corrupted application support files or preferences located in your account. If the application came with an installer file, try running the installer to fix the broken files, or delete the application and reinstall from the Mac App Store. If you don't have an installer file or you didn't purchase the software through the App Store, follow these steps to delete the problem files:

1. Within the Finder, hold down Option and choose Library from the Go menu.

2. In the Spotlight Search field, type the name of the application that is crashing.

3. Choose the Filename selection in the Spotlight Search drop-down menu that appears.

4. Click Library in the Spotlight Search filter bar.

5. Click the + button to add a new search criterion.

6. Choose Other from the first search attribute drop-down menu.

7. Find System Files in the attribute list and check the In Menu checkbox beside it. It doesn't matter if other attributes are checked.

8. Click OK.

9. Select Are Included from the drop-down menu next to System Files.

10. Review the search results. When you select a file in the results, the path where it is located is shown at the bottom of the results window.

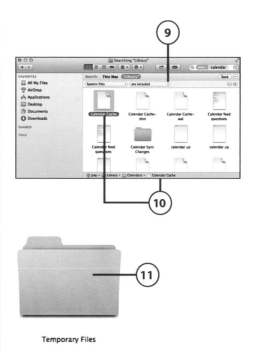

11. Move any files or folders matched by the search results from the Preferences, Caches, or Application Support directories to a temporary location on your desktop. (You can create a Temporary Files folder for just this purpose.)

12. Try running the crashing application again. If the problem is solved, delete the files you removed; otherwise choose Edit, Undo to put the files back, and then contact the software publisher.

Temporary Files

Restarting and Correcting a Frozen Machine

On very rare occasions, your system might freeze entirely, forcing you to reboot. If you find yourself in this situation, first determine if the problem is a fluke, or if it will happen with each restart.

Power down your frozen Mac by holding the power button for five or more seconds. After it turns off, disconnect any peripheral devices that are plugged into your computer. Press the power key to restart the Mac—if it freezes again, begin following the instructions in this section, beginning with "Starting in Safe Mode."

Starting in Safe Mode

When you encounter problems, Mavericks allows you to start up in Safe Mode, which disables non-Apple additions to the system and prevents applications from automatically launching when you log in.

1. With your Mac powered down, hold down the Shift key.

2. While continuing to hold down the Shift key, press the Mac power button (not pictured).

3. Continue to hold down the Shift key until your Mavericks desktop appears. Use your computer as you normally would. If the problems you had experienced are gone, you might need to remove non-Apple software that has been installed and is running when the system boots, such as login applications or launch daemons.

Changing Login Applications

When you log into your account, there are a variety of applications that might launch and perform tasks in the background. Sometimes, however, these applications can cause problems that affect other software. To view, add, or remove login applications, follow these steps:

1. Open System Preferences and click the Users & Groups icon.

2. Select your account from the account list.

3. Click the Login Items button to display software configured to launch when you log into your account.

4. Choose any applications that you want to remove and then click the – button to remove them from the list.

5. If you want to add applications back to the list in the future, either drag their icons from a Finder window into the list of items, or click the + button to choose them from a file browser dialog.

6. Close System Preferences.

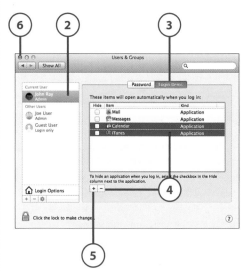

Check to Hide

The Hide checkbox in front of the Login Items is not used to disable them! This can be confusing for individuals who were used to the Extension Manager in the older versions of Mac OS. Using the Hide button for an application simply hides the windows after the application launches.

Removing Startup Applications and Launch Daemons

Login items and restored applications aren't the only things that run automatically when you start your Mac. There are several locations where software packages might install tasks that need to be run when your system is booted. These tasks are referred to as launch daemons, launch agents, and startup items. To find and disable these invisible applications, follow these steps:

1. Choose Go, Go to Folder from the Finder menu bar.

2. Type one of the following paths into the field that appears: ~/Library/LaunchDaemons, ~/Library/LaunchAgents, /Library/LaunchDaemons, /Library/LaunchAgents, /Library/StartupItems.

3. Click Go.

4. Review the contents of the directory for a file or folder with a name that matches a software title or software publisher name for the software that you've installed.

5. Move any matched files to the Trash can.

6. Provide an administrator username and password if prompted,
   and click OK.

7. Repeat steps 1–6 for all of the
   listed directories.

8. Restart your computer from the
   Apple menu. The background
   processes will no longer run when
   you boot your system.

Remove Unneeded Files

If you're content with the result,
you can now delete the files you
removed. If necessary, reinstall the
software to correctly re-enable the
background processes.

Disabling Extensions

After installing a new piece of software, you might find your computer
is acting up. The cause may be an
extension—a small piece of software
that runs at a very low level to provide a service to your system (the
equivalent of a Windows driver). To
remove an extension that the software installed, follow these steps:

1. Choose Go, Go to Folder from the
   Finder menu bar.

2. Type the path /System/Library/
   Extensions into the Go to the
   Folder field.

3. Click Go.

4. Review the contents of the directory to positively identify an extension (.kext) file that matches a device or device manufacturer that you want to remove.

5. Drag the matching file to the Trash can.

6. Provide an administrator username and password when prompted, and click OK.

7. Restart Mavericks.

8. Delete the extension file if you have confirmed it's causing the problem, or move it back to the Extensions folder to re-enable it.

Avoid the System Folder!

If at all possible, you should avoid modifying any folder within the System folder. Only use the steps described here if your system is consistently crashing after you've installed a piece of hardware or software!

Removing System Preference Panes

Frequently, system features are added through System Preference panes that are installed for your account or for all accounts on the system. If you suspect that a System Preference item that you installed is causing a problem, you can remove it by doing the following:

1. Open the System Preferences application.

2. Right-click (or Control-click) the Preference pane that you want to remove.

3. Choose Remove (name of application) Preference Pane.

4. Close the System Preferences application.

Fixing Disk Problems with Disk Utility

Disk errors, when they occur, can be an upsetting problem to diagnose. Applications might freeze, the system might slow down, and so on. It's difficult to predict how a given piece of software will behave if it encounters a disk problem that it wasn't expecting. Thankfully, Mavericks provides a tool, Disk Utility (found in the Applications folder under Utilities/Disk Utility), for verifying and correcting problems with file permissions and disk errors.

Repairing Permission Problems

Despite your computer seeming very "personal," it is actually capable of supporting many different users and relies on a set of file owners and permissions to maintain proper security. As you install software, these permissions might begin to stray from their original settings. To quickly fix the permissions, complete these steps:

1. Open the Disk Utility application, found in the Utilities subfolder of the Applications folder.

2. Choose your Mac disk from the list of disks that appears on the left side of the window.

3. Click the First Aid button near the top-middle of the window.

4. Click Repair Disk Permissions.

5. Your disk is scanned for permission problems, and any problems are repaired. This process can take several minutes, depending on how much software is on the drive.

6. When the scan completes, quit Disk Utility by closing the window.

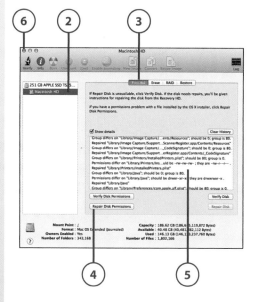

It's Not All Good

WHY SHOULDN'T I USE THE VERIFY PERMISSIONS FUNCTION?

You can choose to verify rather than repair permissions, but this function takes almost the same amount of time as repairing and either tells you that you need to repair the system or that you don't.

Because the repair permissions feature won't try to fix anything that isn't an issue, there's no harm (and no time lost) using Repair instead of Verify.

Verifying and Repairing Common Disk Errors

In the event of a power surge or serious system crash, your Mac might incur a low-level disk error that can worsen with time. If you suspect that your system has a disk error, you should first verify that there is an error and then attempt to repair it.

Verifying Your Disk Has an Error

To verify that your disk is, or isn't, suffering from an error, follow these steps:

1. Open the Disk Utility application found in the Utilities subfolder of the Applications folder.

Pain-Free Fusion

Do you have a nifty new Fusion drive in your Mac? Think you might need a disk repair? Just proceed as if you had a normal hard drive. The Fusion drive is *completely* transparent to the end user. There are no user-configurable options, and it presents itself in Disk Utility just like a normal non-Fusion drive.

2. Choose your Mac disk from the list of disks that appears on the left side of the window.

3. Click the First Aid button near the top-middle of the window.

4. Click the Verify Disk button to begin checking your disk for errors.

5. If errors are detected, they are shown in red and should be repaired. Follow the steps in the next task ("Repairing Your Disk") if a repair is needed.

6. Exit Disk Utility by closing the window.

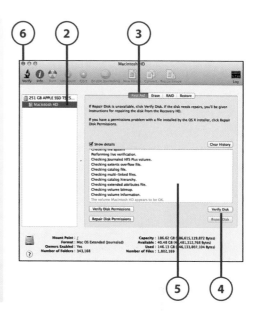

Repair Using Your Mavericks Recovery Partition

Notice that you can't use the repair function on your internal (boot) disk. To repair problems with your startup disk, you need to boot from another drive or from the recovery partition installed automatically when you installed Mavericks. You can boot into the recovery partition by holding down Command+R when starting your Mac.

Even if the partition is damaged, most Macs made since 2010 can boot from Apple's Internet restore site using the same command sequence.

Repairing Your Disk

Repairing disk errors requires that you boot from your Mavericks recovery partition. Follow these steps to repair your disk:

1. Reboot or start your Mac while holding down Command+R.

2. In the utilities window that appears, choose Disk Utility.

3. Click Continue.

4. Choose your Mac disk from the list of disks that appears on the left side of the window.

5. Click the First Aid button near the top-middle of the window.

6. Click the Repair Disk button to begin checking for and fixing errors on your disk.

7. After several minutes, the results of the repair display in the details area. If repairs could not be made, they are highlighted in red, and you should test your system with a third-party tool or take your Mac to an Apple Store for diagnostics.

8. Close the Disk Utility window to exit.

9. Reboot your computer to re-enter Mavericks.

BUILDING A REPAIR TOOLKIT

Disk Utility is only capable of fixing common problems. In the case of a serious issue, Disk Utility warns that it can't solve the problem, but it makes no suggestions for how to proceed.

If you have experienced a serious drive error, you should consider investing in DiskWarrior (www.alsoft.com/DiskWarrior/) or TechTool Pro (www.micromat.com/). These third-party tools provide much more robust diagnostic and recovery features than Disk Utility does.

>>>Go Further

Gathering Information About Your Mac

Sometimes, the best way to figure out what is going on with your computer is to ask it. Your Mac can provide a great deal of information about its current operation by way of the built-in monitoring and reporting software. These tools can also help you prepare a report to hand over to the Apple Store Genius or other technicians in the event you need to take in your equipment for service.

Monitoring System Activity

The Activity Monitor (found in the Applications folder under Utilities/Activity Monitor) delivers instant feedback on the software that is running on your system, the amount of memory in use, and how much of your processing power is being consumed. To use Activity Monitor to identify processes with excessive resource consumption, follow these steps:

1. Open the Activity Monitor application found in the Utilities subfolder of the Applications folder.

2. A list of processes is displayed.

3. Track down resource hogs by using the column headings to sort by CPU usage, the amount of virtual memory, or the threads being used.

4. If an offending process is located, click to highlight it, and click the stop sign icon in the toolbar to force it to quit.

5. Use the buttons above the process list to show overall CPU, Memory, Disk Activity, Disk Usage, and Network activity in the graphs at the bottom of the screen.

>>>Go Further

HOW IS USING THE ACTIVITY MONITOR DIFFERENT FROM FORCE QUITTING WITHIN THE FINDER?

In addition to the detailed information on the processes that are running on your system, the Activity Monitor also enables you to see background processes that are active. These processes might have been started by an application or script and, without any visual warning in the Finder or Dock, have hung or crashed. Using the Activity Monitor, you can identify these troublemakers and kill them.

Generating a System Profiler Report

If you've ever been asked to "describe your computer" for the purposes of obtaining technical assistance, it's hard to know what information to provide. Using Mavericks's System Information utility, however, you can quickly create reports on your hardware, peripherals, and even software installations.

1. Open the System Information application found in the Utilities subfolder of the Applications folder.

2. Use the list on the left side of the window to choose an information category.

3. Click the category you'd like to view information on, such as Memory or Applications.

4. Details of the chosen category display on the right.

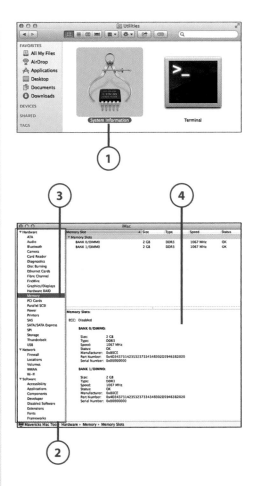

5. Save a copy of the report by choosing File, Save.

6. Choose a report name and save location.

7. Click Save.

8. Alternatively, Choose File, Send to Apple to send your system information to Apple for technical support.

9. When prompted with the Privacy Agreement, click the Send to Apple button.

Lengthy Reports

Although System Information offers a Print option, be careful when choosing it! A full system report can be more than 400 pages long!

Viewing the System Logs

To get a view of any errors that your system might be logging "behind the scenes," you need to take advantage of the Console utility. Console enables you to monitor the various system logs that are generated when Mavericks logs errors or other information. To view your system logs through Console, follow these steps:

1. Open the Console application found in the Utilities subfolder of the Applications folder.

2. The current console error and warning messages are displayed in the content area to the right.

3. A list of available application- or feature-specific logs and filtered logs displays on the left.

4. Click a log/filter name to display the contents of that entry.

5. As new entries are added to the log, the display automatically updates.

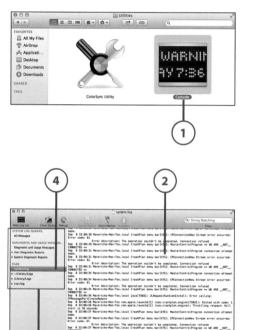

Review Your System Log

Many application errors and warnings are logged to the file system.log. To help diagnose a problem with a specific application, try running the application while the Console utility is open and displaying system.log.

There's a good chance you'll see hidden errors being generated by the software.

Remember Your Backups!

If all else fails, remember your backups! Chapter 13 includes methods for backing up your data. If your system reaches an unusable state or files have become corrupted beyond recovery, you should always have your backups ready to come to the rescue. If you're reading this and don't have a backup plan in place, turn to Chapter 13 and start reading now.

Viewing System Support Options

Ever wonder about your support options for your Mac? Mavericks makes it simple to find out what your warranty options are, as well as how to access community support resources for OS X. To access these features, follow these steps:

1. Choose About This Mac from the Apple menu.

2. Click the More Info button in the window that appears.

3. Use the Support link in the upper-right corner to access online support resources for Mavericks.

4. Use the Service link (also in the upper-right corner) to check on repairs, service, and AppleCare extended protection.

Index

Numbers

1Password, 382
3D flyover (Maps), 269
802.11ac, 3

A

About This Mac, 499
accepting invites, 291
accounts
    adding, 122-124, 216
    configuring, 217
    editing, 218
    email accounts. *See* email accounts
    logging into, 221
    multiple IM accounts, 220
    updating account information, 242-243
    user accounts. *See* user accounts
activating. *See* enabling
Activity Monitor, 495-496
addresses
    IP addresses, 89
    printing, 266
    updating, 242-243
Adium, 381
Administrator accounts, 448
Adobe Flash, 155
ads (iTunes Radio), 331
AFP, 185-187
AirDrop
    compatibility, 183
    file sharing
        overview, 180
        receiving files, 182-183
        sending files, 181-182
        Share Sheets, 183
AirParrot, 432
AirPlay, 432-436
Airport printers, 438
Album view (iTunes), 314
alerts, 409
All My Files group, 31
annotations (iBooks), 355
AppCleaner, 381
Apple IDs, 14, 372
Apple TV
    mirroring to, 432-433
    sending audio to, 435-436
    setting resolution, 433

applications. *See* apps
apps. *See also* specific apps (for example, Adium)
    application data, hiding, 466
    application spaces. *See* spaces
    auto open feature, 76
    browsing for, 373-374
    deleting, 75
    dropping files into, 67
    finding, 71
    force-quitting, 480-481
    hiding, 377-378
    installing
        App Store apps, 376-377
        non-App Store apps, 378-380
    limiting execution of, 463
    login applications, 486
    navigating with Mission Control, 59-60
    purchasing, 375
    removing corrupted apps, 482-484
    searching for, 374
    signatures, 466
    testing with Guest account, 481-482
    uninstalling, 75
    updates, 382-385
App Store, 9, 372
    browsing apps, 373-374
    hiding apps, 377-378
    logging in to, 372-373
    purchasing apps, 375
    reinstalling apps, 376-377
    searching for apps, 374
Arrange By feature (Finder), 32
Ask Me Before Allowing Others to Use My DVD Drive option, 202
Ask to Keep Changes When Closing Documents option, 78
assigning
    permissions, 455-456
    tags, 33
attachments (email)
    previewing, 136
    saving, 137
    sending, 143
audio. *See also* music
    alerts, 52
    audio chat, 231-232
    recording, 413-414
    sending to Apple TV, 435-436
audio in connection, 2
audio out connection, 3
authentication, 87, 180

authorizing computer
in iBooks, 347
in iTunes Store, 316
AutoFill data (Safari)
credit card data, 169
managing, 167-168
names and passwords, 168
auto-installing apps, 377
automated network assistance
Diagnostics, 100-101
setup assistant, 101-103
Automatically Hide and Show the
Dock option, 25
Automatically Rearrange Spaces
Based on Most Recent Use
option (Mission Control), 67
automatic downloading apps,
377
auto open feature (applications),
76
A/V chats, 231-232

B

Back to My Mac, 109
backups, 499
Time Machine backups, 467,
509
activating, 468-469
adding menu items, 470-471
customizing, 469-470
recovering data from,
471-472
restoring computers from,
473-474
to CD/DVD, 467
Versions backups
restoring file versions,
475-476
saving versions, 474-475
Badge App Icon with Notification
Count option, 51
battery, 4, 424
birthdays (Calendar), 284
Bluetooth devices
explained, 3
pairing
Bluetooth status menu,
426-427
headsets, 425-426
keyboard, 424-425
mouse/trackpad, 422-424
bookmarks
iBooks bookmarks, 356
Safari bookmarks, 156-159

books
annotations, 355
bookmarks, 356
browsing, 349-351
organizing into Collections,
352-353
purchasing, 347-348
reading, 353-354
Boot Camp, 14
booting from recovery partition,
493
brightness, 404
browsing
apps in App Store, 373-374
games, 366
iBooks library, 349-351
network shares, 191-192
web. See web browsing
buddies (iMessages), 225
buddy lists, 225-226
built-in battery, 4
buying
apps, 375
books in iBooks, 347-348
from iTunes Store, 316-317

C

Calendar app, 108, 277-278
birthdays/holidays, 284
calendars
creating, 278-279
printing, 293
viewing, 285
checking availability, 290
connecting to iCloud, 280-281
connecting to other calendar
servers, 281-283
events, 285
accepting invites, 291
adding, 286
attributes, 289
creating, 286
editing, 288
Quick Event, 287
searching, 292
sending invites, 289-290
local versus network, 280
subscribing to public shared
calendars, 283-284
calibrating display, 406-407
call list (FaceTime), 241

calls
placing, 237-239
receiving, 240
cards, merging, 261
CDs
backing up data to, 467
importing into iTunes, 318
sharing, 202
changing. See customization
chats
A/V chats, 231-232
starting
Messages, 229-230
Notification Center, 230-231
checking availability in Calendar,
290
Chrome compatibility, 16
classifying spam, 141
Close Windows When Quitting an
Application option, 77
closing
desktop spaces, 63
Mission Control, 58-59
cloud. See iCloud
Coda, 381
Collections (iBooks), 352-353
color profiles, 405
comments (iBooks), 355
configuration. See
also customization
Apple TV, 433-436
app updates, 383
Bluetooth devices. See
Bluetooth devices
Dashboard, 41-44
dictation, 396-397
display
brightness, 404
calibration, 406-407
color profiles, 405
resolution, 403
Do Not Disturb mode, 53
Dock folders, 22
email accounts
account setup, 129-130
advanced account settings,
131-133
file sharing, 185
FileVault, 460-462
Finder. See Finder
firewall, 464
folder access permissions,
189-194
general account security, 454

iCloud
 first-time configuration,
 106-107
 iCloud services, 108-109
IM identities, 222
iTunes, 312
iTunes Match, 341-342
Guest accounts, 450
keyboard. *See* keyboard
Magic Mouse, 401-402
Messages accounts, 217
Mission Control, 67-68
monitor arrangements,
 428-429
network connections, 89
 PPPoE (Point-to-Point
 Protocol over Ethernet),
 92-93
 TCP/IP and Proxy settings,
 89-91
Photo Sharing, 118-119
PPPoE (Point-to-Point Protocol
 over Ethernet), 92-93
printers. *See* printers
private browsing, 171
scanners, 442-445
screen sharing, 204-207
sleep mode, 389-390
sound
 alerts, 409
 for input devices, 411-412
 for output devices, 410
 volume, 408
stacks, 22
status messages, 224
text shortcuts, 393-395
Time Machine backups,
 468-469
Twitter, 244-245
wireless networking, 88
trackpad, 398-399
USB input devices, 419-421
confirming file transfers, 233
connections (network).
 See network connections
Connect to Server command
 (Go menu), 193
Contacts, 252
 connecting to iCloud, 262
 connecting to other contact
 servers, 263-264
 creating, 253, 256-257
 detecting duplicates, 261
 editing, 258-260

finding in Maps, 271
 groups, 253-254
 iCloud, 108
 images, 258
 merging, 261
 My Card, 259
 printing, 266
 searching, 260
 sharing, 265
contact servers, syncing with
 Contacts, 263-264
contextual menus, 12
controls (window), 11
conversations (email), 139-140
corrupted apps, removing,
 482-484
Crashplan, 381
credit card data, adding to
 AutoFill data, 169
CrossOver, 381
cross-platform video
 conferencing, 225
Curio, 381
customization. *See also*
 configuration
 iBooks, 357
 Do Not Disturb mode, 54
 Dock, 24-25
 Finder, 25-28
 gestures, 13
 login applications, 486
 notifications, 51-52
 Spotlight searches, 46
 Time Machine backups,
 469-470

D

Dashboard
 activating, 41
 overview, 40
 shortcuts, 41
 web content, adding, 173-175
 widgets
 adding, 42-43
 configuring, 43-44
 finding, 44
 removing, 42-43
deleting
 applications, 75
 folders, 74, 302
 mailboxes, 148
 reminders, 298

desktop
 extending, 428, 434
 showing, 66-67
desktop spaces. *See* spaces
Diagnostics, 100-101
dictation, 12, 396-397
directions (Maps), 275-276
disabling
 extensions, 488-489
 FaceTime, 241
 wireless networking, 88
disk errors
 repairing, 493-494
 troubleshooting, 490-494
 verifying, 492-493
disk images, 380
Disk Utility, 490
 disk errors
 repairing, 493-494
 troubleshooting, 490-494
 verifying, 492-493
 permission problems,
 repairing, 491
display
 configuring arrangements,
 428-429
 Apple TV
 extending desktop to, 434
 mirroring to, 432-433
 setting resolution, 433
 sharing multimedia to, 435
 calibrating, 406-407
 configuring
 brightness, 404
 color profiles, 405
 resolution, 403
 external displays
 configuring monitor
 arrangements, 428-429
 extending desktop, 428
 mirrored display usage, 431
 mirroring menu, 430
 requirements, 427
 iBooks, 357
 multiple monitors, 429-445
 Retina displays, 3
 sleep mode, 389-390
DisplayPort, 2
Displays Have Separate Spaces
 option (Mission Control), 68
DNS (Domain Name Service), 89
Dock, 5-6
 adding items to, 20-21
 customizing, 24-25

files/folders
  configuring, 22
  navigating in Grid mode, 23
  stacks, 22
hiding, 25
overview, 20
rearranging items in, 21
removing items from, 20-21
Documents and Data feature
  (iCloud), 113
iCloud files
  opening in iCloud, 116
  opening on Mac, 114-115
Mac files
  moving to/from iCloud, 117
  saving to iCloud, 113-114
Documents & Data service
  (iCloud), 108
Dolly Drive, 382
Domain Name Service (DNS), 89
Do Not Disturb mode, 53-54
downloading podcasts, 321-324
Downloads folder, 378
dragging files to Finder window
  tabs, 30
drives
  optical drive sharing
    DVD and CD sharing, 202
    optical drive access, 203-204
Dropbox, 381
dropping files into applications,
  67
DSL connections, 92-93
DVDs
  backing up data to, 467
  sharing, 202

E

editing
  AutoFill data
    credit card data, 169
    names and passwords, 168
  Calendar events, 288
  contacts, 258-260
  iMessage account settings,
    218
email
  attachments
    previewing, 136
    saving, 137
    sending, 143
  changing how often mail is
    retrieved, 142

conversations, 139-140
email accounts
  account information,
    gathering, 128
  adding, 129-130
  advanced account settings,
    131-133
  multiple email addresses, 133
filing in mailboxes, 149
mailboxes
  creating, 147
  deleting, 148
  filing messages in, 149
  renaming, 148
  Smart Mailboxes, 150-151
  VIP Mailboxes, 151-152
multiple email addresses, 133
rules, 154
searching for, 152-153
sharing, 265
signatures, 145-146
sorting, 135
spam filtering, 141
stationery templates, 144
viewing web pages in, 138
enabling. See configuration
encryption, FileVault, 460-462
Energy Saver, 388-389
Ethernet, 2, 82-83
events (Calendar), 285
  accepting, 291
  adding, 286
  attributes, 289
  creating, 286
  editing, 288
  Quick Event, 287
  searching, 292
  sending invites, 289-290
ExFAT, 507
exporting vCards, 265
Express Card, 3
extending desktop, 428, 434
extensions
  installing, 175-176
  disabling, 488-489
  managing, 177
external displays
  Apple TV, mirroring to,
    432-433
  configuring monitor
    arrangements, 428-429
  extending desktop, 428
  mirrored display usage, 431
  mirroring menu, 430
  requirements, 427

F

F1-F12 keys, 4
Facebook, 246-247
FaceTime, 235
  addresses, 242-243
  call list, 241
  calls
    missed calls, 240
    placing, 237-239
    receiving, 240
  disabling, 241
  setting up, 236
  updating, 242-243
FaceTime HD video camera,
  414-416
Fast User Switching, 482
favorites list, 239
files
  adding to Dock, 20-21
  All My Files group, 31
  backing up. See backups
  dragging to Finder window
    tabs, 30
  dropping into applications, 67
  iCloud files
    opening in iCloud, 116
    opening on Mac, 114-115
    organizing, 118
  moving to/from iCloud, 117
  navigating in Grid mode, 23
  permissions, 455-456
  previewing, 40
  receiving, 182-183
  removing from Dock, 20-21
  saving
    to iCloud, 113-114, 477
    manually, 78
  searching for, 45-48
  sending, 181-182
  sharing
    with AirDrop, 180-183
    with Share Sheets, 194-197
    traditional file sharing,
      184-194
  stacks, 22
  StuffIt, 379
  tags, 33-37
  transferring, 233
  uploading to online services,
    195-197
  versions. See Versions

viewing
  all files, 31
  by category, 32
  with Quick Look, 38-39
  Zip files, 379
file transfers, confirming, 233
filing email messages in
  mailboxes, 149
filtering
  iTunes searches, 325
  spam, 141
Finder, 6, 25
  All My Files group, 31
  Arrange By feature, 32
  files, previewing, 40
  posting from, 248
  Sidebar, 26-27
  tags
    assigning, 33
    managing, 35-37
    removing, 34
    viewing, 34-35
  toolbar, 28
  window tabs, 29-30
Finder window, 192
finding
  applications
    in App Store, 374
    in Launchpad, 71
  email, 152-153
  Find My Mac option, 111-112
  Map locations, 270-271
  reminders, 298
  widgets, 44
  wireless networks, 84-85
Find My Mac, 111-112
firewall, 464-466
Firewire, 2, 510
Flash plug-in, 155
folders
  creating, 302
  configuring in Dock, 22
    adding to Dock, 20-21
    deleting, 302
    Downloads, 378
    Launchpad folders, 73-74
    managing, 301
    navigating in Grid mode, 23
    removing from Dock, 20-21
  tags
    assigning, 33
    managing, 35-37
    removing, 34
    viewing, 34-35

traditional folder sharing, 184
  enabling, 185
  folder access permissions,
    189-194
  folder selection, 188
  network shares, connecting
    to, 191-192
  protocols, 185-187
  remote shares, connecting
    to, 193
  Windows passwords, 187
force-quitting apps, 480-481
fraud protection in Safari,
  172-175
friends (Game Center)
  challenging, 367-368
  recommendations, 363
  responding to friend requests,
    362
  sending friend requests, 361
  viewing stats, 364-368
Front Row, 345
frozen Macs, troubleshooting,
  484
  changing login applications,
    486
  disabling extensions, 488-489
  removing System Preference
    panes, 490
  starting in Safe mode, 485
full-screen application spaces,
  creating, 64
function keys, 4, 392

G

Game Center, 357
  browsing games, 366
  friends
    challenging, 367-368
    friend requests, 361-362
    recommendations, 363
    viewing stats, 364-368
  Me screen, 360
  signing in, 358-359
games, browsing, 366
gathering information
  system activity, 495-496
  system logs, 498
  system profiler reports,
    496-497
general account security, 454
generating system profiler
  reports, 496-497

Genie animation effect, 24
Genius Recommendations,
  318-321
gestures
  changing, 13
  explained, 12
  of Magic Mouse, 401-402
  on trackpad, 399-400
gift cards, redeeming in iTunes
  Store, 316
Grid mode (Dock), 23
groups (Contacts)
  adding, 253
  creating, 453, 254
  emailing to, 253
  permissions, 455-456
  smart groups, 255
Guest accounts
  enabling, 450
  explained, 448
  testing apps with, 481-482

H

hardware, 2, 387
Hazel, 381
headphones, 411
headsets, 232, 425-426
hiding
  apps, 377-378
  Dock, 25
  location information and app
    data, 466
highlighting in iBooks, 355
holidays (Calendar), 284
Home Sharing (iTunes), 339-340

I

iBooks
  annotations, 355
  authorizing your computer,
    347
  bookmarks in, 356
  browsing library, 349-351
  Collections, 352-353
  customizing display, 357
  purchasing books, 347-348
  reading in, 353-354
  searching, 353
  starting, 345-346

iCloud, 106, 252
  accounts, 122-124
  applications, 110-111
  browser tabs, 166
  configuring for first time,
    106-107
  explained, 13-14
  files
    moving to/from iCloud, 117,
      477
    opening in iCloud, 116
    opening on Mac, 114-115
    organizing, 118
    saving to iCloud, 113-114
  integration, 106
  iTunes Match. See iTunes
    Match
  Photo Sharing, 118-122
  reminders, 300
  services
    activating, 108-109
    Back to My Mac, 109
    Calendars, 108
    Contacts, 108
    Find My Mac, 111-112
    Keychain, 108
    Mail, 108
    Notes, 108
    Photos, 108
    Reminders, 108
    Safari, 108
  syncing
    Calendar app, 280-281
    Contacts, 262
    Notes app, 307
icons, Launchpad, 72
IM accounts, 221
Image Capture utility, 444
iMessage, 216
  buddies, 225
  buddy lists, 225-226
  editing, 218
  Messages app, 227
IM identities, 222
importing
  CDs, 318
  vCards, 265
incoming chat, responding to,
  228
incoming services, configuring
  with firewall, 465-466
information gathering
  system activity, 495-496
  system logs, 498

system profiler reports,
  496-497
input devices
  configuring sound, 411-412
  USB input devices, 419-421
installing
  apps
    App Store apps, 376-377
    non-App Store apps, 378-380
  Flash plug-in, 155
  Safari extensions, 175-176
instant messaging, 216. See also
  chats
  adding traditional accounts,
    219-220
  A/V chats, 231-232
Internet Accounts panel, 247
Internet Accounts System
  Preferences panel, 123-124
Internet connections, sharing,
  211-212
invitations
  accepting, 291
  sending, 289-290
IP addresses, 89
iTunes, 311
  Album view, 314
  CDs, importing, 318
  configuring, 312
  controls, 315
  Home Sharing, 339-340
  iTunes Match
    accessing music, 343-344
    activating, 341-342
    connecting iTunes library to,
      342-343
    cost, 341
  iTunes Radio, 331
    ads, 331
    creating stations, 332-333
    fine-tuning stations, 334
    identifying songs, 335
    listening to, 331-332
    sharing stations, 335
    viewing recently played
      songs, 335
  iTunes Store
    authorizing computers, 316
    Genius Recommendations,
      318-321
    gift cards, 316
    podcasts, 321-324
    purchasing from, 316-317
    rented movies, 317

iTunes U, 324
Library, 313, 324-325
mini player, 330
playlists
  accessing, 329
  creating, 326-327
  smart playlists, 328-329
syncing
  between devices, 337-339
  purchases, 336

J-K

Junk icon (Mail), 141
keyboard
  configuring
    Bluetooth devices, 424-425
    function keys, 392
    key repeat rate, 391
    shortcuts, 392-395
    USB keyboards, 420
  function keys, 4
Keychain Access
  adding data to keychain, 458
  adding keychain menu items,
    460
  creating keychains, 459
  explained, 456
  iCloud, 108
  viewing keychain items, 457
Kindle app, 348

L

launching. See starting
Launchpad, 8
  applications, deleting, 75
  folders
    creating, 73
    deleting, 74
  icons, rearranging, 72
  navigating, 70-71
  searching, 71
  starting, 69
library
  iBooks, 349-351
  iTunes, 313
    connecting to iTunes Match,
      342-343
    searching, 324-325
    sharing, 339-340
    syncing between devices,
      337-339

limiting application execution, 463

Linux compatibility, 16

listening to music. *See* music

lists (Reminders), 295

local Mac screens, sharing, 207-208

locations
adding, 98-99
hiding, 466
Reminders app, 297

logging into accounts, 221

login applications, 486

logs, system logs, 498

M

Mac App Store, 9
browsing apps, 373-374
hiding apps, 377-378
logging in to, 372-373
purchasing apps, 375
reinstalling apps, 376-377
searching for apps, 374

MacUpdate, 380

Magic Mouse, 401-402

Magnification setting (Dock), 24

Mail, 128
application workspace, 134
attachments
previewing, 136
saving, 137
sending, 143
email. *See* email
iCloud Mail, 108

mailboxes
creating, 147
deleting, 148
filing messages in, 149
renaming, 148
Smart Mailboxes, 150-151
VIP Mailboxes, 151-152

Managed with Parental Controls accounts, 448

managing
AutoFill data (Safari), 167-168
folders, 301
multiple monitors, 429-445
Reading List, 161
Safari extensions, 177
tags, 35-37

Maps, 267
directions, 275-276
finding yourself, 270
navigating, 267
points of interest, 272-274
searching, 271-272
starting, 267
traffic, 277
viewing, 269
view mode, 268
views, 268

media center software, 345

menu bar, 5
volume control, 408

merging Contacts, 261

Me screen (Game Center), 360

Messages app, 216
accounts
adding, 216
configuring, 217
logging into, 221
chats, 229-230
configuring, 224
file transfers, confirming, 233
iMessages, 227
IM identities, 222
pictures, 222-223
responding to incoming chat, 228
screen-sharing sessions (IM), 234
status menu, 221
traditional IM accounts, 219-220
transferring files, 233

Messages buddy list window, 220

microphones, 232, 411-412

Microsoft Remote Desktop, 381

Mini DisplayPort, 2

Minimize Windows into Application Icon option (Dock), 24

mini player (iTunes), 330

mini TOSLINK adapters, 411

mirrored display, 430-431

mirroring to Apple TV, 432-433

missed calls (FaceTime), 240

Mission Control, 8, 57
applications, navigating, 59-60
closing, 58-59
configuring, 67-68
desktop, showing, 66-67
docking, 59
opening, 58-59
spaces
closing, 63
creating, 60-61
full-screen spaces, creating, 64
populating, 60-61
switching between, 62
windows
choosing between, 65
navigating, 59-60

monitoring
battery, 424
system activity, 495-496

monitors. *See* display

mouse, configuring
Bluetooth devices, 422-424
gestures, 401-402
speed, 401
USB mouse, 421

movies, renting, 317

moving
files to/from iCloud, 117
notes between folders, 304

multimedia
purchasing from iTunes Store, 316-317
sharing to Apple TV, 435

multiple email addresses, 133

multiple IM accounts, 220

multiple monitors, 429-445

multiple network connections, 96-99

music
iTunes
Album view, 314
mini player, 330
syncing, 336-340
iTunes Match
accessing, 343-344
activating, 341-342
connecting iTunes library to, 342-343
cost, 341
iTunes Radio
creating stations, 332-333
fine-tuning stations, 334
listening to, 331-332
sharing stations, 335
viewing recently played songs, 335
iTunes Store
Genius Recommendations, 318-321
purchasing from, 316-317
media center software, 345

playlists
    accessing, 329
    creating, 326-327
    smart playlists, 328-329
    sharing, 339-340
My Card, 259

N

names, adding to AutoFill data, 168
navigating
    apps, 59-60
    files/folders in Grid mode, 23
    Launchpad, 70-71
    Maps, 267
    windows, 59-60
nesting Smart Mailboxes, 151
network connections, 81
    configuration, 89
        PPPoE (Point-to-Point Protocol over Ethernet), 92-93
        TCP/IP and Proxy settings, 89-91
    diagnostics, 100-101
    Ethernet (wired) networks, 82-83
    multiple connections, 96-99
    setup assistant, 101-103
    VPNs (Virtual Private Networks), 94-96
    wireless networks
        authentication, 87
        connecting to, 84-86
        enabling/disabling wireless networking, 88
        finding, 84-85
        Mac compatibility, 84
        security, 84
network shares, connecting to, 191-192
optical drive sharing
    DVD and CD sharing, 202
    optical drive access, 203-204
printer sharing, 438
    enabling, 198
    network printer access, 200-201
    permissions, 199-200
screen sharing
    enabling, 204-205
    local Mac screens, 207-208

permissions, 205-207
remote computers and non-Macs, 209-210
No Access permissions, 190
non-App Store apps, installing, 378
    accessing disk images, 380
    unarchiving Zip files, 379
non-Mac computers, screen sharing, 209-210
notes
    adding, 303
    displaying, 304-305
    moving between folders, 304
    searching, 304-305
    sharing, 306
Notes app, 301
    connecting to other note servers, 308
    folders
        adding, 302
        deleting, 302
        managing, 301
    iCloud, 108
    syncing with iCloud, 307
Notification Center, 10
    chats, 230-231
    posting, 249
    responding to incoming chat, 228
    viewing, 49-50
notifications
    customizing display, 51-52
    Do Not Disturb mode, 53-54
    Notification Center, 10
        chats, 230-231
        posting, 249
        responding to incoming chat, 228
        viewing, 49-50
    overview, 48
    receiving, 49

O

opening
    Finder window tabs, 29-30
    iCloud files on Mac, 114-115
    Mission Control, 58-59
optical drive sharing
    DVD and CD sharing, 202
    optical drive access, 203-204

organizing
    bookmarks, 158-159
    books, 352-353
    email, 139-140
    iCloud files, 118
    Top Sites, 160
output devices, 410

P

Page Setup feature, 440
pairing Bluetooth devices, 422-427
    Bluetooth status menu, 426-427
    headsets, 425-426
    keyboard, 424-425
    mouse/trackpad, 422-424
Parallels Desktop, 16
parental controls, 450-452
passwords
    adding to AutoFill data, 168
    Keychain Access
        adding data to keychain, 458
        adding keychain menu items, 460
        creating keychains, 459
        explained, 456
        viewing keychain items, 457
    Windows file sharing, 187
PDFs
    printing to, 441
    viewing online, 164
permissions
    assigning, 455-456
    folder access permissions, 189-194
    printer sharing, 199-200
    repairing, 491
    screen sharing, 205-207
    verifying, 492
Photo Booth, 417
Photo Sharing
    enabling, 118-119
    sharing photos, 120-122
    viewing shared photos, 119-120
Photos (iCloud), 108
placing calls
    from contacts list, 237-238
    from favorites list, 239

playlists
  accessing, 329
  creating, 326-327
  smart playlists, 328-329
Play Sound for Notifications
  option, 52
Plex, 345
podcasts
  downloading, 321-324
  unsubscribing, 324
points of interest (Maps), 272-274
Point-to-Point Protocol over
  Ethernet (PPPoE), 92-93
populating desktop spaces, 60-61
posting
  from Finder, 248
  via Notification Center, 249
PPPoE (Point-to-Point Protocol
  over Ethernet), 92-93
Preview, 443-445
previewing
  email attachments, 136
  files, 40
Print command (File menu), 200
Printer dialog box, 201
printers
  configuring, 436-441
    network printers, 438
    USB printers, 436-439
  printing to, 440-441
  sharing, 197
    enabling, 198
    network printer access,
      200-201
    permissions, 199-200
printing
  addresses, 266
  calendars, 293
  to PDF, 441
  to printers, 440-441
private browsing, 171
profiles, color, 405
protected printers, printing to,
  201
protection. See security
protocols, 180, 185-187
Proxy settings, 89-91
public shared calendars,
  subscribing, 283-284
purchases, syncing in iTunes, 336
purchasing
  apps, 375
  books in iBooks, 347-348
  from iTunes Store, 316-317

Q-R

Quick Event (Calendar), 287
Quick Look, 37
  slideshows, 39
  viewing files with, 38-39
radio. See iTunes Radio
Reader (Safari), 164-165
reading books, 353-354
Reading List (Safari), 156-157, 161
Read Only permission, 190
Read permission, 190
rearranging
  Dock items, 21
  Launchpad icons, 72
receiving
  calls, 240
  files, 182-183
  notifications, 49
recently played songs, viewing
  on iTunes Radio, 335
recommendations for friends
  (Game Center), 363
recording
  audio, 413-414
  screen actions, 416
  video, 414-416
recovering data from Time
  Machine backups, 471-472
recovery partition, booting
  from, 493
redeeming gift cards, 316
reinstalling apps, 376-377
Remember This Password in My
  Keychain option, 195
Reminders, 294
  adding, 296
  attributes, 296-297
  completing, 298
  deleting, 298
  finding, 298
  iCloud, 108, 300
  lists, 295
  searching, 300
  viewing by date, 299
remote computers, screen
  sharing, 209-210
remote shares, connecting to,
  193
removing
  corrupted apps, 482-484
  files/folders from Dock, 20-21
  System Preference panes, 490

tags, 34
widgets, 42-43
renaming mailboxes, 148
rented movies, 317
Reopen Windows When Logging
  Back In option, 76
repairing
  disk errors, 493-494
  permission problems, 491
repair toolkit, building, 494
repeat rate for keyboard, 391
reports, system profiler reports,
  496-497
requests. See friend requests
resolution
  of Apple TV, 433
  configuring, 403
responding
  to Game Center friend
    requests, 362
  to incoming chat, 228
restoring
  computers from Time Machine
    backups, 473-474
  file versions, 475-476
  windows, 77
Retina displays, 3
ripping CDs into iTunes, 318
routers, 89
rules (email), 154

S

Safari
  account information, saving
    and sharing, 167
  AutoFill data
    credit card data, 169
    managing, 167-168
    names and passwords, 168
  bookmarks, 156
    adding web pages to, 157
    organizing, 158-159
  extensions, 175-177
  iCloud, 108
  overview, 155
  PDFs, viewing online, 164
  private browsing, 171
  Reader, 164-165
  Reading List, 156-157, 161
  searches, 157
  security, 172-173
  Share Sheets, 170

tabs
  adding, 162
  iCloud tabs, 166
  viewing, 163
  Top Sites, 156
    adding web pages to, 157
    organizing, 160
  web content, adding to
    Dashboard, 173-175
Safe mode, 485
saving
  account information in Safari,
    167
  email attachments, 137
  files
    manually, 78
    to iCloud, 113-114, 477
  Spotlight searches, 47-48
  versions, 474-475
Scale animation effect, 24
scanners, configuring, 442-445
scheduling sleep mode, 390
screen actions, recording, 416
screen sharing
  enabling, 204-205
  local Mac screens, 207-208
  Messages app, 234
  permissions, 205-207
  remote computers and
    non-Macs, 209-210
SD card slot, 2
SD (Secure Digital) RAM cards, 2
searching
  apps in App Store, 374
  contacts, 260
  email, 152-153
  events, 292
  files, 45-48
  iBooks, 353
  iTunes library, 324-325
  Launchpad, 71
  Maps, 271-272
  notes, 304-305
  reminders, 300
  Spotlight searches
    customizing, 46
    saving, 47-48
    starting, 45
  web, 157
Secure Digital (SD) RAM cards, 2
security, 447. See also backups
  apps, limiting execution of,
    463
  FileVault, 460-462

firewall, 464-466
groups, 453-456
Keychain Access
  adding data to keychain, 458
  adding keychain menu items,
    460
  creating keychains, 459
  explained, 456
  viewing keychain items, 457
private browsing, 171
Safari, 172-173
user accounts
  creating, 449
  general account security, 454
  groups, 453
  Guest accounts, 450
  parental controls, 450-452
  permissions, assigning,
    455-456
  types of, 448
Versions
  restoring file versions,
    475-476
  saving versions, 474-475
wireless networks, 84
sending
  attachments, 143
  files with AirDrop, 181-182
  friend requests, 361
  invitations, 289-290
server-based reminders, 300
services (iCloud)
  activating, 108-109
  Back to My Mac, 109
  Calendars, 108
  Contacts, 108
  Find My Mac, 111-112
  Keychain, 108
  Mail, 108
  Notes, 108
  Photos, 108
  Reminders, 108
  Safari, 108
setup assistant, 101-103
Share Sheets, 170, 183, 194-197
sharing
  account information with
    Safari, 167
  contacts, 265
  files
    with AirDrop, 180-183
    with Share Sheets, 194-197
    traditional file sharing,
      184-194

Home Sharing (iTunes),
  339-340
Internet connections, 211-212
iTunes Radio stations, 335
multimedia to Apple TV, 435
notes, 306
optical drive sharing
  DVD and CD sharing, 202
  optical drive access, 203-204
Photo Sharing
  enabling, 118-119
  sharing photos, 120-122
  viewing shared photos,
    119-120
points of interest (Maps), 274
printer sharing, 197
  enabling, 198
  network printer access,
    200-201
  permissions, 199-200
screen sharing
  enabling, 204-205
  local Mac screens, 207-208
  permissions, 205-207
  remote computers and
    non-Macs, 209-210
web pages, 170
Sharing Only accounts, 448
shortcuts
  Dashboard, 41
  keyboard shortcuts, 392-395
  Mission Control, 67-68
  text shortcuts, 392-393
Show Desktop feature (Mission
  Control), 66
Show Indicator Lights for Open
  Applications option (Dock), 25
Show Notifications on Lock
  Screen option, 51
Show Wi-Fi Status option, 86
shutdown, scheduling, 390
Sidebar (Finder)
  modifying manually, 27
  system shortcuts, 26
signatures, 145-146, 466
signing in Game Center, 358-359
signup for iTunes Match, 341-342
sleep mode, 390
slideshows with Quick Look, 39
Smart Folders, saving Spotlight
  searches as, 47-48
smart groups, 255
Smart Mailboxes, 150-151
smart playlists, 328-329

SMB, 185-187
social networking, 249
software. *See* apps
Solaris compatibility, 16
songs. *See* music
sorting email, 135
sound. *See* audio
spaces
    closing, 63
    creating, 60-61
    full-screen spaces, creating, 64
    populating, 60-61
    switching between, 62
spam filtering, 141
speakers, 411
special keyboard keys, 4
speech feedback, configuring, 398
speech recognition, 12
speed
    of Magic Mouse, 401
    of trackpad, 398
spelling correction, 392-393
Spotlight, 44-45
Standard accounts, 448
starting
    chats
        Messages, 229-230
        Notification Center, 230-231
    Diagnostics, 100-101
    iBooks, 345-346
    Launchpad, 69
    Maps, 267
    in Safe mode, 485
    screen-sharing sessions (IM), 234-235
    setup assistant, 101-103
    Spotlight searches, 45
startup, scheduling, 390
stationery templates, 144
stations (iTunes Radio)
    creating, 332-333
    fine-tuning, 334
    sharing, 335
status menu
    Bluetooth, 426-427
    Messages app, 221
status messages (Messages app), 224
StuffIt, 379
subnet masks, 89
subscribing to public shared calendars, 283-284

SuperDrive, 3
switching between spaces, 62
syncing
    Calendar app
        to iCloud, 280-281
        with other calendar servers, 281-283
    Contacts with other contact servers, 263-264
    iCloud and Contacts, 262
    iTunes
        between devices, 336-339
        purchases, 336
    Notes app, 307
system activity, monitoring, 495-496
System Information utility, 496-497
system logs, 498
System Preferences, 10
    Dock, 24-25
    removing, 490
    unlocking, 448
system profiler reports, generating, 496-497
system support options, 499

T

tabs
    Finder window tabs, 29-30
    Safari
        adding, 162
        iCloud tabs, 166
        viewing, 163
tags, 7
    assigning, 33
    managing, 35-37
    removing, 34
    viewing, 34-35
TCP/IP and Proxy settings, 89-91
templates
    Contacts, 259-260
    stationery templates, 144
Terminal application, 204
testing apps with Guest account, 481-482
text shortcuts, 392-393
Thunderbolt, 2, 510
TightVNC, 210
Time Machine backups. *See* backups
toolbars, Finder toolbar, 28

Top Sites, 156
    adding web pages to, 157
    organizing, 160
TOSLINK adapters, 412
trackpad, configuring
    Bluetooth devices, 422-424
    gestures, 399-400
    speed, 398
traffic (Maps), 277
transferring files, 233
trimming video, 197
troubleshooting, 479
    3D Maps, 270
    apps
        force-quitting, 480-481
        removing corrupted apps, 482-484
        testing with Guest account, 481-482
    Bluetooth passkeys, 425
    disk errors, 490
        permission problems, 491
        repairing errors, 493-494
        verifying disk errors, 492-493
    frozen Macs, 484
        changing login applications, 486
        disabling extensions, 488-489
        removing System Preference panes, 490
        starting in Safe mode, 485
    repair toolkits, 494
    system activity, 495-496
    system logs, 498
    system profiler reports, 496-497
    system support options, 499
Twitter, enabling, 244-245

U

unarchiving Zip files, 379
uninstallers, 75
uninstalling applications, 75
Universal Serial Bus (USB), 2
unlocking system preferences, 448
unsubscribing podcasts, 324
Update All button, 385
updating
    apps, 382
        applying manually, 384-385
        automatic downloads, 383
        configuring, 383

FaceTime
  account information,
    242-243
  addresses, 242-243
uploading files to online services,
  195-197
USB (Universal Serial Bus), 2
  USB input devices, 419-421
  USB printers, 436-439
  USB scanners, 442
user accounts
  creating, 449
  general account security, 454
  groups, 453
  Guest accounts
    enabling, 450
    explained, 448
    testing apps with, 481-482
  parental controls, 450-452
  permissions, 455-456
  types of, 448

V

vCards, 265
verifying
  disk errors, 492-493
  permissions, 492
Versions
  restoring file versions, 475-476
  saving versions, 474-475
VersionTracker, 380
video
  media center software, 345
  recording, 414-416
  rented movies, 317
  trimming, 197
  video calls. See FaceTime
  video chat, 231-232
  video conferencing, 225
viewing
  browser tabs, 163
  calendars, 285
  files
    all files, 31
    by category, 32
    with Quick Look, 38-39
  friends' stats on Game Center,
    364-368
  keychain items, 457
  Maps, 268-269
  Notifications Center, 49-50
  PDFs online, 164

recently played songs on
  iTunes Radio, 335
reminders by date, 299
shared photos, 119-120
system logs, 498
tags, 34-35
web pages in email, 138
views
  iTunes
    Album view, 314
    Library view, 313
  Maps, 268
VIP Mailboxes, 151-152
VirtualBox, 16, 382
virtualization, 15-16
Virtual Network Computing
  (VNC), 210
Virtual Private Networks (VPNs),
  94-96
VMWare Fusion, 16
VNC (Virtual Network
  Computing), 210
voice recognition
  configuring, 396-397
  dictation, 12
volume, 408
VPNs (Virtual Private Networks),
  94-96

W-X-Y-Z

wake/sleep mode, 390
web browsing
  account information, saving
    and sharing, 167
  AutoFill data
    credit card data, 169
    managing, 167-168
    names and passwords, 168
  bookmarks, 156
    adding web pages to, 157
    organizing, 158-159
  extensions, 175-177
  iCloud, 108
  overview, 155
  PDFs, viewing online, 164
  private browsing, 171
  Reader, 164-165
  Reading List, 156-157, 161
  searches, 157
  security, 172-173
  Share Sheets, 170

tabs
  adding, 162
  iCloud tabs, 166
  viewing, 163
Top Sites, 156
  adding web pages to, 157
  organizing, 160
web content, adding to
  Dashboard, 173-175
websites
  MacUpdate, 380
  VersionTracker, 380
When Switching to an
  Application, Switch to a Space
  with Open Windows for the
  Application option (Mission
  Control), 67
widgets
  adding, 42-43
  configuring, 43-44
  finding, 44
  overview, 40
  removing, 42-43
windows
  choosing between in Mission
    Control, 65
  controls, 11
  navigating with Mission
    Control, 59-60
  restoring open windows, 77
Windows compatibility
  Boot Camp, 14
  virtualization, 15-16
Windows file sharing, 187
window tabs (Finder)
  adding, 29
  opening with one click, 30
wired networks, connecting to,
  82-83
wireless networks, 84
  authentication, 87
  connecting to, 84-86
  enabling/disabling wireless
    networking, 88
  finding, 84-85
  Mac compatibility, 84
  security, 84
Write Only permission, 190
Write permission, 190
Zip files, unarchiving, 379

Your purchase of *My iMac®, Mavericks Edition,* includes access to a free online edition for 45 days through the **Safari Books Online** subscription service. Nearly every Que book is available online through **Safari Books Online**, along with thousands of books and videos from publishers such as Addison-Wesley Professional, Cisco Press, Exam Cram, IBM Press, O'Reilly Media, Prentice Hall, Sams, and VMware Press.

Safari Books Online is a digital library providing searchable, on-demand access to thousands of technology, digital media, and professional development books and videos from leading publishers. With one monthly or yearly subscription price, you get unlimited access to learning tools and information on topics including mobile app and software development, tips and tricks on using your favorite gadgets, networking, project management, graphic design, and much more.

Activate your FREE Online Edition at
informit.com/safarifree

STEP 1: Enter the coupon code: RPSBXAA.

STEP 2: New Safari users, complete the brief registration form. Safari subscribers, just log in.

If you have difficulty registering on Safari or accessing the online edition, please e-mail customer-service@safaribooksonline.com